LE FRANGLAIS

On the authors

Philip Thody is Professor Emeritus of French Literature at the University of Leeds. His publications include books on Anouilh, Barthes, Camus, Genet, Aldous Huxley, Laclos, Proust and Sartre. He is also the author of *French Caesarism from Napoleon 1e to Charles de Gaulle* and *The Conservative Imagination*. He is joint author, with Howard Evans, of *Faux Amis and Key Words: A Dictionary-Guide to French Language, Culture and Society through Lookalikes and Confusables* (Athlone, 1985).

Howard Evans is Senior Lecturer in French at the University of Leeds. He has published widely on French local government and the contemporary French language.

Michelle Pepratx-Evans, Agrégée de l'Université, is Senior Research Fellow at Trinity and All Saints, University of Leeds. She has published widely on French and comparative education.

Le Franglais

Forbidden English, Forbidden American
Law, Politics and Language in Contemporary
France

A STUDY IN LOAN WORDS AND NATIONAL IDENTITY

PHILIP THODY
with the assistance of
Howard Evans & Michelle Pepratx-Evans

ATHLONE
London & Atlantic Highlands, N. J.

First published 1995 by
THE ATHLONE PRESS
1 Park Drive, London NW11 7SG
and 165 First Avenue,
Atlantic Highlands, NJ 07716

British Library Cataloguing in Publication Data
A catalogue record for this book is available from the British Library

ISBN 0 485 11476 3 hb
0 485 12115 8 pb

Library of Congress Cataloging in Publication Data

Thody, Philip Malcolm Waller, 1928–
    Le Franglais : forbidden English, forbidden American : law,
politics, and language in contemporary France : a study in loan
words and national identity / by Philip Thody, with the assistance
of Howard Evans and Michelle Pepratx-Evans.
    p.   cm.
    Includes bibliographical references and index.
    ISBN 0–485–11476–3 (hb). — ISBN 0–485–12115–8 (pb)
    1. French language—Foreign words and phrases—English.
2. English language—Influence on French. 3. French language—
Social aspects. 4. National characteristics, French. 5. English
language—Foreign words and phrases—French. 6. French
language—Influence on English. I. Evans, Howard.
II. Pepratx-Evans, Michelle. III. Title.
PC2582.E5T46   1995
442′:421–dc20   95–36701
                                                                     CIP

Typeset by Datix International Ltd, Bungay, Suffolk
Printed and bound in Great Britain by Bookcraft (Bath) Ltd.

To the memory of Ted Hope

Contents

Acknowledgements

Not a word of this book would have reached the printer without the generous help which Janet Kish, Millie Nettleton, Lindsay Pearce and Annette Torode gave us with the mysteries of word processors.

The pleasure of reading French newspapers and magazines was greatly enhanced by the help given by Susan Dolamore and Susan Oldfield of the Modern Languages Library, French Department, University of Leeds.

Introduction

The word 'franglais' was popularised in France by the publication in 1954 of *Parlez-vous franglais?* by the philosopher and literary critic René Étiemble. In it, he criticised what he saw as the excessive use by native speakers of French, and especially journalists, of words of English or American origin. He was not attacking anglicisms in the sense of English words which have been fully absorbed into French. Terms such as 'boulingrin' (bowling green) or 'redingote' (riding coat) did not appear in his book, any more than did 'microphone' or 'téléphone'. Although these words are included in Josette Rey-Debove and Gilberte Gagnon's invaluable *Dictionnaire des Anglicismes*,[1] they can no more be seen as intruders than words such as 'perfume' or 'system' are seen as gallicisms in English. What annoyed Étiemble was what he argued was the constant use of words such as 'business', 'leadership', 'quick lunch' and 'teenager'. Not only did such words, in his view, enable the Americans to export their way of life into France and thus destroy indigenous French culture; they also tended to supplant perfectly good French words by what he called 'le sabir atlantique', Atlantic gobbledegook. They were, moreover, often used not because there was no appropriate term in French, but for purely snobbish reasons.

I shall be using the word 'franglais' in the same sense as Étiemble: 'franglais' words are anglicisms and americanisms which are still visibly recognisable as such, terms which are as clearly foreign in origin as 'joie de vivre' or 'folie des grandeurs' are in English. Part II of this book lists some of the terms of obviously or apparently English or American origin which recur most frequently in the France of the 1990s. While I have taken into account the various government decrees setting out official alternatives to English or American terms said to be in common usage, I have paid more attention to the words used in the books, newspapers, on periodicals listed in the Bibliography (p. 289), as well as to the way people speak on the radio and television. Linguistic inquisitors, like their ecclesiastical forebears, have been known to exaggerate the extent of the heresy which, like Étiemble, they have felt themselves called upon to investigate.

I have also concentrated more on the language used in public by journalists and politicians than on what French people say to one another, or to the visiting foreigner, in private conversation. The debate about 'le franglais' stems largely from objections made to the use of certain words in advertising, the media and business. Not even the most passionate supporters of the laws that were intended to limit the use of English or American expressions in French have suggested that this legislation should apply to the way French people talk to one another in private.

Opinions also vary as to how worried French people in general are about the problems raised by Étiemble. Partly as a result of the impact made by *Parlez-vous franglais?*, but also in response to a more general feeling of concern about the future of French, an agency was founded on 20 March 1970 to enable French-speaking countries to co-operate on cultural and technical matters, under the banner of 'La Francophonie'. It grouped together some thirty French-speaking states, and in the reports of the first summit meeting of these states which was held at Versailles in 1986, great emphasis was placed upon the fact that the only language spoken was French.

Other, comparable meetings have been held regularly since 1986. In 1988 came the publication by J. J. Luthi, A. Viatte and G. Zananini of a *Dictionnaire général de la Francophonie*,[2] a work which supplies a great deal of information about where French is spoken and who the major French-speaking writers are throughout the world, and the movement is, officially, a very popular one. But when, on 18 March 1995, *Le Monde* published an article by Jean-Pierre Péronçel-Hugoz to mark the twenty-fifth birthday of La Francophonie, two facts emerged which cast doubt on just how genuine the support for the movement was. For while 86.3 per cent of those questioned by the public relations institute Lavialle thought that La Francophonie ought to play a more important part in the life of France, 15 per cent of those replying could not name a single francophone country and 59 per cent of those questioned who were under twenty-five also said that membership of La Francophonie had no impact on their lives.

Similarly, according to an article by Bernard Cassin in *Le Monde Diplomatique* for August 1994, a Sofres (*Société francaise d'études par sondages*) enquiry revealed that 80 per cent of those questioned supported the attempt by Jacques Toubon, Ministre de la culture et de la francophonie, to limit the use of 'franglais' terms by law. However, a report in October 1993 in issue no. 13 of *France Journal*, the official journal distributed by the Alliance Francaise, stated that

> dans l'Hexagone, la francophonie ne bénéficie pas, dans le grand public, de toute l'attention qu'elle merite (in France itself, the Francophonie is not given all the attention it deserves by the general public)

and this remark anticipated another point made in *Le Monde* for 18 March 1995: that according a French-speaking journalist from Montreal, Denis Boucher, the predominant reaction of French intellectuals and politicians towards Jacques Toubon's bill had been to make fun of it.

In the light of these conflicting reports, I shall avoid talking about 'the French' in general. It may well be that a majority of French people do object to the presence of obvious anglicisms and americanisms in their language, and even feel guilty at the use which they personally make of them. But it is equally possible that the results of an enquiry into what a representative sample of French people thought about the 'franglais' expressions in common use, as distinct from what they thought about a piece of proposed legislation, would parallel the results obtained when an enquiry was conducted in 1971 in order to discover the attitude of the Czech population towards loan words in their language. This revealed that while some 56 per cent of the 635 respondents 'demonstrated some resentment towards users of foreign words', the general tendency among young people of good education was one of tolerance.[3] Since so many 'franglais' words occur in newspapers and magazines aimed at a readership of under twenty-five, the results in France might be very similar.

My comment above, in the second paragraph, that Part II of this book lists words which are 'apparently' of English or American origin is a reminder of a phenomenon which was noted as long ago as 1921. After his description, in *Le côté de Guermantes*, of M. de Guermantes as 'cet Hercule en "smoking"', Marcel Proust immediately adds the following comment on the word which the French use for what is known in Britain as a dinner jacket and in the United States as a tuxedo:

> puisqu'on donne en France à toute chose plus ou moins britannique le nom qu'elle ne porte pas en Angleterre (since in France, we give everything vaguely British the name which it does not have in England).

When an asterisk * follows a 'franglais' word in the index to Part II, this indicates my awareness of the fact that the word in question is like M. de Guermantes's 'smoking': either it does not exist in present-day English or American, or it has taken on a meaning in modern French which it does not normally have in the United States or the United Kingdom.

'Franglais' words are loan words, terms borrowed from English or American for reasons which vary from snobbery and affectation to a genuine need to fill a specific gap. They will therefore probably either disappear as the fashion for using them fades, or be absorbed into the language and become a normal part of the vocabulary of standard French. When the marker † comes after a word in the index, it indicates that this has already happened, and that the word is included either in the 1992 *Petit Robert* dictionary, or in the 1994 *Petit Larousse Illustré 1995* or the 1994 *Dictionnaire Hachette*. Such words can still, in spite of their inclusion in one of these standard dictionaries, be legitimately classified as examples of 'le franglais'. They do not yet look French enough to be seen as a normal part of the vocabulary of the language. But their presence in one of these dictionaries suggests that they are well on their way to what can, in several senses of the word, be seen as a process of naturalisation. Whenever possible, each word in the index is followed by the date given in the *Petit Robert* for its first attested usage in French.

The term 'le franglais' does not designate an actual language. With only one or two exceptions, of whom Étiemble is the most vociferous, most commentators on the French language agree that neither its syntax nor its morphology has so far been seriously affected. It is easy to see why the one leading expert to express support for Étiemble, Pierre Guiraud, was annoyed by the sentence by a French journalist which he quoted in his *Les mots étrangers* ('Que sais-je?' no. 1166, Presses Universitaires de France, Paris, 1965, p. 122): 'Nous ne sommes pas concernés par le déterrent Nord-Atlantique' (We are not concerned by the North Atlantic deterrent): it is so obviously anglicised a sentence. But even there, the solecisms were in the vocabulary, not in the syntax, and he did not quote any other examples. There are, moreover, so many other influences working on French that it is hard to prove that either English or American is having a more deleterious effect than the style of writing developed by the followers of Roland Barthes or Jacques Derrida. French people do not learn to talk 'le franglais' as they might learn to talk German or Italian. From a linguistic point of view, the argument about 'le franglais' rarely goes beyond a series of quarrels about what words should or should not be used to describe objects, activities and events. Part I of the book explains this aspect of the question in more detail, while at the same time discussing some of the political, social and legal issues raised by the campaign against 'franglais' words in which Étiemble fired the first shot.

Part I also looks in some detail at the role which it is reasonable to expect the law to play in a modern, democratic society, and suggests a number of reasons why there is more concern in France than in any other country over the presence of words of Anglo-Saxon origin or appearance. The words listed in Part II also provide the starting point for an examination of a number of other aspects of French society. Words are always interesting, loan words particularly so. But they become even more interesting if they can be seen as throwing light on the society in which they are used. France is so intriguing a country that no means should be neglected which might lead to a better understanding of it.

Like other students of foreign languages, I have often been struck by how much one can learn about one's own country by looking at what happens elsewhere. The study of the use of American and English words in French has, in particular, made me more aware of how many French words we use on a regular basis in English. Part III of this book lists some of these, and uses them to reinforce one of the suggestions as to why some French people should be so worried by the presence in their language of what many of them see as unwelcome intruders.

The statement on the title page to the effect that this book has been written 'with the assistance of Howard Evans and Michelle Pepratx-Evans' is a recognition of the very considerable debt which I owe to both of them for advice as well as for information. I should nevertheless make two things clear: all mistakes are my own; and I alone am responsible for any disagreement which may be evoked by my treatment of what I am always surprised to discover can be so controversial a subject.

Philip Thody
Leeds, 1995

NOTES
1 Les Usuels du Robert, Paris, 1980.
2 Published by Letouzey & Ané, Paris, 1988.
3 See George Thomas, *Linguistic purism*, Longman, London/New York, 1991, p. 41.

PART I
ARGUMENTS

1 From the language of politics to the politics of language

On 17 February 1993, in a speech at Montlouis-sur-Loire, the then first secretary of the French Socialist Party, Michel Rocard, appealed for what he described as a 'big bang' in the world of French left-wing politics. There should, he said, be a general shake-up, with less insistence on doctrine and on the fortunes of the Socialist Party, and he invited other forces of the left, including the radicals and ecologists, to link their fortunes with the new grouping which he was hoping his speech would produce.

The fact that he sounded, to the English ear, like a man calling for a 'big bong' did not prevent Rocard from being immediately understood. Valéry Giscard d'Estaing, President of the Fifth Republic from 1974 to 1981, predicted what he called 'un big flop'. Raymond Barre, his Prime Minister from 1979 to 1981, was more gnomic, explaining that in the theory of the beginnings of the universe to which Rocard was referring, in which everything first of all shrinks into a black hole, any 'big bang' was preceded by 'un big crunch'.[1] A cartoon in *Le Monde* for 23 March offered a reading of what it saw as the subtext of Rocard's speech. Relations between President Mitterrand and Michel Rocard had often been difficult, and the cartoon showed Mitterrand tied to a large bomb. Standing beside him was Michel Rocard, with the following words coming out of his mouth:

> Pour ceux qui n'ont pas compris ce que c'est que le Big Bang, j'ai apporté un dessin. (For people who haven't understood what the Big Bang is, I've brought a picture.)

In the event, Giscard d'Estaing's prediction about a 'big flop' proved accurate. In the legislative elections of March 1993, the left lost 209 of its 276 seats, with the Socialist Party itself being reduced to 59. For all the ease with which he had made himself understood by the use of a very unfrench word, Rocard himself lost his parliamentary seat at Conflans-Sainte-Honorine, in the outskirts of Paris, to the centre-right Pierre Cardo, a representative of 'les réac' camembert' over 'la gauche caviar'.[2]

The term 'big bang', sometimes hyphenated and sometimes not, sometimes with capitals and sometimes not, stuck to Rocard for some time, often linked with other words of such ostentatiously Anglo-Saxon origin that they were obviously being used as something of a joke. After the second round of the parliamentary elections had revealed the extent of the socialists' defeat, another cartoon in *Le Monde* showed him staggering around with a black eye, the balloon coming out of his mouth reading: 'Je me suis ramassé un Big Baffe' (I got myself a right thumping). When Jacques Delors finally announced, on 12 December 1994, that he would not be a candidate for the presidential elections of 1995, *Le Monde* for 22 December placed part of the blame on

> 'l'homme trop pressé qui, un soir de février 1993, à Montlouis-sur-Loire, avait annoncé prématurément la mort du Parti Socialiste en préconisant le 'big bang' (the man who was in too much of a hurry when, on a February evening in 1993, at Montlouis-sur-Loire, he prematurely announced the death of the Socialist Party by recommending his 'big bang').

The use of an English term in an electoral contest raises a nice legal point. The loi Bas-Lauriol, unanimously approved in the Chambre des Députés on 31 December 1975, and registered in the *Journal Officiel de la République Française* for 4 January 1976, clearly stated that

> Dans la désignation, l'offre, la présentation, la publicité écrite ou parlée, le mode d'emploi ou d'utilisation, l'étendue et les conditions de garantie d'un bien ou d'un service, ainsi

que les factures et quittances, l'emploi de la langue française est obligatoire. (French must be used when describing, offering or presenting goods or services for sale, in describing their use, defining their guarantee, in any advertising, written or oral, as in bills and receipts.)

Rocard, so a pernickety lawyer (un juriste qui cherche la petite bête) might have argued, was offering a new product to his fellow citizens, a series of measures which, if adopted, would fundamentally change their way of life. He ought, therefore, to have used French. By not doing so, he was offending against the spirit and the letter of a law passed with no dissenting voices when he was already a member of the legislative assembly.

Had Rocard been called upon to defend himself against a prosecution brought under the loi Bas-Lauriol – something which has so far happened mainly to commercial companies guilty of advertising products such as hamburgers and milk shakes[3] – he might have argued that he was justified in using the term 'big bang' because no equivalent French term existed. He had, he could have claimed, got his message over in a fairly striking way, something which he might not have done if he had talked about 'un profond remaniement du paysage politique français' (a complete restructuring of the French political landscape), or 'une réorganisation de fond en comble des structures essentielles de la gauche' (a reorganisation from top to bottom of the essential structures of the left). He might also have said that since there seems to be no official translation of 'big bang' either, even when it is used in its scientific sense, he was actually improving the language by helping it to express certain ideas more economically. The fact remains that the law was still there when Rocard made his speech, that what turned out to be an unsuccessful attempt was made to reinforce it by the loi Toubon in April 1994, and that a number of French people do seem very worried about what they see as the invasion of French by words of foreign origin, especially when those words come from English, and even more when they are American.

The intensity of this concern may seem very odd to the

native speaker of English, and the making of laws to forbid the use of words of English or American origin is clearly open to a number of objections based on the very nature of language. Since people talk in order to be understood, nobody is going to use an expression which he or she knows an audience will find incomprehensible. The expression 'big bang', which nobody said they did not understand, and which Rocard's fellow politicians criticised only by the irony which they put into their use of it, had been in French since at least the 1980s, when anyone who had been following the financial pages could not have failed to notice it as a term for the abolition by the London Stock Exchange on 27 October 1986 of the distinction between stock-brokers and stock-jobbers.[4] On 3 November 1988, *Le Nouvel Observateur* no. 1252 had published a long article on its original, scientific meaning of a vast explosion giving birth to the universe, and the reaction to Rocard's speech showed that he was quite right to assume a thorough familiarity with the term. Language itself, it could be argued, has its own self-regulating mechanisms which make it unnecessary and inappropriate to use the law as an instrument of control, and a number of French writers and journalists have expressed disapproval of the attempt which Jacques Toubon and the conservative government of Édouard Balladur made to try to protect the purity of French by legal means.

'Monsieur le ministre', wrote a journalist in *Le Monde* on 6 April 1994, after Toubon's bill had been passed by a comfortable majority, the socialists and other parties abstaining, 'vous avez fait une connerie' (made a right balls-up), and a letter from Alain Gresse, in *L'Événement du jeudi* for 5 May, no. 496, was even more forthright, comparing the attempt at linguistic purification with what was happening in the former Ygoslavia and writing: 'On commence par la purification étymologique et on finit par Drancy' (You start by etymological cleansing and you end up with Drancy).[5] In the same number of what seems, in the light of the laws forbidding the use of English and American terms, to be the defiantly named supplement to the same fortnightly periodical, *L'Événement Junior*, the most interesting and original of contemporary French novelists,

Michel Tournier, claimed that 'le franglais' presented no problem since all languages enriched themselves by loan words, and

> l'anglais lui-même n'est en grande partie qu'un créole français, puisqu'il vient de l'anglo-norman, un dialecte de la langue française du XIe siècle (English itself is to a large extent nothing but a French creole, since it comes from Anglo-Norman, a dialect of eleventh-century French).

Tournier was not alone in his criticisms, and the case for loan words in English was made as early as the sixteenth century when Richard Carew asked the rhetorical question:

> Seeing that we borrow (and that not shamefully) from the Dutch, the Briton, the Roman, the Dane, the French, the Italian and the Spaniard, how can our stock be other than exceeding plentiful?[6]

In an apparently more frivolous vein, the popular weekly magazine *Vendredi Samedi Dimanche* printed on 12 August 1993 a page originally intended for one of the Astérix volumes but not included in the published version. It showed Astérix and Obélix being criticised by a Druid for talking Latin. 'Auditorium', he told them, should be replaced by 'salle pour auditions publiques' (room for public hearings); 'ultimatum' by 'proposition n'admettant pas de contestation' (statement admitting no argument or reply); and 'aquarium' by 'réservoir destiné aux animaux d'eau douce ou d'eau salée' (reservoir for fresh-water or salt-water animals). René Goscinny's text was dated March 1973, and was introduced by the following comment from *Vendredi Samedi Dimanche*:

> Les années 60 ont vu l'invasion du vocabulaire étranger dans la langue française. Cela a donné le franglais. Mais ce n'est pas la première fois que cela arrive. Déjà en Gaule vers les années 60, avant J-C, *of course* .... (The sixties saw our language invaded by a foreign vocabulary. It gave le franglais. But it isn't the first time that this has happened. Already, in Gaul in the sixties, BC *of course* ....)

A number of other French writers and commentators have

nevertheless been worried for some time about what they see as the unwarranted intrusion of English and American words into their language, and not all the journalists who discussed the question in 1993 and 1994 were critical of Jacques Toubon's initiative. Bernard Cassin, writing in *Le Monde Diplomatique* in August 1994, highlighted one of the political issues in 'la querelle du franglais' by objecting to an article in the *Wall Street Journal* which argued that since the principles of free market economics were just as applicable in the realm of language, the state should play no part in either area.[7] On the contrary, Cassin maintained, the state had the right as well as the duty to play a much wider and more active role in all areas of life than it did in English-speaking countries, and he put forward three other arguments in favour of using the law to regulate linguistic behaviour. One of these was that this was what the majority of French people wanted to happen, and he quoted the public opinion poll mentioned in my Introduction. The second was that France had already moved into what was effectively a bilingual society, with English playing as much of a part as French in areas such as finance and applied science, and that unless something was done, English would take over completely. The third was that it was wrong to see the preference of the young for American culture and American expressions as the result of a free choice. They had simply been brainwashed by the media, and consequently needed the protection of the state against an insidious and powerful take-over bid by the worst aspects of transatlantic culture.

Such arguments were not new in France, and go back at least to the nineteenth century. In 1845, François Wey devoted a chapter of his *Remarques sur la langue française au XIXe siècle, sur le style et la composition littéraire* to what he called 'L'invasion des mots anglais dans la langue française' (the invasion of French by words from English), and in 1855, Marcel Viennet complained in his *Epîtres et satires à Boileau* of the way French was being corrupted by English.[8] Rémy de Gourmont also had some harsh words to say about the popularity of English words in his 1899 *L'esthétique de la langue française*, but it was not until after the second world war that the publication of

Étiemble's *Parlez-vous franglais?* brought the issue to the attention of a wider public and away from the relatively narrow circle of academicians and literary critics where it had been discussed until then.

Parlez-vous franglais? was based on a series of articles which had originally appeared in Sartre's *Les Temps Modernes*. The first of them, published in December 1949 under the title 'Nouvelle Défense (mais non point illustration) de la langue française' (New Defence – but in no way an illustration – of the French language), announced one of the main political themes of Étiemble's campaign by talking about how Mexico was 'menacé par l'impérialisme yanqui' (threatened by Yankee imperialism), and the second, which appeared in August 1952, talked about the way French was being enslaved by 'le sabir atlantique' (Atlantic jargon). After calling for government intervention to protect France against the invasion of an 'American way of life' which he described as 'cocalcoolique' (cocacolaholic), Étiemble placed the issue firmly in a Cold War framework when he concluded by accusing the United States of preparing a preventive war against the Soviet Union and wrote:

> On veut bien se faire tuer, à la rigueur, mais pour que les survivants conservent le droit de parler notre français, car qu'est-ce qu'une patrie qui n'a plus de langage? (We're quite prepared to get ourselves killed, if it is really necessary, but so long as the survivors keep the right to speak our French. For what is a country which has lost its language?)[9]

Parlez-vous franglais? has remained sufficiently popular to be republished in 1973, 1984 and 1991, this time with the ironic sub-titles 'Fol en France'/'Mad in France' and 'La Belle France'/'Label France'. It is a long, vigorously written work, with 381 closely printed pages, and with what seems at first sight a plethora of examples about words such as 'businessman', 'boss', 'crack' (in the sense of expert), 'deb' (in that of a young girl making her first appearance in society), 'establishment' (in that of 'les gens en place, les deux cents familles')[10] 'fast food', 'girl', 'hot dog', 'ice-cream', 'jet-clipper', 'long

rifle', 'milk-bar', 'nursery', 'quick-lunch', 'remake', 'scratches'
(in the sense of visible defects on a film), 'tennis', what
Étiemble spells as 'yatching', and 'zoom'. These words were
all, in Étiemble's view, signs of the progress which what he
called 'l'impérialisme yanqui' (Yankee imperialism) was
making in its destruction of French as a language, and he
accused the Americans of imposing the word 'design' on the
French as part of what he described as 'a deliberate attempt
to kill a section of our industry'. The effort which 'les Yanquis'
were making to colonise France, he argued, involved brain-
washing followed by 'le bourrage de crâne', a term first used
in the 1914–18 war to describe filling people's heads with
government propaganda. Indeed, he presented 'la civilisation
cocal-coolique' as an organised plot to replace French, which
he described as being, until the twentieth century, 'la langue
de l'homme blanc civilisé' (the language of the civilised white
man), by what he had already called 'le sabir atlantique'.[11]

SOME TENTATIVE DEFINITIONS

The implicit definition of a 'franglais' word, as I suggested in
my Introduction, is that of a term which is of visibly English
or American origin but which has not been fully assimilated
into the language. Such a definition clearly differentiates
'franglais' words from ordinary anglicisms. A noun such as
'jury', for example, which came into the language from English
in 1790, has for over a century been as thoroughly French a
word as the verb 'jurer' (to swear), from which it was originally derived, and which has existed in French since the ninth
century. The same thing is true of 'impérialisme', borrowed
from English in 1880, but not mentioned by Étiemble as a
word which has no right to figure in the French language.
Like 'compétition', borrowed from English in 1759, or
'humour', which dates from 1725, and which still provides an
essential alternative to the French word 'humeur', 'jury' and
'impérialisme' are loan words which are interesting in their
own right. They tell us something about the way French and
English have evolved, and about the relationship the two
cultures have had with each other over a longish period. The

French borrowed imperialism from English in the nineteenth century because Britain was an imperialistic nation in a sense that they, at the time, were not.[12] The adjective 'impérial' had different connotations. It referred either to the régime of one of the Napoleons, or to the soldiers or supporters of the Holy Roman Empire. The word 'jury' came in because it evoked an institution which the French did not have at the time, which they began to adopt in practice only with the people's juries of 1791, and which was not formalised until after the July monarchy of 1830. 'Humour' was needed because 'humeur', dating back to the eleventh century, had when used by itself acquired the meaning of a mood, generally a bad one. 'Compétition', a sporting term introduced in the eighteenth century, seems in no danger at the moment of replacing 'concurrence' in a commercial context.

'Franglais' words, in contrast, are much less interesting. They clearly are intruders, even though they may sometimes be necessary ones which stand a good chance of finishing up by being fully assimilated. At the moment, however, they tend to have little or no history behind them, and to be interesting for often fairly transient social reasons. Only loan words which have been fully absorbed into the language offer a degree of linguistic and intellectual interest in their own right, and it is not always words of English origin which are most informative about the way cultures as well as languages enrich one another. 'Douche', for example, came into French as a result of the description which Montaigne published of the visit he had made to Italy in 1580, and where he had encountered 'una doccia' (a shower). It is perhaps an indication that the Italians, a more cultured people than the French in the sixteenth century, also washed themselves more frequently. In another context, as T. E. Hope observes in his *Lexical Borrowings in the Romance Languages: a Critical Study of Italianisms in French and Gallicisms in Italian from 1100 to 1900*,

> The whole contribution of Italy to the fifteenth-century military scene is called up by the word 'soldat' (1451). It replaced 'homme d'armes', 'sergent', and other words evocative of feudal levies, just as the Italian professional private

soldier replaced the liegeman of the feudal host. On the one hand, we have the Crusades; on the other Machiavelli.[13]

There is little in 'la querelle du franglais' which is as intriguing as the way in which words of similar appearance take on different meanings in different languages. The word 'gentilhomme' in French has always meant a nobleman, and nothing more. In Italian, in contrast, as Professor Hope also observes, 'gentiluomo' was already being used by Boccaccio, in 1348, in the sense of 'a man of worth', just as it was to take on a comparable meaning in English in the eighteenth century. It is a linguistic difference which reflects the greater importance in French society of the hereditary aristocracy, where the feudal order was not shaken, as it was in Italy, from the fifteenth century onwards, by the rise of the cities, or fundamentally changed, as it was in Britain, when the revolutions of the seventeenth century followed on from the social impact of the Tudors and the demographic effects of the Wars of the Roses. In France, where feudalism was not formally abolished until after 1789, the concept of the gentleman never developed, the term used to indicate approval being 'honnête homme', an expression with different associations.[14] 'Gentilhomme' continued to mean an aristocrat – as in Molière's *Le Bourgeois Gentilhomme*, the would-be nobleman – and the word 'gentleman' did not come into common usage until the nineteenth century.[15]

In his exhaustive study of the words which the French and English have borrowed from one another, *Les Relations de la France et de l'Angleterre d'après le vocabulaire* (1939), Professor Fraser Mackenzie emphasises the complementary nature of our two cultures. He argues that the debt which English civilisation owes to France is, like the vocabulary of English itself, even greater than the French debt to England and to English, and that both countries have benefited immensely from the exchange. France took from Britain, especially in the eighteenth century, the terms needed to create a democratic system of government – 'tolérance' in 1722, 'balance des pouvoirs' in 1734, 'législature' and 'opposition' in 1745 – while virtually every word in English which describes ecclesiastical organisation and polite behaviour, to say nothing of fashion or food, is of French origin.[16]

There are, in contrast, relatively few 'franglais' terms which offer a comparable intellectual or social interest, or which support Professor Fraser Mackenzie's contention that the study of the words that English and French have given each other suggests the existence of

> une civilisation anglo-française où la différence de mentalité des deux peuples riverains de la Manche ne serait pas plus sensible que celle qui existe entre les habitants du nord et du midi de la France (an Anglo-French civilisation in which the difference in mentality of the two peoples on either side of the Channel is no more perceptible than the one separating the inhabitants of the north of France from those of the south).[17]

There is, on the contrary, some evidence that many of the English and American words which have come into French during the last fifty or sixty years have neither enriched the language nor given a very favourable idea of English-speaking civilisation, and the description of 'le franglais' in *The New York Times* for 14 March 1994 as

> a hybrid born of the French penchant for borrowing English words and adding something to them

underlined the mongrel-like nature of many recent borrowings. Native speakers of French who are sensitive to the beauties of their language may well be right to feel a certain hostility towards words which often epitomise the least attractive aspects of American and English society, and to be less than enthusiastic about the world of pop music, drug-taking and sexual deviance which is so frequently evoked by 'franglais' terms. The two private radio stations in Paris which aim their broadcasts most obviously at young people have the ostentatiously 'franglais' names of Fun Radio and Skyrock. When, on 3 January 1995, a policeman was shot and killed in Nice, one of the presenters on Skyrock commented several times: 'un flic est mort à Nice. C'est plutôt une bonne nouvelle' (a cop dead in Nice. Rather a good piece of news).

On 27 January 1995, Fun Radio broadcast a commentary describing Auschwitz as a pleasant country house which had recently come on to the market and which needed only a few repairs to be made into a very attractive holiday centre.

In 1984, in *Les movements de mode expliqués aux parents.*[18] Hector Obalk, Alain Soral and Alexandre Pasche were more successful in raising a laugh when they set out both to explain the way adolescents behaved in France in the 1980s and to make fun of them. Only in the middle section, devoted to youngsters who set out to be BCBG ('bon chic bon genre'; respectably fashionable) did French terms become more numerous than terms of American or English origin. The words which dominated in the other four sections – significantly entitled 'Le Pop', 'Le Punk', 'La New-Wave Cool' and 'Le Fun' – were not only of very recent import from across the Channel or from the other side of the Atlantic. They were also terms whose associations could send nothing but a shudder of horror up the spine of any parents anxious for their offspring to lead a normal, healthy and successful life.

It may nevertheless be true, as I shall argue, that the law is not the most appropriate instrument for dealing with the matter, and that languages have their own means of solving their problems without state intervention. It may also be that it is as dangerous to meddle with the mechanisms whereby a language develops as it is to interfere with the process of genetic inheritance. It is also the case, as I shall again argue, that it is the least attractive sectors of French society that are sometimes the most vocal in their hostility to 'le franglais', with the result that it is tempting to draw the same kind of conclusions as political commentators in the England of the 1950s when they said that a course of action simultaneously recommended by The Daily Express and The Daily Worker must be wrong. But anyone who thinks that the popularity of 'le franglais' represents a desirable tendency in the development of French should compare the world evoked by words such as 'acid jazz', 'fast food', 'bondage', 'overdose', 'sex shop', or 'zap' with the rich and fertile intellectual exchanges which have taken place over the centuries between our two languages, and which are set out in such detail in *Les Relations de la France et de l'Angleterre d'après le vocabulaire.*

'Franglais' words also tend to have another disadvantage in that the only linguistic interest which they offer lies in the fact that they sound as odd in English as they do in French. Like 'baba cool' for what used to be known as a 'cool chick', 'le footing', in the sense of taking exercise by walking, 'un pressing' to designate a dry-cleaner's, or 'reality show' in the sense of live television, they are as illustrative of the mistakes that people can make about one another's language as the use in English of the term 'palais de danse' to describe what the French call 'un dancing', or the description of the person who used to show you to your seat in the cinema as an 'usherette' when the French call her 'une ouvreuse'. Most English readers of Sartre's *Les chemins de la liberté* are as baffled by what might have gone into the drink known as 'un cherry cobbler – in fact, a mixture of sherry, lemon and sugar – as they are by the behaviour of the main character Mathieu, and as long ago as 1784 Beaumarchais was able to raise a laugh at the expense of popular stereotypes by giving Figaro a speech in which he claimed that all you needed to say in English was 'Goddam'.[19] The kind of English or American words which are most noticeable as intruders in modern French often have as little intellectual content and are as remote from actual usage in the United Kingdom or the United States of the late twentieth century as Figaro's expletive is from modern English.

The publication in 1994 of a dictionary which provided officially acceptable French words to replace the 'franglais' words which were seen as intruders in the language was nevertheless not an unqualified success, and stands as a warning as to what can happen when the state tries to interfere in an area where its qualities are less evident than they are in providing a well-drilled army, a properly organised police force, or an efficiently run social security system. The *dictionnaire des termes officiels de la langue française*, which appeared under the auspices of the Délégation Générale de la Langue française and as one of the publications of the *Journal Officiel de la République Française*, gives a wealth of scientific terms to replace the English expressions which have either taken the place of indigenous French terms, or, more frequently, been borrowed to satisfy an immediate need. In this respect, it follows on from two other substantial publications: the *diction-naire des néologismes officiels*, published in May 1989 by the Commissariat Général de la Langue française, and the revised version which appeared in March 1993 under the title of the *dictionnaire des termes officiels*.[20]

However, the civil servants who worked on the *dictionnaire des termes officiels de la langue française* – each representing his own ministry – do not seem to have been professional linguists, and it does not stand up to a sustained comparison with any of the three most recent bilingual dictionaries to be produced jointly in France and Britain, the Collins–Robert, the Oxford–Hachette and the Larousse French–English: English–French dictionary. It is, naturally, even more inferior to the *Petit Larousse Illustré 1995* and to the 1992 *Petit Robert*, and a glance at the index on p. 295 of this book will reveal a shortcoming inseparable from all attempts to legislate about language. Before the *dictionnaire des termes officiels de la langue française* had even been published, most of the 'franglais' words currently in use in French had acquired enough respect-ability to be included in the *Petit Larousse Illustré 1995*. The work on this dictionary, an annual publication, which de-scribes itself, with a justification which nobody has ever seri-ously questioned, as containing not only what is acceptable to native speakers of the language but what is in practice ac-cepted by them, is a continous process and would therefore have begun in the early 1990s. The *dictionnaire des termes officiels de la langue française*, published in 1994, cannot there-fore avoid being seen as a sustained pushing-shut of the stable door after the horse has not merely bolted but is gambolling merrily in the field. This dictionary may, as I suggest in more detail later, be useful to the specialists for whom it is obviously intended. But as far as the ordinary speaker of French is concerned, it has at the most a kind of archaeological value, comparable with that of the manuals of polite behaviour published some thirty years ago as guidance to nervous mem-bers of the upwardly mobile petty bourgeoisie. The only difference is that it is hard to imagine native speakers of French being nervous enough about their linguistic ability to want to use it.

The *dictionnaire des termes officiels de la langue française* has other defects, one of which stems from its self-imposed limitations. The words included are all terms given approval by the various ministries who have been charged with the task of finding suitable French equivalents for the often highly technical terms which have come into the language from English. This means that a number of obviously English or American terms such as 'baby boom', 'baby-sitting', 'baskets' (in the sense of tennis shoes), 'businessman', 'briefing', 'dealer', 'junior', 'pedigree', 'pull' (in the sense of pullover), 'sex shop', 'slogan', 'thriller', 'top model' and 'trader' are not there, with the result that the *dictionnaire des termes officiels de la langue française* is a disappointing publication for any readers who might come to it in quest of an answer to Étiemble's more general question of how best the French language can be protected against the invasion by Anglo-Saxon terms.

The absence of so many 'franglais' terms from the dictionary to which the French themselves jovially refer as the Toubon, a term which I shall use from now onwards, may well be explicable in the light of the need which its authors had to justify each of their recommendations by quoting chapter and verse from the *Journal Officiel*, the publication in which all French laws and decrees are officially registered. The contrast between the 'franglais' terms which are missing and those which are there nevertheless creates a very odd effect. In a democratic society, one of the basic features of the rule of law is the idea that where the law is silent, freedom of choice in speech and action is absolute. If, therefore, a word of obviously English or American origin is not included in the Toubon, then the presupposition is that it is perfectly all right to use it. But given the nature of the campaign against 'le franglais', it is strange that the noun 'camping', in the sense of a camp-site, should be absent from the Toubon, while the term 'camping-car', for which the recommended form is 'autocaravane', should be there. It is equally strange that the very common expression from the world of economics, 'stop and go', should not be in the Toubon, while the much rarer and more technical 'stop loss', an insurance term for which the Toubon recommends the translation of 'excédent de pertes', should be included.

There are other imperfections in the Toubon, one of which was emphasised by Gilbert Gantier in a long speech on the loi Toubon in the debate in the Assemblée Nationale on 3 May 1994. Arguing that any issue concerning the French language transcended party interests, but reminding his colleagues that he had for several years been spokesman for his group, the Union pour la Démocratie Française, on financial matters, he warned against what he saw as the excessive number of recommendations in the *dictionnaire des termes officiels de la langue française*. Was it entirely reasonable, he asked, when you saw the word 'Pressing' (a dry-cleaner's) on every street in Paris and the provinces, to impose the Toubon's 'Pressage', or to insist that the short news bulletin that comes on the television at eight o'clock every evening should be called not 'le flash' but 'l'éclair de huit heures'? Requirements of this kind, he argued, might well make the loi Toubon follow its predecessor, the loi Bas-Lauriol, and become 'une loi mort-née' (stillborn),[21] and it would be misleading, as the remarks I have quoted by Michel Tournier and Alain Gresse indicate, to see the French as totally united behind the attempt to use legal means to protect their language.

The apparent desire of the Toubon to abolish words which have been in everyday use for many years is paralleled by its failure to mention some of the more obvious ones for which one would like to see a genuine French equivalent. Some of these omissions are noted in the Introduction to Part II as well as in the individual entries. The Toubon is not free of mistakes. One at least of these is due to sheer ignorance of the different meanings which what seems to be the same word can have in French and English. 'To dope', for example, when used to denote an illegal practice on the racecourse, means in English to inject drugs to make a horse run more slowly. 'Doper' in French means to use drugs to make a horse run faster; or, increasingly, to introduce measures to stimulate the economy. Other entries are misleading through what they miss out, as when 'a walk-over' is rendered as simply as 'forfait', the meaning which the word has when you win because the other team does not turn up. There is no indication of the equally frequent meaning of a walk-over in English, that of a victory by a very large score over poor opposition.

The Toubon is ingeniously constructed. Although the index does not itself give the gender of the French words recommended, the reader can discover what this is by turning backwards to the main body of the text. The fact that the index gives the English terms to be avoided first, in alphabetical order, before offering the official French equivalent, makes the book very useful to the specialists for whom it is primarily intended. The computer scientist, for example, anxious to discover what the official term is for the abbreviation 'wysiwyg' (= what you see is what you get) immediately finds out that it is 'tel écran – tel écrit'. The biologist looking for an acceptable term for 'host cell' also discovers without much difficulty that it is 'cellule hôte', while the marketing manager in search of the correct term for 'blister pack' will be told on official authority that it is 'habillage transparent'. Problems nevertheless start to recur when the terms involved are less arcane. The reader turning from the index to the main body of the text will discover, for example, that the word 'fortin' is masculine when used in the sense of a military bunker, as is also the word 'ensable' when referring to a bunker on the golf course. But were the reader to take this latter suggestion seriously when actually on the golf course, or even to use the alternative, feminine term of 'une fosse de sable', heads might be shaken in wonder as well as in pity. Everyone playing golf in France uses the English terms, just as anyone going in for fencing in England rapidly learns to say 'en garde' or 'touché'.

There are other entries in the Toubon which make it vulnerable to the criticism which Lady Bracknell voiced of the Court Guide when she commented in *The Importance of Being Earnest* that she had 'known strange errors in that publication'. 'At the money' may well be correctly translated as 'à parité'; but it is not a term normally used in English, and does not figure either in the 1990 Chambers or the *Oxford English Dictionary*. The same is true of 'bus mailing', which the Toubon recommends be translated as 'multipostage', a term more commonly rendered into English as 'bulk posting'; or, as Jean-Pierre Colignon claims in his *La cote des mots*, 'direct mail'.[22] Most air travellers have heard of a 'no show', somebody who does not turn up to take their seat. A 'go show', in the sense of a traveller prepared to take a seat which suddenly becomes available, may well be correctly translated into French as 'imprévu'. But the term more frequently used by English-speaking airlines is surely 'stand-by'. The index of the Toubon also includes the term 'touch and go', explained in the body of the text as the equivalent of the French expression 'posé – décollé' used by the pilot of an aeroplane when he aborts a landing, simply touching down and immediately taking off again. It is not the way any native speaker of English uses the expression.

It is true that there is excellent precedence in France for producing strange guides to our two languages. The poet Mallarmé, who taught English for a living, published in 1877 a book called *Les Mots Anglais*. It included a number of allegedly French proverbs which he suggested that his pupils translate into English in order to improve their ability to write the language. These included 'Qui peut raser un oeuf?' (Who can shave an egg?), 'Vous êtes un honnête homme et je suis votre oncle; et cela fait deux mensonges' (You are an honest man and I am your uncle; and that makes two lies), 'Tricotez à mon chien une paire de culottes et à mon chat un habit à queue' (Knit my dog a pair of breeches and my cat a tail coat).[23] But although the Toubon has clearly some way to go yet, its suggested translation of 'acknowledgement' as 'aperçu', of the mysterious 'hasty crossing' as 'franchissement dans la foulée' (it is when you go across a stretch of water without having made sufficient preparation in advance), or its proposal that 'crashworthiness' be rendered as 'résistance à l'écrasement' and 'jerrican' as 'nourrice', have a potentially Mallarmean ring. The French themselves have not failed to notice this, as when a cartoon in *Le Point* for 26 March 1994, no. 1123, showed a motorist who had run out of petrol glaring with fury at his son, who had brought him a lady sufficiently mature and well endowed to perform the functions of what the word 'nourrice' normally means, which are those of a wet nurse. The balloon coming out of the motorist's mouth read: 'J'aurais dû dire Jerrycan' (I should have said Jerrycan) and the caption says simply: 'Parlons français' (Let's speak French).

The authors of the Toubon should nevertheless not be criticised too harshly. They were faced with a very difficult task, and their dictionary was clearly not aimed at the general reader. It was intended less for ordinary French people than for specialists in pure and applied science, economics, engineering, or medicine, who come up against what Lynne Wilcox described in an article entitled 'Coup de Langue' published in *Modern and Contemporary France* in 1994 as

> the practical effects of the growing hegemony of English within France, particularly in the field of commerce, where banks, advertisers and industry resort more and more frequently to the use of English, and in science and technology, as witnessed by the ever-increasing number of scientific conferences held in France but which use English as a working language.[24]

Whether passing laws is the right way to deal with the problem is naturally another question, especially when language changes so quickly.

It is also important not to confuse two issues: the need which some French people have to use English rather than French in certain contexts, and the use of English or American terms in what is ostensibly French. The two issues are naturally connected. Both underline the fact that English-speaking civilisation plays a more important role in the modern world than does French. It is the awareness of how much the French language has declined from its earlier predominance that makes the French so sensitive to the use of English or American terms by native speakers of their language. This is why, although I shall be dealing, in this book, mainly with the questions posed directly by the presence of English and American expressions in modern French, I shall try to look at the problem of 'le franglais' against the wider background of France's relationship to the outside world in general. On 1 December 1994, *Le Nouvel Observateur*, no. 1569, quoted the then Prime Minister, Édouard Balladur, as saying:

> Depuis un demi-siècle, nous sommes taraudés par un doute: sommes-nous encore un grand people? (For half a century,

we have been obsessed by a doubt: are we still a great people?)

The debate about 'le franglais' rarely moves far away from this preoccupation.

The more detailed and specific criticisms to which the Toubon is vulnerable offer another reason for arguing that 'la querelle du franglais' is often only incidentally about language. What appears, at first sight, to be an argument about whether one should say 'jumbo jet' or 'gros porteur', speak of a 'promoteur' rather than a 'promoter', or write 'boum' instead of 'boom', is often the symptom of an uncertainty which the French feel about their national identity and relationship with the outside world, especially when this involves the United States of America. If the French were primarily concerned with 'le franglais' as a purely linguistic phenomenon, and were genuinely interested in the problem of the relationship between English and French, the *dictionnaire des termes officiels de la langue française* would be a much better and much more reliable book than it is. It is because their eye is so much more on a number of political targets, and especially the role of the United States in the modern world, that the various attempts which the French authorities have made to produce convincing alternatives to the 'franglais' expressions which have made their way into the language so often fall short of the mark.

It is significant that the words in the Toubon which the French are recommended not to use all come from English and American. It is English-speaking culture which is seen as a threat, not that of France's continental neighbours. Although there is a brief annexe in the Toubon giving the normal French for the Latin terms still used in a legal context, there is no mention of words from Italian, German, or Spanish. In French, as in English, it is impossible to discuss music without using Italian. But nobody in France seems to find this objectionable, and I have not, in several senses of the word, been able to find a French equivalent to the Percy Grainger who insisted on referring to a piano as a 'keyed-hammerstring' a composer as a 'tone-wright' and who sought to replace the Italian 'fortissimo' by 'louden lots'.[25] The last time that the French tried to discourage the use of Italian words was in the sixteenth century, with the publication in 1578 of Henri Estienne's *Deux dialogues du nouveau langage français italianisé et autrement déguisé*, a work very similar to *Parlez-vous franglais* in the largely invented nature of many of its examples. But it did not, as Professor Hope observes, have much effect, since by the reign of Louis XIV Italian was accepted as the foreign language *par excellence* in France, and what had started off as italianisms had by and large been absorbed into the language.

With the passage of time, something similar will almost certainly happen to 'franglais' words. They may simply fall out of usage because they have become as quaint and old-fashioned as 'cherry cobbler', or the use by Balzac of the word 'fashionable' as a noun when talking about the elegant young men of Restoration France. Or, if this does not happen, they will gradually become as much an integral part of French as words such as 'assistant', 'bar', 'coalition', 'docker', 'entraîner', 'film', 'gramophone', 'hypnotisme', 'international', 'jungle', 'kaléidoscope', 'libéral', 'microphone', 'négocier', 'officiel', 'parlementaire', 'qualifica-tion', 'radical', 'sélection', 'tourisme', 'utilitaire', 'vapeur', or 'wagon'. These all appear in Josette Rey-Debove and Gilberte Gagnon's invaluable 1980 *Dictionnaire des Anglicismes*, together with many more terms which have long since ceased to be seen even as loan words, still less as expressions deserving of censure.

This is very much what has happened to the French words which suddenly came into English during the War of Spanish Succession (1701–13), and which led Addison to formulate a wish in no. 165 of *The Spectator*, on Saturday, 8 September 1712, that there should be in our constitution certain men

> set apart as superintendents of our language, to hinder any words of foreign currency from passing among us; and in particular to prohibit any French phrases from becoming current in this kingdom, when those of our own stamp are altogether as valuable.

For the words which so aroused Addison's ire, almost all of

which dealt with military matters, have either disappeared or become so thoroughly a part of English that there are very few people conscious of the fact that terms such as 'battalion', 'corps', 'reconnoitre' or 'resistance' were originally seen as unwelcome gallicisms.[26] The words which I have chosen to discuss in Part II of this book are, like the words to which Addison took such exception, clearly intruders at the moment. They are words to which a purist might object, and which do, in some cases, seem to be used for reasons of snobbery rather than because the absence of a satisfactory French equivalent creates a genuine need for them.

'Franglais' words sometimes have the advantage of throwing light on what is happening in France. The use of the term 'big bang', for example, is not restricted to the political context in which it was used by Michel Rocard. As is shown by the entry in Section IIa, its occurrence can be used to illustrate the existence of more general tendencies in France society, as well as differences between English-speaking and French-speaking culture which go beyond the merely linguistic. My use of 'franglais' words to discuss these tendencies will, I hope, give to *Le Franglais: Forbidden English, Forbidden American: Law, Politics and Language in Contemporary France* the same place of honour as a book which people place for their guests to browse through in the loo (US john) as was held by the earlier study *Faux Amis and Key Words: a Dictionary-Guide to French Language, Culture and Society through Lookalikes and Confusables* (US *Mistakeable French*) which I published in collaboration with Howard Evans in 1985. This, in turn, will compensate for my discovery that the seeker for examples of 'franglais' words in the French press often feels like the Joe Gargery who described the pleasures of reading to Pip, in Chapter VII of *Great Expectations*:

> Give me a good book, or a good newspaper, and sit me down afore a good fire, and I ask no better. Lord . . . when you *do* come to a J and a O, and says you: 'Here, at last, is a J-O, Joe', how interesting reading is!

Joe must have often thumbed his way through some rather disappointing pages, and the second cultural reference which underlines a central aspect of 'la querelle du franglais' takes place in Conan Doyle's *Silver Blaze*.

'Is here any point to which you would wish to draw my attention?'
'To the curious incident of the dog in the night-time.'
'The dog did nothing in the night-time.'
'That was the curious incident.'

You do not, however, need the genius of Holmes to appreciate the significance of the fact that you can read whole pages in *Le Monde* or *Le Nouvel Observateur* without coming across any more linguistically offensive term than 'management', and listen for hours to the French radio without noticing more than the very occasional 'franglais' word. 'Outsider' naturally occurs from time to time in the racing forecasts by Lionel Ovadia for the 'tiercé', 'quarté' and 'quarté plus'[27] which take up four minutes every hour on the hour on France-Inter. But other English terms are in a way remarkable for their absence, and it is only in relation to the audio-visual media that English or American words occur with any frequency in French in an artistic or cultural context. Apart from the term 'thriller', for which there seems to be no equivalent, discussion of the novel takes place without anglicisms, and this is even more the case with philosophy, poetry and the theatre. There is a marked contrast between the impression given by the 2,400 words listed in the Toubon, and the experience of actually reading French books, newspapers and magazines. There is something obsessional in *Parlez-vous franglais?* which comes out in Étiemble's comment that he spent four and half years building up his set of examples and ten years writing the book, and it is quite easy, on a more amusing note, to produce the kind of cartoon with which Jacques Faizant entertained the readers of *Le Point* no. 1098 for 2 October 1993. This showed a young man explaining to his girlfriend how he had obtained 'un side-job' which required him to 'rewriter des dialogues pour des serials qui passent à la télé' (rewrite dialogues for serials on the telly). He did this, he explained, 'en free-lance' and he described how 'le dernier soap' (the last soap) that he had 'rewrité' (rewritten) was 'l'histoire d'un tycoon dont les fils est un golden boy, washed-out, et qui sniffe' (the story of a tycoon whose son was a golden boy who was washed out because he sniffed cocaine).

The young man carried on in the same vein, talking about 'des hold-ups', evoking somebody who had 'un nervous break-down', and wondering whether the scenario he was writing would turn out to be 'thriller ou love story avec happy end'. He then explained to his girlfriend that the reason why he had been chosen to do the job was that the television critics always complained if the actors did not speak perfect French ('Vous savez comment sont les critiques de télé? Toujours à râler si les acteurs ne causent pas un français impeccable').

Like all Jacques Faizant's cartoons, it was very funny. But it no more represented the way the French normally talk than the exchange of foreign phrases such as 'après vous', 'quel dommage', 'mea culpa', 'j'y suis, j'y reste' that takes up the first two minutes of Tom Stoppard's 1976 play *Dirty Linen* represents the way English people normally speak.

As is shown by the example of Michel Rocard's speech in February 1993, everyone uses words of English or American from time to time. Some groups, such as advertising men or international bankers, may use some of them a great deal, just as chefs the world over use French. But just as the pages of *Le Monde* or *Le Figaro* offer few examples of 'le franglais', so you can read a history book such as Henri Mendras's excellent *La Seconde Révolution française, 1965–1984* without coming across any English words apart from 'baby boom' and 'melting pot'.[28] It may be, as I point out later, that 'franglais' words become slightly more frequent when you go down the social and intellectual scale, as well as when you look at publications aimed at the under twenty-fives, but this is not always the case. In 1961, seven years after the appearance of *Parlez-vous franglais?*, and consequently at the very time when the French language had, according to Étiemble, been totally overrun by 'franglais' words, Christiane Rochefort published a highly successful novel called *Les petits enfants du siècle* (Grasset, Paris). It was a first-person narrative, ostensibly told by a working-class teenager, and was widely praised for the accuracy with which it reproduced current colloquial French. It enjoyed, in particular, the status of a novel which French teenagers read without being told to do so by their teachers. But it was also as free of words of English or American origin as the stable in *Silver Blaze* was of the warning barks of the watch-dog.

The impression that 'franglais' words are relatively rare when French is looked at as a whole was confirmed in 1980, when the best-known firm specialising in the publication of dictionaries in France, la Société du Nouveau Littré produced its *Dictionnaire des Anglicismes*. In their preface, its compilers, Josette Rey-Debove and Gilberte Gagnon, pointed out that the number of words of obviously Anglo-Saxon origin currently in use in French did not constitute more than 2.5 per cent of its total vocabulary. They also quoted a study made of the issues of *Le Monde* between January and May 1977 which showed that only one word out of every 166 was of American or English origin, and pointed out how many words which had started off as anglicisms had long since ceased to be recognised as such.

On 11 November 1994, in a review in *The Times Higher Educational Supplement* of the recently published Routledge's *French Technical Dictionary/Dictionnaire Technique Anglais*, Martin Ince commented:

> The domination of English in all fields of science and technology might be expected to have produced a particularly vicious influx of English words in technical French. But this appears not to have happened. Computers are *ordinateurs*, tape-recorders are *magnétophones* and bursters (the X-ray sort found in astronomy) are *sources à sursaut*.

As might be expected, Étiemble's *Parlez-vous franglais?* tells a different story, though not one which is very believable. His claim in 1954 was that there were from 3,000 to 5,000 words of obviously English or American origin currently in use in French, without counting those which were modelled on Anglo-Saxon expressions.[29] Although this may be the case if one were to count every single one, including every hapax legomenon such as Michèle Fitoussi's 'Daddy blues',[30] it is clearly impossible on purely practical grounds, since nobody would understand what was being said. Étiemble's other claim that more than a quarter of the average young person's vocabulary is made up of words of American origin,[31] which have replaced the normal French words, is also difficult to prove statistically, and even a radio station such as Fun Radio does not use anything like that number of 'franglais' words. Neither is there much support in daily life for Étiemble's vision of Anglophone culture as nothing but a menace. The initials WC, designating a water-closet, came into French in 1923. The thing itself, as visitors to France at the time of the publication of *Parlez-vous franglais?* will recall, often seemed of more ancient and unsatisfactory origin. It is only in the last fifteen years that the loos in most French hotels have begun to reach an acceptable standard, and that an 'en suite' bathroom – an expression equally absent from the Toubon and from the French language – has become as easy to obtain in a Paris hotel as it always has been in the cheapest motel in downtown Phoenix.

The *Dictionnaire des Anglicismes* is not the only publication to cast doubt on the claim made by other people in addition to Étiemble that French is being swamped by an invasion of terms first used in America or Britain. In 1987, one of the most distinguished French linguists, Claude Hagège, published a book entitled *Le français et les siècles*. He was, at the time, Directeur d'Études at the École Pratique des Hautes Études in Paris and Professor of Linguistics at the University of Poitiers, and has since been appointed to the Collège de France, so that his criticism of the French obsession with 'le franglais', and of the associated attempt to use the law to enforce linguistic norms, could not come from a more respectable source. Like all professional linguists who have discussed 'le franglais', Claude Hagège points out that any influence which English might be having on French has not so far affected the heart of its language. Neither its morphology nor its accidence and syntax had, he argued in 1987, been in any way affected, and there is no evidence that the situation has changed. The only example of the use of an English word to fulfil a syntactical purpose which I have come across is the working-class 'Ma mère, elle avait toujours l'estomac détraqué *because* la charcuterie' (Mum always had something wrong with her insides because of the charcuterie), paralleled in the Larousse dictionary by the invented example 'Elle n'est pas revenue *because* sa maladie' (She hasn't come back because of her illness), and the remark in the phonetic spelling affected by Raymond Queneau in *Zazie dans le métro* that everyone drank coffee after dinner '*bicose* Charles et Gabriel bossaient de nuit' (because Charles and Gabriel worked at night).[32]

Jacques Cellard, who for years wrote a regular column in *Le Monde* on linguistic questions, made the same point about the total absence of any impact of English on the grammar of French, and his remark underlines one of the general rules governing language brought out in 1947 by Marcel Cohen in his *Histoire d'une langue: le français*. In any language, he pointed out, grammar and pronunciation 'forment un système impénétrable' (make up an impenetrable system). They have, in other words, a kind of a water-tight quality to them, and can no more be infiltrated by outside elements than can the rules of chess. Vocabulary, in contrast, is what Cohen described as 'inorganisé et pénétrable' (unorganised and penetrable)'[33] as open to either permanent or temporary visitors as the language of clothes. Although his book has a certain period charm, being written from the strongly left-wing viewpoint fashionable in Paris immediately after 1945, it makes no mention of any invasion of American words, while André Thérive's 1954 *Libre histoire de la langue française* considers the allegations that French is being taken over by English, only to dismiss them with the remark that there are not more than about a hundred obvious anglicisms currently in use in French. My own Joe Gargery-like quest for examples of 'franglais' nouns actually used in the French press and radio, as distinct from the technical terms listed in the Toubon, has come up with only about three times that number, and a more diligent search for French expressions in common use in English – these terms are listed in Part III – might well have equalled this figure.

It is not only the reactions of professional linguists, and the uncertainty of the authors of the *dictionnaire des termes officiels de la langue française* as to what is normal English usage, which support the view that the argument about 'le franglais' is more about politics than about language. The political drive of Étiemble's study is particularly visible in his refusal to remove the references to racial discrimination in the Deep South from later editions of *Parlez-vous franglais?* You would never guess, from the 1973 edition, that the declaration of the Supreme Court in Brown v. the Board of Education of Topeka to the effect that 'separate educational facilities are inherently unequal', dates back to May 1954, the year in which *Parlez-vous franglais?* was first published. When the député, Bruno Bourg-Broc, speaking from the benches occupied by Jacques Chirac's *Rassemblement pour la République*, said in the debate in the Assemblée Nationale in May 1994 that the French must

> lutter contre l'hégémonie linguistique, fer de lance d'une hégémonie culturelle et économique (struggle against linguistic hegemony, spearhead of a cultural and economic hegemony)[34]

he was expressing an anti-Americanism that was as virulent in its own way as the attacks on the USA when *Parlez-vous franglais?* appeared at the height of the Cold War. Étiemble's original and highly ironic injunction, in 1954, never to forget that

> le sabir atlantique, c'est la langue du camp de la liberté, celui de Franco, de Salazar, de Tchiang-Kai-Chek (Atlantic jargon is the language of the camp of liberty, of Franco, Salazar and Tchiang-Kai-Chek)[35]

did not disappear from the 1984 edition of his book, when all these particular 'bêtes noires' were dead, and objections to 'le franglais', like the general phenomenon of anti-Americanism in France, are one of several areas in which the extreme right and the extreme left come together. This is shown by some of the quotations in Chapter 2, and Claude Hagège even goes so far as to lay some of the blame on General de Gaulle, speaking of the attacks on 'le franglais' as providing a 'linguistic alibi'[36] for the jealousy felt by the French at the way they have been supplanted as top nation by the Americans. Although this is not something which an Englishman should say off his own bat, there is a temptation to agree with him. Anglophobia has always been a characteristic of the French right, and the end of the Cold War has done nothing to reduce the anti-Americanism of the French Communist Party. The Communist Party newspaper *L'Humanité*, like the Communist *députés* who took part in the debate on the loi Toubon, expressed great support for a move which it depicted as seeking to defend French culture against 'l'impérialisme culturel américain' (American cultural imperialism). But it also offered on 1 August 1994 what may have been one of its rare examples of deliberate humour as well as an involuntary linguistic parallel to the anecdote about the visitor to a Belgian brothel who was anxious to check up that all the girls were free from infection. 'Mais, mon pauvre monsieur,' replied the owner,

> on ne peut jamais savoir, d'un jour à l'autre. Il y a des vérolés partout. Tenez, moi qui vous parle . . . . (But, my poor dear sir, you can never know, from one day to the next. There are people with the pox everywhere. Look, take my own case . . . .)

What *L'Humanité* wrote was:

> Le Conseil Constitutionnel a relooké la loi Toubon sur la langue française, en déclarant out deux de ses dispositions les plus restrictives. (The Conseil Constitutionnel has given a different look to the loi Toubon on the French Language, and rejected two of its most restrictive articles.)

NOTES

1 For Rocard's speech, see *Le Monde*, 18 February 1993. For Barre, idem, 23 March. In a more literary age, Rocard might have expressed the same idea by quoting the remark which Néron makes in Racine's *Britannicus*: 'J'embrasse mon rival, mais c'est pour l'étouffer' (I embrace my rival, but in order to smother him).

2 See *L'Événement du Jeudi* no. 497, 5 May 1994. The term 'camembert' evokes a populist, grass-roots conservatism, as opposed to the Highgate humanist, radical chic associations of caviare. Michel Rocard, a former pupil of the École Nationale d'Administration and a member of the Inspection des Finances, is very

much a member of the French intellectual élite, some of whose
characteristics are mentioned under the entry 'must' in
IIa.

  Unless otherwise indicated, all the expressions connected with
French administration, education, or politics mentioned in this
study of 'le franglais' can be found in Philip Thody and Howard
Evans, *Faux Amis and Key Words: a Dictionary-Guide to French
Language, Culture and Society through Lookalikes and Confusables*,
Athlone Press, London, 1985.

3 See Chapter 3, note 3 for details.

4 See Sarah Tulloch (camp.), *The Oxford Dictionary of New Words:
a Popular Guide to Words in the News*, Oxford Press, Oxford
University 1991.

5 The camp in the north-east suburbs of Paris where, during the
Occupation, Jews were parked on their way to the gas
chambers.

6 Quoted on p. 127 of Volume II of Fraser MacKenzie's *Les
Relations de la France et de l'Angleterre d'après le vocabulaire*, Droz,
Paris, 1939.

7 For the link between opposition to attempts to use the law to
protect the French language and the concept of the free market
in economics, see the entry 'stopper' in IIb; and p. 77.

8 See Fraser MacKenzie, op. cit., Vol. I, p. 49, for details.

9 *Les Temps Modernes*, August 1952, pp. 291–303. For the earlier
article, see 1949, pp. 1690–8.

  Although Étiemble's first name is René, he always omits it in
his published work. He is fond of controversy, and in 1952
created a considerable stir in the French literary world by publishing a long denunciation of what he called the myth of Rimbaud.
Like many of the authors who wrote in *Les Temps Modernes*, he
was very hostile to the United States, and in 1947 wrote a long
review of Camus's *La Peste* (*The Plague*), in which he accused the
Americans not only of being violently racist in their attitude to
Negroes, Mexicans and Jews, but also of preparing to launch an
atomic war (*Les Temps Modernes*, Paris, 1949, pp. 1690–8).

10 p. 244 of *Parlez-vous franglais?*, Gallimard, Collection 'Idées',
Paris, 1973. All references are to this edition. The most frequently
used French dictionary, the *Petit Robert*, gives the definition of
'débutante', in French, as that of 'Jeune fille qui sort pour la
première fois dans la haute société' (young lady going out into
high society for the first time). The shortened form might nevertheless be legitimately considered an example of 'le franglais'

and not a proper French word. For 'les deux cents familles', see IIa, note 2.

11 His term for a language made up of words of American origin. For quotations see op. cit., 1, 190, 285, 312, 311, 230, 194 and 297 ('la langue de l'homme blanc civilisé' [the language of the civilised white man]; not a term which would be acceptable nowadays, whether in circles concerned with political correctness or elsewhere); and for his general argument, *passim*. On the back of the 1991 edition, this became 'le langage de l'homme blanc cultivé'.

12 See 'self-government' in IIa.

13 Blackwell, Oxford, 1971, Vol. I, p. 60. The dedication of this book to the memory of Ted Hope evokes a scholar of distinction, a man of great physical courage, a firm friend and the ideal colleague. His death in 1987 prevented him from undertaking the study of 'le franglais' to which his scholarship fitted him so eminently.

14 Its primary meaning, developed in the seventeenth century, is that of a cultivated, highly civilised person, who showed consideration for his fellows and fitted well into polite society.

15 For an entertaining and instructive history of this concept, see Simon Raven, *The English Gentleman*, Anthony Blond, London, 1961. For a learned and invaluable account of the history of borrowings from English, see the *Dictionnaire des Anglicismes: Les mots anglais et américains en français*, comp. Josette Rey-Debove and Gilberte Gagnon, Les Usuels du Robert, Paris, 1980.

16 op. cit., Vol. I, pp. 160–70 and Vol. II, pp. 51, 163 and *passim*. See also part III of this book.

17 op. cit., p. 155.

18 Best translated as 'The latest fashions explained to parents'. Published by Robert Laffont, Paris, 1984; republished in the Livres de Poche in 1985. In addition to being very amusing, it is a book which arouses feelings of profoundest sympathy for parents of French teenage children.

19 See *Le Mariage de Figaro*, Act I, Scene iii. The use by Shaw's characters of the term 'goddam' to designate the English in his 1923 *Saint Joan* follows a usage established in 1450 in the *Mistère du Siège d'Orléans* where the English soldiers are referred to as 'des godons'.

20 Published as Brochure no. 1468 of the *Journal Officiel de la République française*.
      A more readable guide to correct usage is *Logiciel et épinglette:*

Guide des termes francophones recommandés, compiled by Gina Mamavi and Loïc Depecker, published by the Documentation française in 1992 under the auspices of the *Délégation Générale de la Langue française*. 'Logiciel' is the widely accepted term for 'software', and 'épinglette' for 'pin's' (see the entry for that word in IId).

21 The debates on the loi Toubon took place in the Sénat on Tuesday 11 April, Wednesday 12 April and Thursday 13 April 1994; and in the Assemblée Nationale on Tuesday 3 May 1994. Both debates were fully reported in the *Journal Officiel de la République Française*, the Senate debate on pp. 948–73, 982–1007 and 1078–97, and the debate in the National Assembly (popularly known as the Chambre des Députés) on pp. 1359–71 and 1375–1411. See p. 1394.

22 Le Monde Éditions, 1994, article on 'Mailing'. Jean-Pierre Colignon is chief copy editor on *Le Monde*, and Bertrand Poirot-Delpech, of the Académie Française, points out in his Preface to *La cote des mots* (a title which evokes both the popularity of words and their prestige) how terrifying it is for anyone writing for *Le Monde* to arrive at their desk and see the request to 'ring Colignon'. It is a sure sign that he or she has made a mistake in French.

M. Colignon points out that it took the relevant authorities some ten years to define the term 'publipostage' satisfactorily.

23 See the 1945 Pléiade edition of Mallarmé's *Oeuvres complètes*, p. 1067, 1068 and 1070. I am grateful to my friend and former colleague R. D. D. Gibson for drawing my attention to this aspect of Mallarmé's work.

J. L. Chiflet's *Sky Mr Allgood: Parlons français avec Monsieur Toubon*, Éditions Mille et Une Nuits, Paris, 1994, a successor to the very popular *Sky My Husband!* and other works, is a contemporary example of writing whose humour depends on the literal translation of idioms; e.g. 'Jamais esprit' as 'Never mind'.

24 Lynne Wilcox, 'Coup de langue: the Amendment to Article 2 of the Constitution: an Equivocal Interpretation of Linguistic Pluralism?' *Modern and Contemporary France*, 1994, pp. 269–78.

25 See John Bird, *Percy Grainger*, Elek Books, London, 1976. The composer of 'In an English country garden' also had other eccentricities. He would run to concerts in shorts, gym vest and running shoes, and was an enthusiastic sado-masochist.

For an earlier attempt to replace words of Latin or Greek origin in English by what were deemed to be more authentic Anglo-Saxon terms, see note 5 to Chapter 2 of Part I.

26 This point was not mentioned by those taking part in the debate in the French Sénat on 13 April 1994, when M. Jacques Habert quoted Addison's remark. See the *Journal Officiel*, p. 972.

27 For the meaning of these terms, see the entry 'Bookmaker' in section VII of Thody and Evans, *Faux Amis and Key Words*.

28 Gallimard, Paris, 1988.

29 op. cit., p. 317. I have not dealt with what are known in French as 'des calques linguistiques', terms so obviously modelled on foreign expressions that they look as though they have been copied on to tracing paper. There are a number of these, of which three of the most obvious are 'la majorité silencieuse' (the silent majority), 'garder un profil bas' (keep a low profile) and 'politiquement correct'. The fact that they are examples of morphologically impeccable French nevertheless makes it hard to see them as examples of 'le franglais'.

30 See the entry 'baby blues' in IIb. As will be seen, Michèle Fitoussi's *Le ras-le-bol des Super Women* (Calmann-Lévy, Paris, 1987), from which this example is taken, is a rich source of 'franglais' words, but sometimes a rather inventive one.

31 op. cit., p. 88.

32 Gallimard, Éditions Folio, 1959, Paris, p. 22. Gabriel, Zazie's uncle, is a large, very hairy man who works as a striptease artist in a homosexual bar.

33 See *Histoire d'une langue: le français*, Éditions d'hier et aujourd'hui, Paris, 1947, p. 125. The explanatory comparisons with games and clothes are my own, the second one reflecting an interest which I have in what can conveniently be termed the semiology of everyday life. This is the study of how the wide variety of non-linguistic as well as linguistic signs which we use to communicate with one another actually work on a day-to-day basis, and is illustrated in the entries on 'boots' in IId and 'catch' in IIc.

Just as I can change the image which I project of myself by wearing a different kind of tie or leaving the buttons of my jacket undone, so I can vary my vocabulary. But even if I try to imitate what I imagine is working-class usage, and make what a purist would see as mistakes, I cannot change the basic syntax of the language to anything like the same extent as I can vary my vocabulary. Similarly, while a language can absorb a large number of loan words, and still remain intelligible, it cannot borrow grammatical structures from another tongue.

34 *Journal Officiel*, p. 1381.

35 op. cit., p. 174. For a quick guide to the intermittent nature of

the democratic tradition in France itself between 1789 to 1962, see my *French Caesarism from Napoleon 1e to Charles de Gaulle*, Macmillan, London, 1989. For anti-Americanism, as a more general phenomenon, see Richard F. Kuisel, *Seducing the French: The Dilemma of Americanisation*, University of California Press, Berkeley/New York/Los Angeles/London, 1993. The quotation about Franco, Salazar and Tchiang-Kai-Chek is on p. 209 of the 1991 edition of *Parlez-vous franglais?*, with a slight change in spelling which produces 'sabir atlantyck'.

36 op. cit., pp. 110–11.

2 Loan words, nationalism and the law

THE CUSTOM OF CONTROL
The decision of the Conseil Constitutionnel to restrict the application of the loi Toubon to situations where French was being used as the official language of the state will be studied in more detail at the beginning of Chapter 3. Most of the entries in the 1994 *dictionnaire des termes officiels de la langue française* were based upon decrees issued by the various ministries in the French government. They were therefore intended in the first instance as guidance for civil servants, and this decision fitted in very logically with the intended readership of what I am calling the Toubon. It was also, more importantly, a sensible and logical choice both on constitutional grounds and in the light of the areas in which 'franglais' words are most often used by private citizens going about their lawful occasions. Such words quite frequently evoke activities whose obvious legality and essentially private nature mean that the state has no right to pass any kind of judgement on them. The assertion by the Conseil Constitutionnel of the right of private citizens to speak and write as they liked provided a most welcome recognition of the limits to be placed on the power of the modern state.

Like a number of the longer-established anglicisms, 'franglais' words recur quite frequently in the vocabulary of sport and constitute one of the most obvious acknowledgements of the contribution made by the English-speaking countries in teaching the world to play; just as the vocabulary of ballet and fencing bear witness to aspects of French culture which have spread throughout the world. The role of English in this context was studied by Ian Pickup in an excellent article entitled 'Anglicisms in the French Sporting Press' (which appeared in December 1988 in *Modern Languages*, vol. 69, no. 4, pp. 218–24) and there is also a whole dictionary, *Le Robert du vocabulaire des sports*.[1] I shall not therefore try to include all the words of English origin which are used to describe sporting activities in France, especially since many of them are also listed in the 1980 *Dictionnaire des Anglicismes* by Josette Rey-Debove and Gilberte Gagnon. Instead, I shall follow Dr Pickup's remark about the 'numerous other borrowings from English which have a broad application outside the realm of sport', and deal principally with the sporting terms taken from English which occur with particular frequency in the realm of my own main interest, which is that of politics. Since there is also a Robert-Collins *Dictionnaire du Management*, published in 1992, I shall again not repeat all the information which it provides. As in other areas, I shall limit myself to discussing the words which occur most frequently in non-specialised publications. Interesting though words often are purely for their own sake, lists of them can become very boring, and there is little interest for the non-specialist in the information offered by the Toubon that the correct French for 'afterburner' is 'réchauffe' or 'post-combustion', or that the English term 'zig zag DNA' should be replaced by 'ADN-Z' or 'ADN zigzag'.

Another area in which 'franglais' words recur with almost as much frequency as they do in sport is in the description of the clothes and leisure activities of the young. These words are listed in Part IId, and I have already commented, in my remarks on Hector Obalk, Alain Soral and Alexandre Pasche's 1984 *Les mouvements de mode expliqués aux parents*, on their tendency to evoke activities of such low prestige in the eyes of official society that some adults might well wish that they did not exist at all. A number of these words are also discussed, in a humorous and non-carping manner which provides a welcome contrast with Étiemble's *Parlez-vous franglais?*, by Pierre Merle in his *Dictionnaire du français branché* (Éditions du Seuil, Paris, 1986), and it is reassuring to be reminded that not all French commentators see the use of 'franglais' words as a potentially hanging matter. The fact nevertheless remains that it is virtually impossible to discuss the world of drugs, popular music, teenage sexuality, or homosexuality without using 'franglais' words, however few these may be in number, and there is an obvious contrast with the kind of French words which occur in English. One of the reasons why the English-speaking peoples have never made any serious objection to the large number of French expressions currently in use in their language lies in the highly favourable associations that such words tend to enjoy. Like 'avant-garde', 'bourgeois', 'chef d'oeuvre', 'dernier cri', 'élite', 'fait accompli', 'hors de combat', 'jeunesse dorée', 'lèse-majesté', 'mélange des genres', 'nouveau riche', 'objet d'art', 'pièce à thèse', 'qui vive', 'raison d'état', 'soi-disant', 'trompe l'oeil', or 'vernissage', they are very valuable from an intellectual point of view. Indeed, it seems at times impossible to analyse cultural phenomena or political events without what Professor Fraser Mackenzie calls the 'nuances de pensée que la France a imposées à l'Angleterre' (the shades of thought which France has imposed on England).[2]

At the same time, other French words in common use in English also have a tendency to evoke activities or ideas of high social prestige. 'Après-ski', 'crème brûlée', 'douceur de vivre', 'embarras de richesse', 'filet mignon', 'gourmet', 'hors d'oeuvre', 'insouciance', 'juste milieu', 'de luxe', 'maître d'hôtel', 'nouvelle cuisine', 'obeisance', 'plat du jour', 'de rigueur', 'tenue de ville' are only a few of the examples which spring immediately to mind. Others are listed in Part III of this book, and even more will occur spontaneously to the native speaker of English, as indeed they did on one occasion to the French ambassador to NATO. He was provoked into using them, as Lord Carrington explained in an interview on the BBC in 1992, by the action of the Italian ambassador, who chose to give his retirement address in English, justifying his choice not only by the fact that he spoke English better than he did French, but by the claim that English was a much richer language. The French ambassador, in fury, made a speech theoretically in English, but in fact composed exclusively of the French expressions which we borrow to enrich our language. As Lord Carrington observed, he had, in selecting which words to use, only the untranslatable expression, 'l'embarras du choix'; it is only unfortunate, as Lord Carrington told me when I wrote to ask if there was a printed version of the text, that it was not seen as being sufficiently formal to be minuted.

French expressions also make a contribution to the vocabulary of the United States. When Jacques Toubon's bill was first discussed in France, early in 1994, press comment in the USA was as unfavourable as it was in Britain or in important sections of the French press, and the same techniques were used to criticise what was widely seen as an example of a nationalism which gave every sign of becoming restrictive and parochial. A fourth leader in *The New York Times* for 17 March 1994, entitled 'Plus Ça Change . . .', began by the statement that 'The *éminences grises* of the French cultural *élite* are in a lather once again', and proceeded to argue that

> A *rendez-vous* with reality is in order here: the innovations that mark the late 20th century come not from Paris but from Tokyo and New York and Detroit. If *le databank* and *le hit parade* have become part of the language used *comme d'habitude*, it's because the things they signify started from somewhere else. Americans don't talk about 'fat liver paste' because, for one thing, it sounds stupid, and for another *pâté de foie gras* comes from France. Similarly, 'prime time' is more euphonic than the *maladroit* 'heures de grand écoute'.

An article in a similar vein on 20 March, by Richard Bernstein, used a comparable technique to make the same point, so that one might think at first sight that French expressions are as current in the United States as they are in the United Kingdom. This is nevertheless perhaps not quite the case, and 'écoute' is not the only word to become masculine in the 17 March article when it is in fact feminine. The same happens with 'bête noir', which also becomes oddly masculine, and there is something peculiar about the use of *comme d'habitude* in the sense given to it by *The New York Times*.

French words do tend to behave even more oddly when they cross the Atlantic than they do if they need to travel only twenty-three miles in order to cross the English Channel. They lose their accents: 'hors d'oeuvres' receives a final 's' which it does not have in France, and 'maître d'hôtel' becomes 'maître d''. French words in America also tend to be open to much stronger competition from words of Yiddish origin, terms such as 'klutz', 'schlock', 'schmaltz' and 'chutzpah' being far more frequently used than 'bonhomie' or 'louche'. The fact that American society is more egalitarian and much less class-ridden than its English counterpart also tends to militate against the conscious use of French words as signs of social prestige. This is partly because the situation where French was for centuries the language of the governing élite, and which I discuss in the introduction to Part III, never arose in the United States. But it is also because American culture enjoys a vigour and autonomy which have only recently come to characterise what happens in England. Looking across the Atlantic, French people with an active concern for their language see it as undergoing what they consider a number of deplorable alterations, and as not being used with anything like the same frequency which seems to them to characterise American words in France. If 'le franglais' were to consist solely of words imported from England, the campaigns against it would not have the political edge which gives them their aggressivity and bite. We too have lost an empire, and are a medium-size power which has come down in the world.

This is not to say that the French are the only people to indulge in the activity which George Thomas describes as 'puristic intervention'. Linguistic purism is, as Professor Thomas observes, 'a global phenomenon', at least in the Renaissance and post-Renaissance world, and he points out that the index to his book contains reference to its existence in forty-five languages. 'If a language with the stature of French can feel threatened by English,' he asks, 'what hope can speakers of less widely distributed world languages hold out for the purity of their native idiom?', and it is indeed the case that the pressures on French are as nothing compared with those which Czech has to undergo in its relationship with German or Bulgarian with Russian. The wish to preserve the purity of one's language by protecting it from foreign influence is, Professor Thomas points out, inextricably connected with strongly nationalistic sentiments, and he confirms the thesis that nationalism is essentially a post-medieval phenomenon by remarking that the notion of a language which had to be kept free of foreign words was unknown in the middle ages. 'In this respect', he comments, 'St Augustine may be reckoned to be the first in an illustrious line of anti-purists in European cultural history', and he argues that both Plato and Aristotle also 'seem to reflect a general unconcern about defining the limits of the lexical corpus of a written language'.[3]

However, he comments, Addison was not the only English writer in post-Renaissance England to be worried about the arrival of words from abroad. He quotes an article published by Daniel Defoe in 1708 which presented 'the using and introducing of foreign terms of art or foreign words' as 'an intolerable grievance', and not every English speaker shares Dr Johnson's view that

> sounds are too volatile and subtle for legal restraints; to enchain syllables, and to lash the wind, are equally the undertakings of pride, unwilling to measure its desires by its strength.[4]

The American lexicographer Noah Webster wrote that

> Nothing can be more ridiculous, than the servile imitation of the manners, language, and the vices of foreigners

and part of his aim in compiling his dictionary was to establish a clear distinction between American and English usage. In nineteenth-century England, an amiable eccentric called William Barnes claimed in 1854 that

> the large share of Latin and Greek words in English make it much less handy than purer English would be for the teaching of the poor by sermons and books

and illustrated what his ideas would mean in practice by suggesting that 'fireghost' be used for 'electricity', 'gleecraft' for 'music' and 'statespell' for 'embassy'.[5]

It is true that the English do not often worry about the

presence of foreign words in their language, and in spite of the example of Mussolini's Italy, discussed later in this chapter, there is no mention in George Thomas's *Linguistic Purism* of any other nation apart from the French going as far as to introduce laws which fine people for using foreign words. Indeed, if one of the most popular T-shirts in the north of England for 1994 was anything to go by, the general tendency is to find any foreign terms intrinsically comic. It had a drawing of the actress Sarah Lancashire, from *Coronation Street*, and the words:

Je m'appelle Raquel. Je suis une supermodel.

The 'franglais' books by Miles Kington began life in 1977 as a weekly column in *Punch* and proved so successful that they are now available in a set of four from Penguin: *Let's parler franglais; Let's parler franglais again; Parlez-vous franglais?*; and *Let's parler franglais one more time*. Like the Raquel T-shirt, they set out from the presupposition that far from being dangerous, the presence of French words in English is inherently funny. If the English were ever to start worrying about the presence of foreign words in their language, they might even find some consolation for not being as rich as the Germans in the fact that they have to use the German language to describe such unappealing concepts as 'Angst', 'Blitzkrieg', 'Ersatz', 'Realpolitik', 'Schadenfreude,' or 'Weltschmerz'. They might also draw comfort for their failure to win international football matches from the impossibility of finding an English translation for 'macho', as well as reassurance in more important fields by the lack of a genuine English equivalent for the word 'mafia'. Loan words are not always flattering to the lending language; a fact which can be verified by reflecting on the lack of any alternative in any language to the term 'football hooligan', or by looking at the words connected with drug-taking and pop music collected in section IId of this book.

Not all 'franglais' words, however, are associated with those who have chosen to adopt a life-style and set of attitudes which make it very difficult for them to do very well out of modern society. Others are linked with activities that escape from the control of the state, and which seem therefore to offer a different kind of challenge to its authority than the apparently increasing Americanisation of the young. Thus while it is perfectly possible to talk and read about business and commerce without using words of Anglo-Saxon origin, these do pop up quite frequently in the discussion of free market economics. This is illustrated by the words in IIa, while those in IIb which are concerned with food, drink and travel also deal with activities in which the state is nowadays called upon to play a relatively minor role. The French have always had something of a passion for using the law to impose linguistic norms, and defenders of the loi Bas-Lauriol and the loi Toubon have underlined the precedent offered by the Ordonnance de Villers-Cotterêts, of 2 August 1539, making the use of French instead of Latin obligatory in all legal and administrative proceedings. While this clearly had the advantage of enabling more people to understand what was happening on the legal and administrative front, it was not an unmixed blessing. As Pierre Ecknell pointed out in an article in *Le Nouvel Observateur* on 21 April 1994, no. 1537, the Ordonnance also established a legal system in which the accused was interrogated in secret, with no lawyer to assist him and no clear information of the charges brought against him ('sans avoir communication de son dossier'), and in which the law allowed information and confessions to be extracted by torture. If there was a threat to the French language, argued Pierre Ecknell, it was in the loi Toubon itself, not in the abuses it claimed to remedy, and his argument takes on an additional force if one looks at what has happened to regional languages in France.

The attitude of the revolutionaries of 1789 was quite clear on the matter, and paralleled the determination of the English during the eighteenth and nineteenth centuries to do away with such barbaric tongues as Welsh or Scottish in the British Isles. The title of the Abbé Grégoire's June 1794 *Rapport sur la nécessité et les moyens d'anéantir le patois et d'universaliser l'usage de la langue française* is a clear indication of their attitude towards anything but what they saw as standard French, especially after Bertrand Barrère had declared, in January of the same year, that

Le fédéralisme et la superstition parlent bas-breton; l'émigration et la haine de la République parlent allemand; la contre-révolution parle italien, et le fanatisme parle basque. (Federalism and superstition speak Breton; emigration and hatred of the republic speak German; the counter-revolution speaks Italian, and fanaticism speaks Basque.)

Just as the centralising tendencies of the revolution in administrative matters, as de Tocqueville pointed out in 1859 in *De l'ancien régime et de la révolution*, were merely the policy of Louis XIV writ large, so the linguistic policy of the various French régimes which followed in the wake of the revolution enforced a movement towards linguistic conformity that already existed well before 1789. The official aim of the phrase in the Ordonnance de Villers-Cotterêts of 1539 laying down that all legal and administrative proceedings and decisions be published 'en langue maternelle française et non autrement' (in the French mother tongue and in no other) was to ensure that French replaced not only Latin but also the patois still widely used in France.[6] An equally important ambition was to establish the predominance of French over the various dialects still spoken by the majority of the population, and thus to strengthen the power of Paris over the provinces. The establishment in 1881 and 1882 of a system of state-controlled primary education which was not only free and obligatory but identical in subject-matter and teaching methods throughout France also added immensely to the power of the state, as did the institution in 1872 of five years' military service. The establishment of the Académie Française in 1635, with the specific task of composing a dictionary of words stamped with official approval, anticipated in this respect a system of military training in which only French was used, and which acted as a kind of 'rouleau compresseur' (steam-roller) in a linguistic as well as an ideological sense. Everyone was assumed to be French, to accept the secular republic, and to speak a language acceptable to the Parisian-based middle class.

There is thus, in French history, ample precedent for the attitude inspiring the Bas-Lauriol and Toubon laws, and Étiemble expressed considerable approval, in the 1984 edition of his book, for the way the state had followed up his suggestion of a law banning words of Anglo-Saxon origin. He was clearly following a well-established French tradition in demanding that the state should pass laws to protect the French language, and twice quotes Montaigne to the effect that there should be

> quelque coercition des lois contre les écrivains ineptes et inutiles comme il y en a contre les vagabonds et fainéants (some compulsion of the laws against clumsy and useless writers, as there is against vagabonds and idlers).[7]

Words of Anglo-Saxon origin were, Étiemble argued, so numerous as to need extirpating by legal means, and there is an instructive similarity, in this respect, between a left-wing intellectual such as Étiemble and a fairly right-wing politician and enthusiastic supporter of Jacques Chirac such as Jacques Toubon. Both wish to strengthen the power of the state over the way its citizens speak, something which has not been a particularly visible characteristic of the English-speaking countries. The government of the United States has been even more reluctant to pass laws about language than to establish a state religion, and the only occasion when a formal decision was taken about language in England was in 1362, when Parliament was opened in English, and it was also laid down that all court proceedings should also be in English. In France, in contrast, there often seems to be a natural presupposition that the state has both the right and the duty to regulate the use of language. David C. Gordon's 1978 study *The French Language and National Identity* (Mouton, the Hague/Paris/New York) gives detailed account of these, from the establishment of the Académie Française in 1635, through to the Abbé Grégoire's 1794 *Rapport sur la nécessité et les moyens d'anéantir le patois et d'universaliser l'usage de la langue française*, and the various steps taken after the establishment in 1964 of the Haut Comité pour la Défense de la Langue Française.

There are even more powerful specifics against insomnia in the detailed account which Philippe de Saint-Robert offers in his 1987 *La Cause du français: Du service de la langue française à la naissance de la francophonie*, with its reminder of the support which Georges Pompidou gave to the loi Bas-Lauriol when it was still at the committee stage, as well as to the general need for as many people as possible to speak French. Although M. de Saint-Robert, who from 1984 to 1987 was 'commissaire de la langue française' and 'membre du Haut Conseil de la Francophonie', does not say what the heads of state actually discussed at the meeting held in Versailles in 1986, apart presumably from how marvellous it was to be there all talking French, it would be impolitic as well as unfair for the native speaker of English to be dismissive of La Francophonie. There is a linguistic inventiveness about some of the native speakers outside what the French call the Hexagon which has been well recorded by Loïc Depecker in his *Les Mots de la Francophonie* (Éditions du Seuil, Paris, 1993), and the grouping itself offers a forum for discussion which is akin in some ways to the Commonwealth. M. de Saint-Robert does not, however, talk much about this aspect of this question, preferring to dwell at length on how the number of court cases brought under the 1975 loi Bas-Lauriol quadrupled after the establishment in 1977 of a pressure group known as the Association générale des usagers de la langue française (AGULF), and claiming that it has managed to put a stop to the practice of using the English language when advertising jobs.[8]

The May 1989 *dictionnaire des néologismes officiels* and the March 1993 *dictionnaire des termes officiels* both provide lists of the various laws and regulations passed to protect French and of the committees established to achieve its protection, while the Toubon gives a comprehensive list of the dates at which the various *commissions ministérielles de terminologie* published lists of recommended terms to be used when talking or writing about agriculture, audiovisual activities and advertising, electronics, defence, economics and finance, education, informatics, shipping, nuclear power, care of the aged, health, sport, space exploration, telecommunications, tourism, transport and town planning. If French is not more widely spoken, and in the most correct words, this cannot be attributed to the refusal of the government to spend the taxpayer's money on encouraging and even obliging people to do so. The 1989 *dictionnaire des néologismes officiels* also offers a list of the rules

governing the feminisation of words for the jobs people do or
the official offices they hold, while both the Toubon and the
1993 *dictionnaire des termes officiels* give the correct forms for
foreign capitals and countries. The French for 'ignorance of
the law is no excuse' is 'nul n'est censé ignorer la loi', and
there are few areas in which the French state has tried to take
more upon itself, and to impose more on its citizens, than in
language. It is only unfortunate that the attitude adopted
seems to involve penalties rather than rewards, and to neglect
the area which is so obviously open for the greater spread of
French culture as well as the French language.

Thus in no other area does the English student of French
feel more envious of the opportunities available to the French
student of English than when she or he compares the wealth
and variety of programmes put out on BBC Radio 4 – to say
nothing of those offered to the matitudinal insomniac by the
BBC World Service – with what is available on France-Inter.
The morning 'Revue de Presse', is, it is true, an excellent way
of catching up quickly with what is happening in France. It
comes on for most of the year at 07.30. The evening programme 'Le téléphone sonne' also offers some useful insights
into what ordinary French people think. But for the rest of the
time, the principal diet consists of pop songs – many of them
in English – and football commentaries. And one only needs
to think of 'Woman's Hour', 'Any Questions', 'Medicine
Today', 'Yesterday in Parliament', 'From Our Own Corre-
spondent', or 'Money Box', to say nothing of 'Letter from
America' or 'Gardeners' Question Time', to appreciate what
the English language, as well as British culture in general,
owes to Lord Reith.

The link between the absence of comparable programmes
from the French radio is relevant to 'la querelle du franglais'
in the light which it throws on the social and political life of
France. Until a series of measures was introduced between
1964 and 1972, the service known as Radio et Télévision
Française was under the direct control of the state, with no
buffer organisation comparable with the BBC Board of Gover-
nors to protect it from the interference of the government of
the day. Understandably, especially when one looked at the

other careers open to the intellectual élite created by the *grandes ecoles* (see the entry 'must' in IIa and note 2 in IIa), no tradition developed which was comparable with the custom in England whereby the brightest and best from Oxford and Cambridge went into radio and television. While the French have continued to gain from this in the triumphs of their engineering, or the excellence of their railway and telephone networks, as well as in their higher standard of living and achievements in the export market, they pay the price in the poor quality of their radio and television services. Neither in radio nor in television is the French language revived, enriched and shown to deserve its place as an international language in the way that English is by the programmes offered on the BBC and Channel 4.

It is not because of the power and influence of the United States that 'franglais' words tend to occur in the vocabulary of radio and television. American television is not, in fact, either very creative or very interesting. It is much more because of a failure of creativity on the part of the French themselves. This is paralleled in the area of popular music, and it is significant that *Le Nouvel Observateur* no. 1532 for 17 March 1994 should have described how young people were generally hostile to proposed government regulations requiring Europe 1, Fun Radio, M40 and RMI (Radio Monte-Carlo) to devote 40 per cent of their music programmes to French songs. In a free market, *Le Nouvel Observateur* pointed out, French pop music cannot compete with English or American groups, and another article in the same weekly paper, 11 August 1994, quoted Benoît Sillard, the head of Fun Radio, as saying that the publishing houses producing French rock music could, at the most, supply only 22 per cent of the market. Sillard also pointed out that what he called 'l'Organisation Européenne des radios' had appealed to the European Commission with the request that the European Court of Justice be asked to consider whether the requirement that French radio stations devote 40 per cent of their time to French music did not constitute an attempt to restrict free competition, presumably as defined in articles 85 and 86 of the Treaty of Rome. If the Court ruled in favour of Fun Radio, *Le Nouvel Observateur* commented, then the 'amendement Pelchat', which imposed the 40 per cent, might go the same way as some of the articles in the loi Toubon. This would not please Jacques Chirac, who was reported in *Le Monde* for February 25 1994 as saying that 90 per cent of what you heard on television and radio was American, and asking for the strict application of quotas.

LAWS AND TARGETS

The readiness of the French state to lay down rules for the correct use of the French language, and to impose penalties on backsliders, does not go against the way in which many French people think of themselves. Georges Duhamel once described his fellow countrymen as a nation of grammarians, and there is far more popular interest in language in France than in any other country. This does not always give rise to tremendous support for projects such as the loi Toubon or concepts such as 'la francophonie'. When, on 20 March 1995, La Francophonie officially celebrated its twenty-fifth birthday, press coverage varied from the muted to the critical. It may well be that most ordinary French people are as indifferent to the future of French outside France itself as most English people are to the fact that Britain no longer has an empire. But few journalists and no politician would call into question the truth of M. H. Yvon's remark, in the 1951 number of the appropriately named journal *Le Français moderne*, that 'la langue française est le fondement même de la culture nation-ale' (the French language is the very basis of the national culture), or cast doubt on Max Gallo's observation, reported in *L'Événement du jeudi* no. 494 for 21 April 1994, that

> En France, le rapport à la langue est un peu spécifique. Il a toujours été lié à l'idée qu'on se faisait de la monarchie, puis du gouvernement. (In France, the relationship of people to language is a shade specific. It has always been linked to the idea which people had of the monarchy, and subsequently of the government).

The attitude which the French have towards their language and culture is nevertheless not always free from a certain hypocrisy, especially when it takes the form of what is intended as a compliment. 'Vous parlez très bien le français, monsieur,' they say, 'seulement avec un léger accent belge' (You speak French very well, except that you have a slight Belgian accent); apparently oblivious of the fact that anyone who knows enough French to make himself understood will have already discovered that the Belgians play the same role in French jokes that the Irish do in English ones. 'Je vais raconter une histoire belge' (I'm going to tell a Belgian story), announces a Frenchman at a dinner table. 'Je vous préviens, monsieur,' says his neighbour, 'que je suis belge moi-même' (I should warn you that I am Belgian myself). 'Dans ce cas-là,' replies the Frenchman, 'je vais la raconter deux fois; et lentement' (In that case, I shall tell it twice; and slowly). An article in *Le Point* no. 1144 for 20 August 1994 gave further illustration of the attitude which the French can occasionally have to some of their fellow members of La Francophonie when it commented of Jacques Chirac's responsibility, in 1981, for ensuring that François Mitterrand was elected President of the Republic, as well as his inability to beat Mitterrand in 1988, that

> Chirac a joué à la roulette belge. Toutes les balles sont dans le barillet. (Chirac played Belgian roulette. All the bullets are in the barrel.)

This habit of telling any English person who speaks their language without too many grammatical mistakes that he or she sounds like someone who is a baguette or two short of a picnic is not directly connected to the fact that the civil servants charged with preparing the Toubon did not do anything like as good a job as the compilers of the 1980 *Dictionnaire des Anglicismes*. It is not unusual, in France as in other countries, for books produced by commercial publishers to be more readable and more reliable than anything emanating from the state. The attitude of the French towards the Belgians, as indeed towards other countries, whether French-speaking or not, is nevertheless another pointer to what they mean when they talk about 'le rayonnement français'. Etymologically, the word evokes Louis XIV's vision of himself as the

Sun King, sending out his rays from the centre of a universe
which would otherwise remain in total darkness, and this
vision remained permanent enough to inspire the *académicien*
Jean d'Ormesson, who had played a prominent part in 'la
lutte contre le franglais' (the fight against franglais), with the
title 'Nos lumières éclairent-elles toujours l'univers?' (Does our
light still enlighten the universe?) for an article in *Le Figaro* on
1 August 1994. D'Ormesson's statement:

> Les droits de l'homme sont français. La tolérance est fran-
> çaise. L'ironie est française et le panache est français. (The
> rights of men are French. Tolerance is French. Irony is
> French and 'panache' is French.)

shows that for him, at least, France still stood as much at the
centre of the intellectual and cultural universe as it did in the
days of Louis XIV.

It is because of the vision that the French have of their own
identity, as well as of their relationship to the rest of the
world, that the issues raised by 'la querelle du franglais' are
only incidentally about language as such. They concern the
role of the state, as well as the kind of society which certain
politicians and some literary men would like to see established
in France, and there are times when one feels some sympathy
with their attitude. The fact that 'franglais' words also occur
with some frequency in the world of television advertising is a
reminder of the impact which the mass media have on the
way people think and feel, and on the ideal vision which they
are encouraged to have of themselves and of the society in
which they live. This involves, as critics such as F. R. Leavis
and Richard Hoggart have argued in their analysis of what
has happened in Britain, a reluctance to query the predominance of a wholly materialistic scale of values. Such critics do
not accept the view that this is part of the price which one has
to pay for a society capable of producing the wealth characteristic of late capitalist civilisation. They maintain that it is the
duty of the leaders of society to prevent it from being dominated by the meretricious and dehumanising standards associated with consumerism, and some of the opponents of the
spread of 'franglais' words in French belong to the same

tradition as the essays of Leavis and Orwell, or a book such as Hoggart's *The Uses of Literacy* (Chatto & Windus, London, 1957).

It is still open to question whether laws forbidding the use of certain words offer the best way of fighting against the excesses of the consumer society. One of the defining characteristics of what Karl Popper called the open society is that the law should be used solely to punish specific acts which harm identifiable individuals, or which can be clearly seen to harm the community as a whole.[9] This is why the use of the law to limit the freedom of speech is seen as a peculiarity of totalitarian societies. It is only if it can be proved in a court of law that the use of certain words constitutes a slander which harms a specific person, or is likely to lead to the persecution of a particular racial or religious group, that the law can be invoked to limit freedom of expression. This point was specifically made by the socialist François Autain in the debate in the French Sénat on 12 April 1994 when he drew attention to the fact that

> l'utilisation de mots étrangers, pour regrettable qu'elle puisse être, n'est pas susceptible de nuire à autrui et ne saurait donc autoriser une atteinte à la liberté d'expression (the use of foreign words, however unfortunate it may be, is not likely to hurt anybody, and thus cannot authorise a limitation on the right to free expression).[10]

It is also hard to see how advertisements for hamburgers or milk shakes can do this, or who is actually damaged by being sold an airline ticket printed in English rather than in French,[11] or who is harmed when journalists talk about 'le rewriting' or waiters in restaurants recommend certain areas of the town as 'très bien pour le shopping'. But it is very difficult, as the supporters of the loi Toubon discovered when the Conseil Constitutionnel declared parts of it unconstitutional, to use the law to impose or forbid certain words without at the same time incurring the charge that one is limiting the expression of certain ideas.

One of the advantages of being a secular society, as France has been since the separation of church and state in 1905, is that there is no possibility of anyone being prosecuted by the state on a charge of blasphemy. One of the objections to the loi Toubon, though not one which I saw mentioned among the other criticisms published of the proposed measure in the French press, is that it conferred a quasi-sacred status on the French language. While this status may be justified on aesthetic and cultural grounds, it is hard to see how it can be protected by the law. It could well be argued that some people's feelings can be hurt by the use of the word 'sponsor' instead of 'parrain', and that it is tiresome to hear the word 'sniper' instead of the perfectly adequate French words 'tireur isolé', 'franc-tireur', or 'affûteur'. One of the arguments used to justify the banning of Salman Rushdie's *The Satanic Verses* was that it hurt the feelings of devout Muslims. This argument was often put forward by people who had no religious beliefs at all, as well as by those whose own religious convictions made them hostile to attacks on any religion, and from one point of view it showed a commendable concern for the way that the citizens of a multi-cultural society should behave towards one another. But once the argument is accepted that the law can be invoked to protect people's feelings, whether in matters of religious belief or because they are particularly sensitive to language, there is no means of deciding where the legislator should stop.

It is not primarily with reference to Britain that 'la querelle du franglais' raises the question of the kind of relationship which France ought to have with the outside world. English visitors to France do not need long to realise that while they are very interested in France, the French in general are not very interested in England, though they are interested in Scotland, and very interested in Ireland. If they are interested in any other country outside France, it is Germany which is seen as a model for economic policy and an ally on the political front, and American culture which is seen as a threat. This, again, is understandable, since the American words which have made their way into French are rarely those which present a very attractive vision of transatlantic civilisation. One of the great achievements of the United States has been the establishment of what is known as 'the rule of law'.

This is not, however, a term which has made its way into
French. From the mid-1970s onwards, perhaps in response to
the celebrations of the bicentenary of 1776, the term used was
the equally accurate, evocative but very French expression,
'l'état de droit'. It is not only those who feel reservations
about the use of the law to regulate language who would be
happier if there were more adaptations of Anglo-American
expressions of this kind into French, and less talk of 'les
jingles', 'les remakes' and 'les gays'.

The preoccupation with the United States was very apparent in the debate which took place on 3 and 4 May 1994,
when Jacques Toubon's bill, already approved by the Sénat,
came up for discussion by the *députés* of the Assemblée Nationale. A literal reading of the *Projet de loi relatif à l'emploi de la
langue française* makes it seem a relatively mild and limited
document. Like the loi Bas-Lauriol, which it was intended to
reinforce as well as to replace, its most clearly stated aim is to
protect the consumer and ensure that employment contracts
for people working in France are drawn up in French. It
stipulates that notices in public places must be displayed in
French, that health and safety regulations must be printed in
French, and that advertising on radio and television must not
employ foreign terms if a French equivalent exists; and it
issues the reminder that article 2 of the Constitution clearly
states that 'la langue de la République est le français' (the
language of the Republic is French), a change introduced in
1992, at the instigation of Jacques Toubon and other like-
minded politicians, at the time of the signature of the Maastricht treaty. It also insists on the need for all teaching to take
place in French, except when the direct method is being used
for modern languages. In its first draft, as approved by the
Sénat, the bill stated that all documents distributed at conferences taking place in France must be translated into French.
In response to protests from the Académie des Sciences that
this would mean that a number of scientific conferences would
be held elsewhere – there is no comparable stipulation in any
other country – this requirement was amended so that it
applied only to conferences subsidised by the French taxpayer.
But fines of up to 20,000 francs (£2,400; $4,000) could be

imposed on anyone breaking the other rules, and anyone trying to stop government employees carrying out the necessary checks to ensure that the law was obeyed was liable to a fine of 50,000 francs and six months in prison.

But although the wording of the bill seemed to limit it, as one *député* put it, to ensuring that when he bought a camera, he could be sure that the instructions included with it were in French, or when he bought a tin of fish imported from Hong Kong, he could find out how to open it without knowing that 'left' in English meant 'gauche' in French, there was an important subtext which came out in the debate in the Assemblée Nationale, as it had already done in the Sénat. It was essentially a question, as even one of the bill's critics, the socialist Didier Mathus put it, of refusing

> un monde uniforme où l'anglo-américain hégémonique ruinerait les cultures et les diversités (a uniform world in which a hegemonic Anglo-American would ruin cultures and diversities)[12]

a phrase which echoed what Jacques Toubon himself had said in the debate in the Sénat when he quoted the remark by a former President of the socialist group in the Assemblée Nationale, Louis Mermaz, about

> le monde uniforme et glacé que nous préparons si personne ne résiste à l'hégémonie de l'anglo-américain (the uniform and frozen world which we are preparing if nobody resists the hegemony of Anglo-American).[13]

If the socialists and communists abstained in the final vote, as they had done in the Sénat, it was not because they disagreed about the danger of what several speakers referred to as 'l'impérialisme culturel américain' (American cultural imperialism). Some socialists, like François Autain, were uneasy about the use of the law to regulate language, and it was those who shared his view who took the matter to the Conseil Constitutionnel. But if they expressed reservations, it was more because they thought that the government was not going far enough, and wanted to remind it of its failure to remedy the situation in which one in four French children reached the age of eleven without being able to read and write properly. Apart from some kind remarks about the role played by the BBC in protecting the quality of the English language, nobody had a good word to say for the English, and the Americans were seen only as an enemy. Jacques Toubon himself, when defending his text in the Assemblée Nationale, insisted on the need to fight against the invasion of 'la culture anglo-marchande', a phrase which was perhaps an unconscious echo of Étiemble's assertion that any self-respecting civilisation gave the merchant the lowest place in society.[14] What French people who are hostile to 'le franglais' have against it are its cultural associations, its links with what Étiemble, borrowing the term from Henry Miller, called 'the air-conditioned nightmare'.[15]

SOME UNHAPPY PRECEDENTS

This readiness to use the law to exclude certain words because of their cultural associations implies a concept of the relationship between the state and its citizens which goes beyond mere paternalism. Georges Sarre, speaking in the debate in the Assemblée Nationale on 3 May 1994 on behalf of the socialist group République et liberté, was nevertheless exaggerating when he pointed to the dangers of a system in which there would be three levels of language spoken in France: English and American for anything connected with business and economics; French for cultural activities; and

> un franco-anglais argotique de cinq cents mots pour les classes socio-linguistiquement les plus défavorisées (a demotic mixture of 500 French and English words for those who were least favoured socio-linguistically).[16]

It is indeed true, as I have already suggested, that if you look at a publication such as *Vendredi Samedi Dimanche*, or *20 Ans*, magazines obviously aimed at a young and not over-educated audience, that expressions of obvious and recent American origin become more frequent than they do in *Le Figaro* or *Le Monde*. But one should not exaggerate the number of words involved. The March 1995 issue of the magazine *20 Ans*, for example, contains a number of words which are 'franglais' or of the franglais type: 'Glamforever', 'food fun', 'bondage', 'drag queen', 'groupie', 'grunge' and 'brushing'. But these words do not dominate the articles in which they appear, and are not particularly intrusive in the advertisements either. You have to look for them, as Joe Gargery had to look for his 'J-O, JO'; and you then realise that they form quite a small part of a not particularly impoverished vocabulary in which the vast majority of the words are still French.

The same is true of Philippe Vandel's *Le Dico français-fran-çais* (The French-French dictionary; Éditions Jean-Claude Lattès, Paris, 1993), an entertaining study in eighteen short chapters of the styles of speech currently most fashionable in France. There is only half a page on 'le franglais', and only four examples: 'briefer', 'relooker' (translated as 'modifier l'aspect', to change the appearance), 'driver' – in the sense of to drive a car – and 'surbooké'. Other 'franglais' words do, it is true, occur in the body of the text: 'top secret', 'une balle liftée' (what English-speaking footballers would call a high ball), 'le tennis elbow', 'le rafting', 'les trainers' (see the entry on 'les baskets' in IId) and 'les strings'. But although the statement on p. 269 to the effect that 'on a fumé du shit toute la nuit' (we smoked shit [marijuana or dope] all night) offers a reminder of the least attractive context in which words of American origin are most frequently found in France, and Philippe Vandel is a working journalist in daily contact with the language, his book offers no support for Étiemble's vision of French as totally taken over by 'le franglais'.

A similar point was made in the debate on the proposed loi Toubon in the French Sénat on 12 April 1994 by Madame Françoise Seligman. The minister ought really to be aware, she said, of the fact that the measure he was proposing was likely to prove both dangerous and ineffective. It was dangerous because of the way it would tend to widen the gap between the government and young French people, and ineffective because of the chaos which would inevitably be provoked if the police went into the studios of Skyrock or Fun Radio to try to enforce the loi Toubon in all its rigour. It was, she continued, no accident that these radio stations used a large number of English and American expressions, since they spoke to young people as young people speak to one another, and she made a point about what happens to 'franglais' words after they have been used for some time (a point which can be confirmed in more detail by looking at the words in the index to this book which are followed by the marker †). 'Il suffit', she said:

> de consulter les dictionnaires Larousse et Robert 'de la langue française' pour y trouver nombre de termes étrangers qui ont été tout naturellement intégrés dans leur corpus. C'est le cas, pour ne citer que quelques exemples, de termes comme flash, scoop, score, starter ou timing, qui sont devenus tellement courants dans notre langage que vous aurez du mal à en interdire l'emploi et à imposer les traductions que vous proposez dans votre dictionnaire officiel. (All you need to do is look at the Larousse and Robert dictionaries 'of the French language' to find a number of foreign terms which have been quite naturally included in them. This is the case, to quote only a few examples, of terms such as flash, scoop, score, starter, or timing, which have become so current in our language that you will have a great deal of difficulty in forbidding their use and in imposing the translations which you propose in your official dictionary'.[17])

This is also the point which emerges from the February 1995 issue of *Vendredi Samedi Dimanche*. This may at first sight, by putting a photograph on its cover with the very visible title 'Les femmes GAY', give the impression of a France threatened by an invasion of franglais-speaking lesbians. But an interview later on in the magazine with Josiane Balasko, the maker of the film *Gazon Maudit*, a recently released film about lesbianism, contains no 'franglais' words at all. If it has a linguistic interest, it is in the revelation – to me, at any rate – of the expression 'elle est de la pelouse' (literally: of the lawn) to indicate that a woman is a lesbian. French has a long and rich tradition of highly inventive slang, especially in sexual matters. But relatively few of the words listed in one of the most recent analyses of the phenomenon, the *Dictionary of Modern Colloquial French* (Routledge, London, 1984), by René Hérail and Edwin

Lovatt, are of English or American origin. And were Georges
Sarre to have also looked for examples of 'le franglais' in
Cosmopolitain – the French version of *Cosmopolitan* – or *Elle*, he
would have felt the same disappointment as I did when I
thought I was going to add to my collection of 'franglais'
words by a diligent perusal of *20 ans* or *Vendredi Samedi Dimanche*
and was struck by their absence.

Many of the examples in *Parlez-vous franglais?* are of words
particularly connected with the activities of those young
people whom Étiemble does not like to see described in
French as 'teenagers',[18] and it is tempting to see one of the
aims of the laws which try to ban words of American origin
from the French language as seeking to ensure that young
people do not become alienated from the acceptable linguistic
norms of official French society. It is an example of what the
Italian Marxist Antonio Gramsci called cultural hegemony:
an attempt, by the state, to reinforce its political power by
exercising as much control as possible over the cultural models
which its citizens seek to adopt. The decision of the Conseil
Constitutionnel to restrict the application of the loi Toubon to
those who had voluntarily elected to enter into the full-time
service of the state meant that what Gramsci called 'bourgeois
society' was more respectful of individual liberty than he and
other Marxists would allow.

It is nevertheless unfortunate for the image of France pro-
jected by intellectuals such as Étiemble and politicians such as
Jacques Toubon or Georges Sarre that both in Mussolini's
Italy and Hitler's Germany a comparable attempt should
have been made to purge the language of foreign imports.
The image is misleading in the sense that the decline in
popularity of the French Communist Party, coupled with its
most recent changes in the party line and the unanimity with
which all political parties accept the Constitution of the Fifth
Republic, means that France is further from a totalitarian
take-over than at any period in its history. But there is a
worrying parallel in that the vocabulary of sport in fascist
Italy had to become entirely Italian; and there is an obvious
desire among sections of the French right to do something
similar in France. An article in *L'Action Française* for 23

March 1994, pointed out how, in what it called that newspaper's 'grande époque' (great period), the 1930s, when it
was published every day, not a single word of English appeared in its sporting pages. 'On y parlait', it wrote:

> de 'balle ronde', de 'balle ovale', de 'balle à la raquette'.
> Une loi pour protéger la langue française ne peut donc
> qu'avoir notre adhésion, même si nous pouvons regretter
> qu'il faille une loi pour faire comprendre à nos citoyens que
> notre langue est un patrimoine à protéger. (The words
> mentioned were 'round ball' and 'oval ball', or 'ball to be
> hit by a racket'. A law to protect the French language thus
> inevitably has our approval, even though we may regret
> that a law is needed to make our citizens realise that our
> language is a heritage to be protected.)

On 24 March 1994, the present *L'Action Française* took a stand
comparable with that of its better-selling predecessor. Reminding its readers of what it still stood for by the statement that
there will be

> une civilisation française dynamique et conquérante le jour
> où l'Etat exprimera de nouveau une 'fidélité créatrice'
> incarnée par le sceptre royal (a dynamic and conquering
> French civilisation only when the state once again expresses
> a 'creative fidelity' incarnated by the royal sceptre)

it continued with a passage very reminiscent of the opening
pages of Étiemble's *Parlez-vous franglais?*, not a book containing
many arguments in favour of the restoration of the French
monarchy:

> Walkman sur la tête, Michael Jackson dans les oreilles, je
> sirote un coca cola à la terrasse d'un Mac Donald [*sic*] sous
> l'effigie d'un Mickey géant (a Walkman on my head,
> Michael Jackson in my ears, I sip a coca cola on the terrace
> of a McDonald's under the statue of a giant Mickey
> Mouse)

and commented:

> Ainsi assistons-nous à la victoire apparente d'une culture

étrangère, universaliste, déracinante et déstructurante, une 'idéologie culturelle' importée des Etats-Unis depuis longtemps. (We thus witness the apparent victory of a foreign, universalising, uprooting and destructuring 'cultural ideology' which is destroying our roots, and which has long been amongst us as an import from the United States.)

The supporters of *L'Action Française* would clearly have been very happy in the Italy of the 1930s and 1940s, where fines of 1,000 lire – quite a lot of money in those days – were imposed on anyone using foreign words in print. An even heavier fine, of 6,000 lire, was imposed on anyone failing to change a foreign-sounding name to its Italian equivalent. Neither is there much encouragement, for admirers of the open society, in the example offered by non-totalitarian countries who have tried to use the law to impose linguistic norms. In the 1960s and 1970s, when Apartheid was in full swing in South Africa, a government-appointed committee sat in permanent session in order to find Afrikaans equivalents of words such as 'carburettor'. A country which, like the province of Quebec, chooses the words 'Je me souviens' as the motto to put on the registration plates of its cars does not inspire confidence in its ability to act intelligently in the modern world, and there is little to disagree with in Dennis Ager's verdict on linguistic policy in that part of Canada. It resulted, he wrote, in creating a monolingual Quebec and a bilingual Canada,[19] an interesting variation on Voltaire's summary of the attitude of the Catholic Church to toleration: 'When you are powerful, I will ask you to tolerate me, because that is your policy. When I am powerful I shall refuse to tolerate you, since that is my policy.' While French is taught and spoken everywhere in English-speaking Canada, the only language other than French which is taught in the public schools of the province of Quebec is Latin. In 1977, law no. 101 made French compulsory in all commercial transactions as well as in all aspects of administration. It was only by an appeal to the Supreme Court, in 1982, that English-speaking businessmen and shopkeepers were able to secure permission to advertise their wares in English. In the France of 1994, a similar event was to have an even greater impact on the loi Toubon.

NOTES

1 Published in 1982. Dr Pickup's bilingual *Dictionnaire des Sports* is published by Éditions Ellipses, Paris, 1995.

2 Fraser Mackenzie, *Les Relations de la France et de l'Angleterre d'après le vocabulaire*, Droz, Paris, 1939, Vol. II, p. 279.

3 George Thomas, *Linguistic Purism*, Longman, London/New York, 1991, pp. 209–10.

4 From the 1755 Preface to Johnson's Dictionary, quoted by Thomas, op. cit., p. 111.

5 Thomas, op. cit., pp. 55 and 93. For a list of comparable suggestions by Percy Grainger, see p. 29.

6 The issue is instructively discussed by Michel de Certeau, Dominique Julia and Jacques Revel in their *Une politique de la langue: la révolution et les patois*, NRF, Paris, 1975, as well as in a special number which *Les Temps Modernes* published in August-September 1973 on 'Les minorités nationales en France', especially J. L. Calvet's article 'Le colonialisme linguistique' and Yves Person's 'Impérialisme linguistique et colonialisme'. The debate in the French Senate on 12 April also contained some lively exchanges on the place of regional languages in France, introduced by Henri Goetschy from Alsace.

7 Étiemble, *Parlez-vous franglais?*, Gallimard, Paris, 1984 edn, pp. 257 and 329.

8 For details of some of the prosecutions brought by the AGULF, see note 4 to Chapter 3.

9 Hence the justification for the penalties imposed for the non-payment of taxes and excise duties: other people have to pay more to make up for the shortfall. Fines and prison sentences for what the thoroughgoing libertarian might see as the self-regarding activity of taking certain drugs are defended on the grounds of the cost to the community in terms of increased crime and the need for additional medical care. There is nevertheless some inconsistency here since neither tobacco nor alcohol is classified as an illegal substance, in spite of the harm they do personally to those who consume them to excess as well to the community at large by the higher health charges to which the illnesses they provoke give rise.

10 *Journal Officiel*, p. 966; see above, Chapter 1, note 21.

11 For details on these prosecutions, see Chapter 3, note 4.

12 All the quotations from the debate of 3 and 4 May 1994 are taken from the *Journal Officiel*, p. 1376.

13 *Journal Officiel*, p. 959.

14 op. cit., p. 247. See also the entry 'businessman', in Part IIa.

15 op. cit., p. 322. Étiemble explains in *Parlez-vous franglais?* how he spent five years in the United States, and disliked it intensely. He also offers to make available to any reader who doubts his word a letter from a public relations agency offering him money to stop his campaign (p. 326), reveals something of his background – he is a grandson of a peasant family – and describes how he spent a year assiduously collecting examples of the way French was being corrupted by American English.

16 *Journal Officiel*, p. 1366.

17 *Journal Officiel*, pp. 967–8. For the recommendations made in the Toubon for these words, see the individual entries in Part II.

18 op. cit, p. 84: 'Mais puisque nous on n'a pas thirteen ou sixteen, mais treize ou seize ans, c'est idiot de dire *teen*' (But since we are not thirteen or sixteen but thirteen years old or sixteen years old, it's idiotic to say *teen*).

19 See Dennis Ager, *Sociolinguistics and Contemporary French*, Cambridge University Press, Cambridge, 1988, p. 101. See also pp. 222–3 of Claude Hagège's *Le français et les siècles*, Odile Jacob, Paris, 1987, for details about the role of law 101 in Quebec, and the successful appeal of the shopkeepers of Montreal, in majority English-speaking, against the stipulation in article 58 that goods for sale be described solely in French. The Appeal Court in Montreal declared this article unconstitutional, with the result that goods could be described in English, as well as in the obligatory French.

3 Law, loan words and history

A CALL TO ORDER

It was on 1 August 1994 that an event took place in France which underlined the advantages of having a written constitution, and especially one which separates the legislative from the executive branch of government, and ensures that both come under the control of an independent judiciary. The constitution of the Fifth Republic provides for a special court, the Conseil Constitutionnel, whose role is to say whether or not a 'projet de loi' (government bill) or a 'proposition de loi' (private member's bill) is or is not in keeping with the constitution. The invaluable *Quid*[1] sets out the conditions on which it can be officially called upon to give an opinion, and it is clear from these that at least sixty *députés*, probably from the Socialist Party, were sufficiently unhappy about the loi Toubon to take the matter to the Conseil constitutionnel after the 'projet de loi' had been approved by the Sénat and the Assemblée Nationale in April and May 1994. They had not, significantly enough, expressed any formal opposition during the public debate which had taken place on 3 and 4 May. To have done so would have been the equivalent of electoral suicide. But there was no disputing their right to call upon the Conseil Constitutionnel to give a ruling on the issue which they raised.

On 1 August, the Conseil gave a judgment summed up in a cartoon by Plantu in *Le Monde*. Jacques Toubon is standing rather shamefacedly in front of a group of 'conseillers' and a balloon is coming out of the chairman's mouth:

Monsieur Toubon, on trouve que votre loi, c'est plutôt has

been. (Monsieur Toubon, we find your law a bit of a has-been.)

What the Conseil Constitutionnel said was that while the state had the right to oblige its employees to use a particular kind of language, 'un langage codifié', it did not have the right to impose this on private individuals, non-state organisations – privately owned firms, or other non-public bodies. To do so, the Conseil argued, went against article XI of the 1789 *Déclaration des droits de l'homme et du citoyen*, which read:

> La libre communication des pensées et des opinions est un des droits les plus précieux de l'homme; tout citoyen peut donc parler, écrire, imprimer librement; sauf à répondre de cette liberté dans les cas déterminés par la loi. (The free expression of ideas and opinions is one of the most precious of man's rights; any citizen can therefore speak, write and print freely; on condition that he assumes responsibility for this freedom in cases determined by the law.)

In the view of the Conseil Constitionnel, the manner in which ideas were expressed was just as important as the ideas themselves. The state therefore had no right to require its citizens to express themselves in any one particular kind of language. Freedom of expression involved the free choice of words, irrespective of their origin. Ordinary French citizens could, within the limits imposed by the law of libel, say what they liked how they liked. Only those who had elected to serve the state could be required to use a language officially defined by the state as acceptable French.

There is a clear similarity between article XI of the *Déclaration des droits de l'homme et du citoyen* and the First Amendment to the Constitution of the United States of America, with its statement that

> Congress shall make no law respecting an establishment of religion, or prohibiting the free exercise thereof; or abridging the freedom of speech or of the press; or the right of the people peaceably to assemble, and to petition the government for a redress of grievance.

Indeed, what now seems remarkable is that no group of *députés* had thought of taking the loi Bas-Lauriol to the Conseil Constitutionnel when it was approved in 1975. The *Déclaration des droits de l'homme et du citoyen*, referred to in the Preamble to the Constitution of 1958, enjoys the same respect among ordinary French people as the 1776 *Declaration of Independence of the Thirteen United States of America* does with Americans. And there was, in fact, very little difference between the loi Bas-Lauriol and the loi Toubon.

One of the main interests of 'la querelle du franglais', as the title of this book suggests, lies in the questions which it raises about the role and function of the law in a democratic society. To the outside observer, as well as to most of the journalists who commented on it, the decision of the Conseil Constitutionnel to limit the application of the loi Toubon to those citizens who had freely elected to enter government service seems eminently sensible. It did more than place a barrier on the power of the state to interfere in the lives of ordinary citizens. It also provided an immediate example of what is meant by the rule of law, especially when this is embodied in a written constitution. For the rule of law, in this respect, does not refer merely to the individual laws of a country, which the executive itself must observe in the same way as do the citizens which it governs. It is also, more particularly, a set of rules which are clearly defined in advance, and which a society has decided to set above its immediate political needs. The rule of law places these rules out of the reach of decisions made by the legislative body, in exactly the same way as it protects the decisions of the courts from interference either by the executive or by the legislative branch of government.

It is of course possible, in France as in the United States, to change the constitution, and thus to alter the concept of the rule of law which this embodies. In France, the Constitution of the Fifth Republic can be altered by referendum – as de Gaulle did in 1962, when he obtained a majority for the election of the President by universal suffrage – or by a vote of a two-thirds majority in a joint session of the Sénat and of the Chambre des Députés in what is then known as 'le Congrès'. In the United States, it needs a two-thirds majority in Congress – Senate and the House of Representatives – which then has to be ratified by three-quarters of the individual states. But until the constitution has been changed in this way, any individual laws approved by the legislature must conform to it, something which is not necessarily the case in the United Kingdom. There, the sovereignty of the Queen in Parliament is theoretically unlimited, and the lack of formal restraints on the powers of the legislature in the United Kingdom can be illustrated by what might have happened if an incident which took place in the Houses of Parliament in June 1994 had had a different outcome. Anthony Steen, Conservative member for South Hams, obtained permission to bring forward a private member's bill banning the use of French words in English. It was, he explained, though obviously with his tongue firmly in his cheek, a necessary riposte to the way the French were behaving, as well as a measure which would solve the problem of unemployment. So many extra staff would have to be taken on by the government to make sure that terms such as 'sang froid' were replaced by 'coolness under pressure', and 'omelette' by 'eggs mixed together with water and a little salt and then fried', that three million jobs would be created overnight.

It was obviously a joke and was treated as such, being defeated by 149 votes to 49. But had the impossible happened and the vote been the other way round, and had the bill then been carried in the Lords, any citizen unhappy about the measure would have found that there was no official body to which she or he could appeal on the grounds that it was unconstitutional. While this strengthens the case for the adoption of some kind of written constitution in the United Kingdom, just as there has been one since 1787 in the United States, it could also be argued that the powers of the Conseil Constitutionnel are particularly necessary in France because of an aspect of French political culture which, since the seventeenth century, has tended to separate French political behaviour from what has happened in Britain or the United States. Traditionally, the attitude both of the right and of the left in France has been to say that the law is there to be a servant of the state, and thus by implication of the person or party who happens to be in power. Louis XVI's remark 'C'est légal parce que je le veux' (It is legal because such is my will) anticipates the claim made almost two centuries later by the socialist Louis Mermaz, Minister for Transport in Pierre Mauroy's 1981 government and from 1988 onwards President of the socialist group in the Chambre des Députés. After the Socialist Party had obtained an absolute majority over all other parties in the Chambre des Députés in the legislative elections of 14 and 21 June 1981, he told his right-wing opponents:

> vous avez juridiquement tort parce que vous êtes politiquement minoritaires. (You are legally in the wrong because you are politically in a minority.)

With a tradition like this, it is argued, France needs a body such as the Conseil Constitutionnel for reasons similar to those which lead certain alcoholics to entrust the key of the drinks cupboard to somebody who will refuse to open it except for very short periods.

In 1945, in the debate about what kind of constitution was to replace the Vichy régime, the view on the left was that the French should go back to the tradition embodied in the Convention of September 1792. This was a legislative body whose supremacy was not limited by any system of checks and balances, and it had led within eighteen months to the Jacobin dictatorship of Robespierre. Earlier, on 15 October 1791, the *Assemblée Législative* had decided to exclude the anglicism 'honourable member' from its formal vocabulary'[2] and it is perhaps more than a coincidence that the députés known as 'les Brissotins' were sent to be guillotined on 31 October 1793. It was perhaps the memory of this and other events which led to the post-war proposal to set up an omnipotent legislative body – a proposal strongly supported by the Communist Party – being rejected by referendum on 5 May 1946. In spite of this, however, the Fourth Republic was not given a Conseil Constitutionnel capable of requiring the legislature to respect the constitution. Its introduction was one of the features of the Fifth Republic, which reflected de Gaulle's concern to give the state protection against any excessive use of its power by the legislative body, and the Conseil Constitutionnel in fact came into existence in October 1958, four months before the official inauguration of the Fifth Republic on 1 January 1959.

In the constitution of the Fifth Republic, the nine members of the Conseil Constitutionnel are not full-time professional judges. They are not therefore vulnerable to the kind of political pressure which Jean-Marie Colombani referred to in an article in *Le Monde* for 19 October 1994, when he described how, in 1883, the Third Republic carried out a massive purge of the judiciary in an attempt 'de rendre la justice républicaine' (to make justice republican) and eliminate from the bench all trace of monarchical or Bonapartist sympathies. For although judges in France, as in other democratic countries, enjoy security of tenure and cannot in theory be dismissed by either the executive or the legislative – 'l'inamovibilité des juges est essentielle au bon fonctionnement de tout système démocratique' (the impossibility of removing or dismissing judges is essential to the satisfactory working of any democratic system) is how the French put it – this rule has sometimes in the past been honoured more in the breach than the observance. Objections to the loi Toubon in the courts might not therefore have been successful, and in restricting its application in advance, the Conseil Constitutionnel fulfilled exactly the function entrusted to it: that of enabling changes to be made to proposed legislation in order to protect the private citizen against the excessive and unconstitutional use of its powers by the legislative as well as by the executive body.

The decision of the Conseil Constitutionnel was not welcomed on all sides. Jack Lang, a former Minister of Culture in the Rocard government of 1988, criticised it for being inspired by what he called 'une philosophie ultra-libérale', an expression which has two meanings in French. On the one hand, it implies that too much importance is being given to the rights of the individual as opposed to those of the state. This was clearly what Lang had in mind, since he also spoke of how 'les principes de 89' had been

> largement inspirés par les grands intellectuels de la Révolution qui, eux, concevaient une politique volontariste pour

la langue française (largely inspired by the great intellectuals of the Revolution who, for their part, certainly knew what they wanted the French language to be like).

What Lang meant by this was that thinkers such as Voltaire, Rousseau and Diderot would have supported the attempt of the loi Toubon to impose a kind of French defined as correct by the state, and his remark offers interesting support to the critics of the revolution of 1789 who see it as having, from the very beginning, had the potentially totalitarian ambitions fully if temporarily realised by Robespierre. But Jack Lang also meant, by his use of the word 'libérale', that the decision of the Conseil Constitutionnel had been inspired by an excessive respect for free market economics, and there is some truth in this. By restricting the state's power to control the language to the case of its own servants only, the decision of the Conseil Constitutionnel gives private companies the right to decide on how best to present and sell their own products. However objectionable purists might find it, the manufacturers of Tuborg lager still have the right to advertise it in English on the back page of *L'Express*, as they did on 21 April 1994, no. 2232, by saying 'For generations, Tuborg has been part of the noble art of beer drinking in all European countries'. Nippon Airways are able to carry on advertising themselves in *L'Expansion* as 'Japan's Best To The World', Singapore Airlines to promise '5 vols non-stop de Paris à Singapore, avec plus de 300 correspondances vers l'Asie', and Church shoes to present its 'famous English shoes', as it did in *Le Nouvel Observateur* no. 1569 on 1 December 1994, with the claim that 'les "Classic Boat" en sont l'illustration'. Similarly, the chain of shops which specialises in selling running equipment will keep the right to call itself 'Athlete's Foot', and it may even be that the advertisement for American Express in one of the corridors in the airport Roissy-Charles de Gaulle which so aroused the ire of Jacques Toubon because it was entirely in English will not have to be accompanied by a notice of the same size in French.[3]

Several commentators favourable to the loi Toubon nevertheless pointed out, after the decision of the Conseil

Constitutionnel had been made public, that a number of its provisions remained unchanged. According to *Liberation* for 1 August 1994, French was still obligatory in all advertisements in newspapers, on the radio and television, in notices in the street or on public transport, as well as in all employment contracts and regulations governing practice in the workplace. Although the Sénat had not approved the requirement that French scientists had to publish in French if they wanted to qualify for a government grant, *Libération* – which did not disapprove of the idea – also pointed out that the stipulation that any conference taking place in France had to make a translation of all papers and summaries available in French was still in force. The original proposal that all the proceedings of conferences held in France had to take place in French had been abandoned in response to pressure from the scientists themselves.

So, too, as other commentators pointed out, were the fines. They remained at between 10,000 and 20,000 francs (£1,200, $2,000) for each offence, and 50,000 francs together with a possible prison sentence of six months for anyone trying to stop the law being put into effect. The loi Bas-Lauriol had laid down comparable penalties, and the organisation praised by Philippe de Saint-Robert in his *La Cause du français*, the Association générale des usagers de langue française, took a number of firms to court in the 1980s. These included TWA, fined 800 francs in June 1981 for two boarding cards printed in English, a firm called News, fined 5,000 francs, with 2,500 costs, for the mention of '20 filter cigarettes', and the Opéra de Paris, fined 100 francs, with 2,300 costs, for selling a programme called 'Bubbling Brown Sugar'. In February 1984, Quick had to pay a fine of 300 francs, with 3,000 damages, for using the words 'hamburger', 'big cheese', 'soft drink' and 'Irish coffee', and in January 1983, the advertising agency Technicon had to pay 4,000 francs for publishing a job advertisement in English in *Le Monde*.[4]

It would nevertheless be misleading to see the population of France as having gone in fear and trembling for its pocket book between 1975 and 1994 in case it infringed the loi

Bas-Lauriol by using the verb which the Toubon gives as 'décripter' instead of the acceptable 'transcrire', or talking about 'sourcing' when it really meant 'sourçage'. As Claude Hagège pointed out in *Le français et les siècles*, in 1987, the financial consequences of enforcing the loi Bas-Lauriol in all its rigour would have brought in more money to 'les caisses de l'état' (the public purse)

> que les redressements d'impôts ou les procès-verbaux pour contraventions au code de la route (than collection of unpaid taxes and fines for motoring offences)[5]

and there has been no reduction in the money which the French state has taken from its citizens by these more orthodox means. In spite of the attempts to limit the spread of English and American expressions, French people are likely to continue to use the words which seem most immediately appropriate to them, and the main linguistic interest of 'le franglais' remains the way it confirms all the commonplaces about the role of loan words in general. Languages borrow words from one another because there is an idea or experience which people wish to express and for which no term exists in their native tongue. Terms such as 'week-end', 'sandwich', 'baby-sitting', or 'parking' are used quite spontaneously by native speakers of French for the same reason that people in England or America talk about 'au pair girls', 'finesse', 'joie de vivre, or 'tour de force': because that is the quickest way to say it, and because the language they normally speak doesn't have quite the right word.

It is very difficult, in this respect, to accept Jacques Toubon's claim in the debate in the Sénat on 13 April 1994 that it was his law which expressed the idea of free speech incarnated in the *Déclaration des droits de l'homme et du citoyen*. While he seemed to be replying in advance to the ruling by the Conseil Constitutionnel which was going to limit the application of his law to individuals and organisations speaking of behalf of the state and in an official capacity, his argument depended upon a very curious use of the verb 'interdire' (to forbid). As far as international conferences were concerned, he declared,

il n'est pas question d'interdire: la loi a pour objectif
d'interdire qu'on interdise. Je crois que nous sommes là en
plein dans la liberté de l'expression et des droits de l'homme!
(It is not a question of forbidding: this law is aimed at
forbidding people to forbid. I think that this puts us fully in
the tradition of freedom of expression and the rights of
man!)[6]

and he clearly meant what he said. But the situation in
international conferences, whether held in France or elsewhere, is not quite what he suggested. It is not that French is
forbidden in the way that Welsh was forbidden in the conduct
of official business in the United Kingdom of the nineteenth
century; or, presumably, since article 2 of the Constitution
now states that 'la langue de la République le français' that a
speaker in the Sénat or the Assemblée Nationale would not be
allowed to use Breton or Occitan. It is merely that international conferences, especially in the sciences, tend to be
conducted in English because this is the language best known
to those taking part and the best way of making yourself
understood. The aim of the loi Toubon, before it was revised
by the Conseil Constitutionnel, was to impose fines on people
using what were deemed to be non-French expressions,
whether the people listening to what they said or reading
what they had written understood them or not.

THE WEIGHT OF HISTORY

When Philippe de Saint-Robert claimed in *La Cause du français:
Du service de la langue française à la naissance de la francophonie* that French has become 'le bien commun de presque deux
cent millions d'hommes' (the common property of almost 200
million men)[7] he was not presenting matters quite as they
stood. The same number does indeed occur in David Crystal's
The Cambridge Encyclopedia of Language, but in brackets; an
indication that this is a rough estimate of the number of
people using French as a second language. David Crystal
gives the figure of 60 to 70 million using French as a first
language, as against between 300 and 350 million for English

(between 700 and 1,400 million as a second language), 350 million for Spanish as a first language, and 1,000 million who quite spontaneously speak Chinese. Étiemble's twice-repeated claim that 120 million people speak French[8] also has to be interpreted with some care. What he is including is the use of French in Africa or the Far East by people for whom it is the second or even perhaps the third language.

French writers and politicians who recommend the use of the law to restrict the use of English or American expressions are also vulnerable to the uncharitable suggestion that if their own language is not more widely spoken than it is, this is much more because of the way they behaved in the past than the result of any twentieth-century Anglo-Saxon plot. As Janet Flanner Genêt observed in 1965 in her *Paris Journal 1944–1965*, it is not the Anglo-Saxons who export English but the French who import it, and her remark anticipated a comment made by the Communist *député* Ivan Renar in the debate in the French Sénat on 12 April 1994. He quoted the French philosopher Michel Serres, who has taught at Stanford since the 1970s, to the effect that:

> Ce n'est pas l'Amérique qui nous envahit: c'est nous qui l'adorons, qui adoptons ses modes et surtout ses mots, des mots que souvent nous ne comprenons pas. (It is not America who is invading us: it is we who worship her, who adopt her fashions and above all her words, words which quite often we don't understand.)[9]

Neither is there is any evidence to sustain Étiemble's claim that the Americans deliberately set out to sabotage French. Another speaker in the debate in the Sénat on 12 April 1994, M. Philippe Richert, from Jacques Chirac's Rassemblement pour la République, commented that

> Force est de reconnaître que, depuis vingt ans, nous avons pris du retard dans ce qu'on appelle l'innovation. Ainsi le *fast food* nous est directement arrivé d'outre-Atlantique sans qu'on ait eu la volonté de trouver un équivalent français à ce mode de restauration typiquement américain. De la même façon, les Anglo-Saxons nous ont apporté le *marketing*,

le *design*, le téléfilm ou le *spot* publicitaire. Dans tous ces domaines, nous n'avons guère été les pionniers et nous nous sommes laissés aller au rêve américain. (We have to acknowledge that, over the last twenty years, we have fallen behind in what can be called innovation. Thus *fast food* has come to us from across the Atlantic without our having had the will to find a French equivalent for this typically American style of eating. Similarly, the Anglo-Saxons have given us *marketing, design* and advertisements on the television. In all these areas, we have scarcely been pioneers, and have let ourselves be carried away by the American dream.)[10]

His remark is particularly interesting in the light of the new meaning taken on in French by the word 'image' (see the entry in IIa).

His comments are also a reminder that 'la querelle du franglais' can sometimes be seen as another example of what the French themselves call 'les guerres franco-françaises', quarrels among themselves about what kind of society they ought to have. These include the contest for predominance between Armagnacs and Bourguignons in the middle ages, the wars of religion in the second half of the sixteenth century, the *Fronde* of the mid-seventeenth century, which unlike the English civil war of the same period ended with the defeat of the rebels and the strengthening of the powers of the Crown, the war between republicans and royalists sparked off by the revolution of 1789, the loss of 10,000 lives in the street-fighting in Paris in June 1848, and of 20,000 more in the repression of the Commune in May 1871, as well as the opposition between supporters of the Vichy régime and members of the resistance movement between 1940 and 1944 and the dispute between 1954 and 1962 as to whether or not Algeria should remain French.

'La querelle du franglais' has nothing of either the short-term or the long-term interest and importance of these conflicts. It has not led to any bloodshed, and is most unlikely to do so. It does not have the ideological importance of the Dreyfus case of 1894 to 1906. What was at stake then was whether France should go back to being a Catholic society dominated by the aristocracy, with perhaps a restoration of the monarchy, and one in which Jews would very definitely be second-class citizens, or whether it should become a secular republic which respected the idea of the equality of all citizens before the law. But the dispute sparked off by Étiemble in 1954 does illustrate what de Gaulle, in his *Mémoires de Guerre*, called 'notre vieille propension gauloise aux querelles et divisions' (our old Gallic propensity for quarrels and divisions), with battle-lines drawn up on fairly identifiable ideological and even political grounds.

Thus I have already pointed out that those who are most vehemently opposed to 'franglais' words, and who are most eloquent in their support of laws to forbid them, tend to belong politically to the far right or the far left. This is visible in the account in the *Journal Officiel* of the debates in the Sénat in April 1994 and in the Assemblée Nationale in the following month, with most of the applause recorded coming from the benches occupied either by the Rassemblement pour la République (RPR) or the Parti Communiste Français, while most of the seats occupied by the socialists and representatives of the centre remained silent. In spite of his readiness to concede that it was the French who were imitating American customs and language and not America which was invading France, Ivan Renar had no doubts about what was happening and what ought to be done. 'Nous avons perdu notre language scientifique', he declared in his speech to the Sénat on 12 April 1994,

> et nous sommes en train de perdre notre langue commerciale et celle de nos chansons. Si nous n'y prenons garde, nous perdrons bientôt notre langue philosophique et même notre langue éducative. C'est intolérable. J'ai soixante ans et quand je vois tous ces mots américains sur les murs de Paris j'ai envie de faire de la résistance. (We have lost our scientific language, and we are in the process of losing our commercial language and the language of our songs. If we are not careful, we shall soon lose our philosophical language and even the language in which we educate our children. It is intolerable. I am sixty and when I see all

these American words on the walls of Paris, I want to join
the resistance.)[11]

Maurice Schumann, old enough to have been in the resistance
during the Second World War, and who had received the
signal honour of becoming one of the 1,059 'Compagnons de
l'Ordre de la Libération', uttered a heartfelt 'Bravo', as did
also the RPR senator Jacques Legendre. But while those who
see themselves as the true heirs of Charles de Gaulle are
moved to express considerable enthusiasm for the loi Toubon,
French people who are closer to the political centre tend to be
relatively indifferent to the matter, and doubtful as to the
usefulness of using the law to regulate language. They read *Le
Monde*, *L'Express* or *L'Événement du jeudi* rather than *Le Figaro*,
Le Nouvel Observateur or *L'Humanité*, and it is easier to imagine
them, in the presidential election of 1995, voting for the
socialist Lionel Jospin rather than the Communist Robert
Hue, for Édouard Balladur rather than for Jacques Chirac,
and certainly not for the right-wing, clerical and nationalistic
Philippe de Villiers or the vociferous Jean-Marie Le Pen.

Such an analysis does, it is true, depend on what the
French now call 'le look' (see the entry in IIa) of the personali-
ties and political groupings involved, and on what is also
known, in a fairly obvious anglicism, as their 'image' (see the
entry in IIa). It can nevertheless be supported by the fact that
ideological positions in France, as in Britain or the United
States, are particularly noticeable in attitudes to foreign influences, entanglements and commitments. If the legendary
United States senator who refused to say more about foreign
policy than that there was too much of it ever existed, he
certainly belonged to the extreme right of the Republican
Party. On the other side of the Atlantic – and of the ideological
divide – there are few more embarrassing scenes in the English
theatre of the twentieth century than the one which takes
place in Arnold Wesker's 1962 *Chips With Everything* in which
the RAF conscripts are made to express their defiance of the
American-based culture which their officers try to impose on
them via an Elvis Presley record, by singing a peculiarly
tuneless English medieval ballad. But in both cases, as in

xenophobia in general, the hostility is directed as much if not more against the fellow-countrymen whom you are disappointed to discover are traitors within the gates than at what is actually coming at you from abroad. Foreigners are pretty wicked anyway, and there is no reason to feel any surprise at their knavish tricks. But you had, at least, thought you could count on your own chaps not to let the side down.

This attitude of hostility directed to your own countrymen is particularly visible in Étiemble's remark that the French bourgeoisie, 'qui n'avait pas réussi à devenir colonie allemande, ne rêva plus que du protectorat yanqui' (having failed to become a German colony, dreamed only of becoming a Yankee protectorate).[12] It is a harsh judgement, even if a predictable one from a member of the French left, and places 'la querelle du franglais' very firmly in the debate about French national identity which runs parallel to the concern which Édouard Balladur voiced on 1 December 1994 when he wondered whether France was still a great nation. The first part of Étiemble's attack against the lack of patriotism of the French middle class is nevertheless supported by a remark in Michel Tournier's autobiographical *Le Vent Paraclet* where he comments on the enormous increase, between 1940 and 1944, of French pupils studying German as their first foreign language.[13] After the war, English resumed its traditional place as the main foreign language studied in French schools and universities, and there is nothing particularly odd about what happened either during the occupation of France or afterwards. Languages, like trade, follow the flag, and are highly sensitive to political changes. The place of Russian in the schools and universities of the United Kingdom, and perhaps even of the United States, would be a good deal different from what it is now if the Soviet Union had been allowed to win the Cold War.

Some political changes which influence the status of languages are also entirely home grown, and those that affect French took place such a long time ago that it is very difficult to do anything about them. Thus, while individual French explorers showed as much initiative in the sixteenth century as their Portuguese or English contemporaries in travelling to the New World, there was much less enthusiasm for exploiting their discoveries on a permanent basis. In 1534, Jacques Cartier sailed all the way up the St Lawrence to what is now Quebec, and in 1541 returned to try to found a colony there. He failed, partly because of the climate, but also because the French were more interested in fur-trading than in establishing a permanent settlement. It was not until 1608, the year after the English established their first colony at Jamestown, that Samuel de Champlain founded Quebec, but even then the French showed little enthusiasm for establishing settlements of the kind set up by the English in the 1630s and 1640s on what is now the Eastern seaboard of the United States. The defeat of the French in the North American campaigns of the Seven Years War (1756–63) was due partly to political and military factors. The French had no leader with the determination of the younger Pitt, and nobody with his ability to recognise the long-term importance of the American colonies. The French navy was inferior to the British, and the Iroquois, temporarily allied to Britain, had virtually wiped out the Hurons, the tribe which the French Jesuits had had most success in converting to Christianity, before the official beginning of the war in 1756. But even without the military genius of Wolfe, an English victory was virtually certain on demographic grounds alone. Fewer than 90,000 French-speakers faced a rapidly expanding population of more than 1,500,000 speakers of English. It was not only that the French of the *ancien régime* were voting with their feet and staying at home. They were being actively encouraged to do so, with Louis XIV forbidding Protestants who left the country after the revocation of the Edict of Nantes in 1685 from going to live in French settlements in the New World.

The refusal to leave for the colonies of those Frenchmen who had not been deprived, as the Protestants were in 1685, of the freedom to practise their own religion was nevertheless fully understandable. A number of commentators hostile to the loi Toubon quoted a remark which Voltaire made to Madame du Deffand in a letter of 1759:

Ce qui fait le grand mérite de la France, son seul mérite,

son unique supériorité, c'est un petit nombre de génies sublimes ou aimables qui font qu'aujourd'hui on parle français à Vienne, à Stockholm et à Moscou. Nos ministres et nos intendants n'ont aucune part à cette gloire. (The great merit of France, its only merit, its sole superiority, stems from a few sublime or amiable men of genius, thanks to whom French is spoken in Vienna, in Stockholm and in Moscow. Our ministers and senior civil servants make no contribution to this glory.)

What nobody pointed out, however, was that it was Voltaire himself who expressed the Eurocentric attitude which led to North America becoming an English-speaking and not a French-speaking continent. In Chapter IV of his best-known work, *Candide*, he dismissed the Seven Years War of 1756–63 as a quarrel over 'quelques arpents de neige vers le Canada' (a few acres of snow over towards Canada). His remark was picked up by André Delacroix, in *France-Observateur* for 20 July 1961, when he wrote:

Il n'y a jamais eu dans notre histoire une grande idéologie impériale, une exaltation de la présence française comparable au sentiment impérial britannique. La France n'a pas eu de Disraeli ni de Kipling, mais un Clemenceau et un Barrès. Auparavant, ses rois avaient abandonné le Canada aux applaudissements de Voltaire . . . Le nationalisme français est essentiellement continental et européen. C'est Louis XIV, c'est Napoléon, c'est Austerlitz et c'est Verdun. (There has never, in our history, been a great imperial ideology, a celebration of the French presence comparable with the feeling the British have for their empire. France has had no Disraeli, no Kipling. It has had Clemenceau and Barrès. In former days, its kings had given up Canada to the applause of Voltaire . . . French nationalism is essentially continental and European. It is Louis XIV, it is Napoleon, it is Austerlitz and Verdun.)

The article was entitled 'De Gaulle est-il cartiériste?', a reference to the views of Raymond Cartier, the founder of *Paris-Match*. De Gaulle's decision, which became effective on

1 July 1962, to withdraw from Algeria, was fully consistent not only with Cartier's view that France should give up its empire and concentrate on Europe, but also with the whole tendency of French policy since the end of the sixteenth century. The France of the seventeenth and eighteenth centuries was the richest and most powerful nation in the world, whose future obviously lay in the Europe which no military defeat could prevent the French from dominating with relative ease, and where French was the universal language of civilised society.

But in spite of his possession of what was still the leading language of Europe, there was little advantage for a French nobleman in going to provide leadership for French-speaking settlers, either in Quebec or in the Louisiana which had been claimed for France in 1682 and named after the Sun King. In both, he found his powers as limited by the Paris-appointed *intendant* as he did if he had stayed at home. The Huguenots whose skill as merchants and artisans made them immediately acceptable anywhere went to Holland, Germany and England. Since Louis XVI would not allow them to go to Quebec, those who did choose to leave Europe went to the Dutch settlements in South Africa. In the Abbé Prevost's *Manon Lescaut*, first published in 1729, it is clear that virtually the only way in which French women could be persuaded to go to Louisiana was by being shipped out as convicted prostitutes. While Australia was initially peopled in a very similar way, with the First Fleet going out in 1789 and the men and women, who had been carried in separate ships, enjoying a splendid orgy in the pouring rain when it finally reached Botany Bay,[14] English-speaking North America was the product of the free choice to emigrate; even though it may have been a choice forced upon a large number of migrants by the need to find something to eat.

Initially, the prestige of French language and culture suffered little from what turned out to be a set of unfortunate political decisions. As late as 1830, John Stuart Mill was writing to de Tocqueville that

    Ideas seldom make much way in the world until France has

recast them in her own mould and interpreted them to the rest of Europe

and Gibbon's decision to ignore the advice given to him by David Hume, and write *The Decline and Fall of the Roman Empire* in English and not in French, did not seem as obviously sensible at the time as it has since proved. Although events have, as he predicted, given 'a superior stability and devotion to the English language',[15] Gibbon was still writing *Decline and Fall* when Rivarol, in 1784, won a royal pension, as well as a prize from the Academy of Berlin, for writing an essay entitled *Sur l'universalité de la langue française*. For the subject which Rivarol and his competitors were asked to discuss was not whether there was a universal language, and whether this might possibly be French. It simply assumed that French was the universal language, and Rivarol explained this on the grounds that

> Ce qui n'est pas clair, n'est pas français. Ce qui n'est pas clair, cela peut toujours très bien être du latin, de l'anglais et du grec. (What is not clear is not French. What is not clear can still perfectly well be Latin, English or Greek.)

In 1802, Étienne Molard expressed an even greater admiration for the clarity of French when he told the readers of his *Dictionnaire grammatical du mauvais usage*, a work originally published in 1792 in order to denounce the number of expressions peculiar to the Lyons area which he claimed were destroying the purity of French, that

> La langue française qui a, sur toutes les autres, l'avantage d'être universelle, mérite particulièrement vos soins. Elle est l'organe de la politique et de la vérité, dont elle a la marche simple et naturelle. (The French language which has, above all others, the merit of being universal, is particularly deserving of your care. It is the organ of expression for politics and for truth, and it shares their simple and natural demeanour.)[16]

In 1800, Baron Czartoryski, Foreign Minister to the Emperor Alexander I of Russia, made the use of French obligatory in all diplomatic correspondence throughout the Russian Empire, and it is clear from Tolstoy's novels that Russian aristocrats tended to speak to one another almost as frequently in French as they did in Russian. In spite of the beginning of the political decline of France brought about by the career and defeat of Napoleon I, the French language retained much of its prestige until after the First World War. Although the Triple Alliance of 1887 between Austria, Germany and Italy was aimed primarily against France, its terms were drawn up in French, a language whose prestige in a sporting context was still great enough for Baron Pierre de Coubertin, when he revived the Olympic games in 1896, to give priority to French over English in any argument about the meaning of words. Since the late eighteenth and early nineteenth centuries, however, French has gradually lost prestige as an international language. In 1648, it was on a par with Latin as the international language in which the Treaty of Westphalia putting an end to the Thirty Years War was drafted. From 1714 onwards, with the Treaty of Rastadt, the French version of treaties took precedence over the Latin, and this remained the case until 1919, when French had to accept joint first place with English in the Treaty of Versailles. And in 1945, the French had to fight hard to have their language accepted alongside Chinese, English, Spanish and Russian as one of the working languages for the United Nations Organisation, only to see the Bandung conference of newly independent, uncommitted states conduct all its proceedings in English in 1955.

It is the apparent absence of any immediate consolations for this loss of predominance which is one of the main reasons why there is so much concern in certain French circles about the number of English or American terms which are making their way into their language. The Germans seem rather to welcome new additions such as 'talkmaster', and do not, in any case, look back to a period in which their language was freely chosen as the privileged means of communication by the most highly educated members of British, Italian or Russian society. The Spaniards also tend to absorb American English terms into their language with relative equanimity, and a report in *Le Monde* for 11 November 1994 of a meeting recently held in Valladolid suggested a number of reasons why this should be so, and why, in Argentina, a writer called Jorge Asis, who had produced a series of measures aimed at defending the purity of Spanish against anglicisms, had to withdraw it in the face of the many protests directed against his ideas.

The main reason was summed up in another article, this time in The Independent for 3 January 1995, under the title 'Spanish Takes el Futbol in its Stride'. Phil Davison wrote:

> Unlike in France where the Académie Française is très fâché over the English invasion, the Spanish Royal Academy is taking a suitably *mañana* view.
>
> After all, Spanish is spoken by around 300 million people throughout the world, so why should they worry about the introduction of such phrases as 'full English breakfast' in remote areas such as Benidorm?

'A man with fifty millions in his kick', as Bertie Wooster remarked of J. Washburn Stoker in *Thank You, Jeeves*, 'does not need to wear the mask', and if French were the first language of 300 million people, Étiemble might have found a less receptive audience for a book which he claimed alerted the French government to the danger of what was happening on the linguistic front and spurred it into action. Unlike the French, the Spaniards did not have what many French people seem to regard as the humiliation of being liberated in 1944 by what a speaker on France-Inter for 21 December 1994 described as 'un peuple bon enfant mais barbare' (a cheerful but barbarous people). No French commentator on the debate surrounding the loi Toubon made the point that without the action of the American armed forces in 1917 and 1944, and the cool nerves of American political leaders during the Cold War, the discussion might well have been taking place in German or in Russian. It is nevertheless a fact that one of the main ingredients in 'la querelle du franglais' is the persistence of an attitude of hostility to the United States which made Roger Vailland say in 1956 that refrigerators were an American invention aimed at destroying French culture,[17] and which led to the comment in *Le Nouvel Observateur* no.

1568, on 24 November 1994, after riots had recently broken out in certain working-class districts of Paris, to the effect that

> Après la culture rock et la culture Disney, la civilisation américaine vient d'exporter en France une autre de ses facettes: la culture de l'émeute. (After rock and Disney culture, American civilisation has just exported another side of its existence to France: the riot culture.)

No other European nation has quite such a well-established tradition of anti-Americanism as the French,[18] and it is certainly not something found in Spain. But there are also linguistic factors which lead the Spaniards to take a more relaxed attitude towards the presence in their language of words of Anglo-Saxon origin, and which reinforce the self-confidence which they derive from having kept, through the Spanish language, a cultural empire to replace the political one which they lost in the nineteenth century. One obvious factor is the wide variety of the different versions of Spanish currently spoken. It would clearly be impossible to produce an authorised version which proved equally acceptable to Argentinians, Chileans and Cubans, to inhabitants of Costa Rica, Venezuela, or Paraguay, as well as to the original 'castillohablantes' of the Iberian peninsula. There is no chance whatsoever of producing an equivalent to the Toubon whose recommendations would obtain immediate assent.

A number of speakers at the Valladolid conference mentioned the ease with which Spanish had, in the past, enriched its vocabulary with words of Arabic origin, and cited more recent words such as 'liderazgo' (leadership), 'perrito caliente' (hot dog) and 'champa' (shampooing) as illustrations of how this capacity for absorption had remained intact. A comparable point was made by Ross Smith in *The Linguist*, Vol. 33, No 5, 1994, describing in an article entitled 'Spelling English Words in Spanish' how the Spanish Real Academia de la Lengua had tried to introduce some consistency into the use of loan words by recommending 'guisqui' for whisky, 'bolanpié' for football, 'baloncesto' for basketball and 'balonvolea' for volleyball. 'The sporting public's response', he wrote, 'was typically anarchical: they accepted one (baloncesto) and rejected the other two' – i.e. 'balanpié' and 'balonvolea'. The Academia then recommended 'futbol' which is having some success. But Ross Smith's comment that the only positive result of the Academia's efforts is to have shown that 'language springs from below and can only be imposed from above in the most superficial cases' is clearly one that can be applied to the fortunes and misfortunes of 'le franglais' at the same time as it points to an important difference in national temperament. As Antonio Dominguez-Rey pointed out in the conference at Valladolid, the Spaniards tend to speak their language with greater gusto than the French. This went hand in hand, he commented, with a more easy-going and less proprietorial attitude towards the Spanish tongue, which enabled it to absorb and to transform foreign words more easily. Spaniards also, Dominguez-Rey observed, had a fairly tolerant attitude towards foreigners who still made the occasional mistake when speaking their language; an attitude which, as the reporter in *Le Monde* admitted, was found less frequently among the French.

COUNTING YOUR BLESSINGS

'La querelle du franglais' does not always show the French people taking part in it at their best. *Parlez-vous franglais?* is a bad-tempered book, in which what Étiemble would clearly regard as righteous indignation leads him not only to fail to provide chapter and verse for the examples he quotes, but also to treat historical events in a way which is distinctly cavalier. His remark about the most decisive individual event which ensured that English would remain the dominant language in North America, the Louisiana purchase of 1803, is a particular example of this, and to be treated with considerable scepticism. It is true that the agreement struck between Bonaparte and Thomas Jefferson, whereby France received 15 million dollars for the area containing not only Louisiana but also present-day Arkansas, both the Dakotas, Iowa, Kansas, Missouri, Montana, Nebraska and Oklahoma, was not a good bargain for Napoleon. Only the sale of Manhattan island to the Dutch by the Native Americans in 1624 for the equivalent of 24 dollars rivals it for lack of foresight. It was not, however, a treaty imposed by American threats on a France which Étiemble describes as being 'aux abois' (at bay).[19] In 1803, Napoleon's military domination of Europe was at its height, and he was about to make himself Emperor. He was, it is true, discouraged by his failure to crush the revolt of Toussaint L'Ouverture in Haiti, and anxious to remain on good terms with the United States in what he could see would soon be a renewal of hostilities with England. But his decision to give up the possibility of a continued French presence on the North American continent was fully in the logic of a preference for Europe which had always been at the heart of French foreign policy, and which had already shown itself in the readiness of Louis XV to sign away French Canada in the Treaty of Paris of 1763.

There is an important sense in which this Eurocentric policy has paid off, though not in a way mentioned by any speaker in the debate on Jacques Toubon's bill. From its beginnings, in 1950, as the European Coal and Steel Community (ECSC), through its transformation in 1958 into the European Economic Community, its subsequent change of name to the European Communities in 1987, and then to the European Union in 1992, the organisation still most frequently referred to in England as the Common Market has used French as its main administrative language. Many documents are still drafted in French, which also has the advantage of being the *lingua franca* in which the Spaniards, the Portuguese, the Greeks and the Italians can communicate most easily with one another as well as with the French themselves and with the Belgians and the Luxembourgeois. Germany may well be the most powerful country economically, the paymaster of the Community. But the German language has not recovered from the fact that in 1950, when Germany first linked its fortunes with those of France, Italy and the Benelux countries through the Treaty of Paris establishing the Coal and Steel Community, it was still seen as the language of Belsen and Buchenwald. When the British declined to join the ECSC in 1950, repeated their refusal in 1957 when the European Economic Community was established, and were kept out of the

Community by General de Gaulle between 1963 and 1973, French continued to strengthen its place in Community matters and France its influence in Europe. The Danes, the Dutch and the Germans may well have found it convenient, from 1973 onwards, to use English among themselves as well as with members of the British delegation in the informal discussions that take place in the bars, corridors and restaurants. But when it comes to discussing draft proposals, anyone without a good knowledge of French is at a serious disadvantage; and until the entry on 1 January 1995 of Austria, Finland and Sweden, the daily press conferences were always given in French.

The institutions of the European Community are also based on French administrative practice. This is particularly true of the European Court of Accounts, which is modelled on the French Cour des Comptes, and the terms for the various officers of the European Court – Advocate General, Assessors – are direct translations from the French. Small though the number of permanent administrators in the European Community may be – there are more people working in the Scottish Office, and the largest single group of European Union employees in Brussels consists of translators and interpreters – the pattern is that of the continental administrative system, and thus very much a reflection of what is done in France. Valéry Giscard d'Estaing may have suffered only slightly in the public opinion polls when it became known that he conducted his conversations with Helmut Schmidt in English. He owed his defeat by François Mitterrand in the presidential election of May 1981 much more to the refusal of his rival, Jacques Chirac, to support him by telling the members of the Rassemblement pour la République to vote for him in the second ballot. But it would be a bold fonctionnaire who risked his promotion prospects by defying the rules set out in the *dictionnaire des termes officiels de la langue française* and wrote 'software' instead of 'logiciel', or who dared to refer to a 'navire inférieur aux normes' as a 'substandard ship'.

If, as it is often tempting to think, the obsession with words of English or American origin to be found in certain French writers and politicians is the symptom of a national neurosis, of an identity crisis which refuses to recognise itself as such, it also has another feature which links it with private individuals afflicted with comparable problems: a refusal to count one's blessings. This is noticeable in the way Philippe Richert, speaking in the debate in the Sénat on 12 April 1994, acknowledged that the Americans had got there first with the invention of 'le fast food', but failed to mention how much better the French had done in the chain of restaurants known as 'La Courte Paille'. The French commentators who claim that the popularity of 'franglais' marks the end of French inventiveness make little mention of the triumphs of the French car industry. Similarly, it is unusual to find any recognition of the fact that the French are quite capable of ruining their language, and especially of abandoning the clarity so much admired by Rivarol, without any help from the English or even from the Americans. On 7 May 1993, for example, Luc Ferry wrote in *Le Point* no. 1077 that

> Le sujet métaphysique est mort – la déconstruction a donc gagné, plus grâce à Nietzsche et Heidegger qu'à leurs épigones français – mais la nécessité d'une subjectivité responsable, d'une maîtrise de soi, est acceptée.

The fact that Luc Ferry was described as the co-author of a book entitled *La Pensée 1968* is only one of the reasons why any attempt to translate his statement into English is as meaningless as the original French. One might indeed write:

> The metaphysical subject is dead – deconstruction has therefore won, thanks more to Nietzsche and Heidegger than to their French imitators – but the need for a responsible subjectivity, for a certain self-control, is accepted.

But this doesn't mean anything either, and this is fully consistent with Roland Barthes's formal rejection in 1953 of the ideal formulated by Rivarol. 'La clarté', he wrote in *Le Degré zéro de l'écriture (Writing Degree Zero)*,

> est un attribut purement rhétorique, elle n'est pas une qualité générale du langage, possible dans tous les temps et tous les lieux, mais seulement l'appendice idéal d'un certain

discours, celui-là même qui est soumis à une intention permanente de persuasion. C'est parce que la prébourgeoisie des temps monarchiques et la bourgeoisie des temps post-révolutionnaires, usant d'une même écriture, ont développé une mythologie essentialiste de l'homme que l'écriture classique, une et universelle, a abandonné tout tremblement au profit d'un continu dont chaque parcelle était *choix*, c'est-à-dire élimination radicale de tout possible du langage. (Clarity is a purely rhetorical attribute, it is not a general quality of language, attainable at all times and in all places, but merely the ideal appendix to a certain discourse, the one subjected to a permanent attempt to persuade. It is because the pre-bourgeoisie of the period of the monarchy, and the bourgeoisie of the post-revolutionary period, using the same kind of writing, have developed an essentialist mythology of man, that classical writing, one and universal, has given up all trembling in favour of an unbroken tissue of which each element represented a voice, that is to say the radical elimination of every possible in language.[20]

Barthes's influence, like that of Michel Foucault, reached its height in the 1968 student rebellion, and has since been strengthened by that of Jacques Derrida. Together, these writers have popularised a style of writing in France of which Luc Ferry's statement is a characteristic and by no means isolated example. Its principal aim seems to be to render the authors who use it invulnerable to criticism by making it impossible for anyone to understand what they are trying to say. Any attempt to disagree can be immediately parried by the reply that the critic has not understood, and any request for evidence rejected on the grounds that this is bourgeois empiricism. Karl Popper's view that statements are meaningful if it is possible to devise experiments or find examples which would falsify them is as far as it is possible to get from fashionable French intellectual discourse. Just as the awareness that the *Declaration of Independence of the Thirteen United States of America* preceded the French revolution by thirteen years is something which the world vision of Jean d'Ormesson cannot take into account.

There is nevertheless, for the French, some cause for comfort and self-congratulation in the fact that the style of writing popularised by Barthes and Derrida has now so penetrated the discussion of literature in academic circles in the United Kingdom and the United States of America that even Étiemble might see it as a suitable revenge.

NOTES

1 Published annually by the Éditions Robert Laffont. A Kind of expanded version of Whitaker's *Almanack*.

2 See Fraser Mackenzie, *Les Relations de la France et de l'Angleterre d'après le vocabulaire*, Paris, 1939, vol. I, p. 117.

3 *Journal Officiel*, p. 988; see above, Chapter 1, note 21. For the link between free market economics and a laissez-faire attitude towards language, see the entry on 'stopper' in IIb and note 7 to Chapter 1. For Jacques Toubon's claim that it was his law which was in the true tradition of the *Déclaration des droits de l'homme et du citoyen*, see below, note 6.

   It should nevertheless be noted that American Express are now taking the precaution of making all their advertisements and notices in France bilingual; something which they are not doing in Germany, Italy, or Spain.

4 See *L'Express*, 23 November 1984. Quoted by Malcolm Offord in *Varieties of Contemporary French*, Macmillan, London, 1986. For a more detailed discussion of the legal situation, see Roderick Munday, 'Legislating in Defence of the French Language', *Cambridge Law Journal*, July 1985, pp. 218–35.

5 See C. Hagège, *Le français et les siècles*, Odile Jacob, Paris, 1987, p. 124.

6 *Journal Officiel*, p. 984.

7 Philippe de Saint-Robert, *La Cause du français; Du Service de la langue française à la naissance de la francophonie*, Éditions La Place Royale, Paris, 1987, p. 6.

8 Étiemble, *Parlez-vous franglais?*, Gallimard, Paris, 1973, pp. 120 and 296.

9 *Journal Officiel*, p. 968.

10 *Journal Officiel*, p. 963. It will be noted that one of M. Richert's 'franglais' words, 'spot', is what N. C. W. Spence calls a false anglicism (*Forum for Modern Languages Studies*, vol. XVIII, no. 2, April 1987, pp. 169–83). Such words are marked with an asterisk in the index.

11 *Journal Officiel*, p. 969.
12 Étiemble, op. cit., p. 287.
13 Michel Tournier, *Le Vent Paraclet*, Gallimard, Paris, 1977, p. 78. While it is of course possible that neither the pupils themselves nor their parents had much choice over the matter, Tournier gives the impression that it was a result of a deliberate decision to back the horse which seemed to be winning at the time. He himself, he comments, was taking German at school before the war, and thus very conscious of the increase in the number of pupils joining him at the beginning of the new school year in September 1940.
14 See Robert Hughes, *The Fatal Shore: A History of the Transportation of Convicts to Australia, 1787–1868*, Pan Books, London, 1988, pp. 88–9.
15 For both quotations, see David C. Gordon, *The French Language and National Identity*, Mouton, The Hague/Paris, New York, 1978, pp. 36. A good account of the movement known as La Francophonie is given in the book of the same name by William W. Bostock, published by River Seine publications, Melbourne, Australia, in 1988.
16 Quoted by Rodney Ball in his article 'Plus Ça Change? The Enduring Tradition of French Linguistic Conservatism', *French Cultural Studies*, vol. 6, 1995, pp. 61–78.
17 See Tony Judt in *La Croix*, 31 July 1994.
18 For a recent study of the phenomenon, see Richard F. Kuisel, *Seducing the French: The Dilemma of Americanisation*, University of California Press, Berkeley/New York, 1993.
19 Étiemble, op. cit., p. 325.
20 My own translation of p. 43 of the 1972 'Collection Points' edition of *Le Degré zéro de l'écriture*, Éditions du Seuil, Paris, 1953.

PART II
EXAMPLES

Introduction

Parlez-vous franglais? does not always give chapter and verse
for the words which Étiemble finds so objectionable. I have
not therefore mentioned all the terms which he criticises,
especially since some of them have now gone out of circulation.
As Colin Asher quite rightly comments,

> The reader of the 1990's can only view with puzzled amaze-
> ment Étiemble's outrage at *le climb*, *le hully-gully* and *le
> madison*[1]

and there is another disadvantage to the generalised attacks
against 'le franglais' of which Étiemble's is the best known. It
is the fact that words such as 'le rewriting', 'activated sludge',
'kid' and 'chaps' seem to occur only in satires or denunciations
of the phenomenon. When I have not been able to find
chapter and verse for such expressions being used as terms in
their own right, I have included them only when they seemed
either to raise a linguistic point, or to throw an instructive
light on a particular aspect of French society.

I have concentrated instead on words which occur in recent
French publications, and which might therefore indicate the
extent to which 'franglais' terms are in current usage. I can
see how a different classification system from the one I have
adopted might give a different impression. Indeed, I toyed at
one stage with the idea of arranging the examples in increasing
or decreasing order of usefulness to native speakers of French.
This would have produced a list in which words such as
'baby-sitting' or 'week-end', for which there is no French
equivalent, led all the rest, and terms such as 'shopping',
which can easily be replaced by 'faire les courses', or 'boss',
synonymous with 'patron', came in last. It was nevertheless
not long before I realised that this was an operation best
carried out by each individual reader.

The same is true of another taxonomic system which might
be adopted, that of the degree of snobbery involved in the use

of certain words. This is very evident in terms such as 'gentle-man farmer', discussed in section IIa, 'drink', in IIb, 'gossip' and 'glamour' in IId. While there may not always be an immediate French equivalent, such words are not used pri-marily to communicate an idea. Their aim is to show that the speaker is not so old-fashioned as to use a French term when an English or American one is available. Such a classification would, however, reflect my own value system rather than any objective standard. It might also provoke readers into making over-hasty judgements or pre-empt views which they would prefer to develop for themselves.

In his article '*Faux amis and Faux anglicismes*: Problems of Classification and Definition,'[2] N. C. W. Spence implicitly suggests another way in which 'franglais' words might be classified: that of their distance from either indigenous French or correct English. His comment that

> an enthusiasm for English unmatched by competence in the language must explain the introduction of *footing* and the now obsolete *shake-hand*, *starter* in the sense of 'choke', *snow-boot* in that of 'overshoe', and *racing* instead of 'running'

runs parallel to one of the reasons lying behind the use in the index of the asterisk * to indicate that the word in question has changed its meaning when passing from English into French. One of the most valid objections against 'le franglais' is that of the extreme oddity of some of the words ostensibly borrowed from English or American usage. Not only do they reflect the phenomenon also noted by Professor Spence when he com-ments that 'loanwords rarely have the same sense as their sources'. They also create an involuntarily comic vision of England and the English language in which an extraordinarily large number of words end with the suffix -ing,[3] so that *des clubmen* with a high concern for their *standing* take the clothes they have dirtied while taking part in *le footing, le racing, le jogging*, or *le wading* (river fishing) to be cleaned at *un pressing*, or deposit *un bristol* (visiting card) before putting on *un smoking* in order to meet wives who have made themselves look more elegant than usual by having *un brushing* (blow-dry) and putting on *du blush* (rouge) to improve their complexion.

It is true that this slightly nineteenth-century vision of her or his culture is more reassuring for the native speaker of English than the idea of life in the United States given by some of the 'franglais' words collected in IId. There are, fortunately, other ways in which Americans occupy their time apart from taking drugs, wearing weird clothes and indulging in unorthodox sex, and another of the objections to 'le franglais' is that it transforms language from a means whereby different cultures understand one another into the source of considerable misunderstandings. It would nevertheless be very difficult to classify 'franglais' words in terms of how improbable they sound to the native speaker of English – as, indeed, to the many French people who have an impressive mastery of our language – and would distract attention from the fact that they belong, for all their occasional strangeness and sociological interest, to the more general linguistic category of anglicisms.

In his very enthusiastic review in *Le Monde* for 16 May 1981 of Josette Rey-Debove's and Gilberte Gagnon's *Dictionnaire des Anglicismes*, Jacques Cellard argued that most anglicisms could be placed in one of three main categories. First of all, there were the words which designate objects and activities that do not exist in France. The examples which Jacques Cellard gives are 'attorney', 'lawyer', 'base-ball', 'muffins' and 'mint-julep'. These, he points out, can no more be avoided in a normal conversation than can names of towns, and readers might like to consider whether or not terms as different as 'rock music' and 'self-government', which are listed in the index, fall into the same category. I have, again, included such terms only when they raise interesting questions about French society.

Secondly, there were what Jacques Cellard saw as genuine anglicisms: terms such as 'attaché case', 'rugby ball', 'leasing', 'sandwich', or 'starter'. These describe objects which are found in France, and for which a perfectly valid French word obviously exists: 'porte-documents', 'ballon oval', 'location-vente', 'casse-croûte' and 'démarreur'. I have included these only occasionally, deliberately omitting the 'volley-ball', which Jacques Toubon gives as one of his hobbies in the 1995 edition

of *Who's Who in France*, and have been even more economical
with the highly technical terms which take up so much of the
May 1989 *dictionnaire des néologismes officiels*, and of the March
1993 *dictionnaire des termes officiels*, or which are listed in such
profusion in the book which I have referred to as the Toubon,
the January 1994 *dictionnaire des termes officiels de la langue
française*.

This is first of all because these technical terms are so
specialised. The Toubon's 'wet standpipe' (colonne en charge),
is likely to come up frequently only in the conversation of
someone who is an architect concerned with the construction
of precautions against fire, just as 'Shine Dalgarno sequence'
(séquence Shine Dalgarno) will tend to occur only in the
remarks made by a specialist in molecular genetics. It is thus
hard to see how, in either case, the English term could be
considered a serious threat to the purity of French, or be very
interesting in its own right. The same is true of other terms
such as 'saturated boiling', an expression used in nuclear
engineering, and for which the 1993 *dictionnaire des termes
officiels* recommends 'ébullition nucléée saturée', or 'somatic
hybridization', a technique used in agricultural engineering
and whose official French form is given in the 1989 *dictionnaire
des néologismes officiels* as 'hybridation somatique'.

It is the fact of these words being included in the Toubon
which is significant, not the words themselves. It is clearly of
great importance to the French authorities to maintain the
status of French as a scientific language, and their attitude is
fully understandable. It is nevertheless a matter of common
experience that whenever you see an article in a newspaper
which talks about a subject of which you have some knowledge, it is never very accurate. This is certainly true of what
the Toubon has to say about the vocabulary of golf.[4] I hope,
for their sake, that the microbiologists, electrical engineers
and other specialists at whom the Toubon is primarily aimed
find its recommendations a more satisfactory guide to the way
the terms are actually used.

It is Jacques Cellard's third category which is the most
interesting. This consists of words which are in common usage
in French, which clearly come either from the other side of

the Channel or from across the Atlantic, but for which no obvious French substitute exists. It is these which create, for the purist, the problem of deciding whether are not they are so unacceptable that a substitute has to be found for them. One of the main linguistic issues in 'la querelle de franglais' is that of deciding when a word borrowed from English or from American has been in the language long enough no longer to count as an intruder.

I have already touched in Part I of this book on the problem of when a word which is not originally French ceases to be an anglicism and becomes an integral part of the language. I come back to this question in some of the examples quoted in the four sections into which Part II is divided: IIa, *Business, commerce and politics*; IIb, *Food, drink and travel*; IIc, *The arts, the media and sport*; IId, *Youth, clothes and entertainment*. These categories are not watertight, and there is inevitably some overlap. They nevertheless seem to me to be justified in the light of what I am trying to do. This is not to duplicate the work of other linguists, especially not of Josette Rey-Debove and Gilberte Gagnon, but to study the phenomenon of 'le franglais' in the context of French society.

My four categories represent areas of life in which everybody is interested, and in which, traditionally, language has most tended to evolve. Learned words are generally fixed expressions created from Latin or Greek to fulfil a precise function and satisfy a specific and well-defined need. One of the defects of the Toubon, and of all comparable attempts to codify language, is that they take a technique which is perfectly satisfactory for highly technical terms and apply it to the language of everyday intercourse and experience. Because this is the part of language which has always been most subject to change, it is very difficult to codify. The Toubon is unusual among dictionaries in that instead of taking as its starting-point a set of examples which illustrate how the language is used by native speakers, it adopts the prescriptive approach of saying what ought to be the case. This is another reason why the 2,400 words listed in its index are not always a reliable guide to usage.

Another possible way of classifying the 300 or so examples

which I have found would indeed be to have tried to arrange them in some kind of order of seniority, putting those which deserve the linguistic equivalent of a long-service medal at the front, followed by a long and less respectable tail of those which have, as the saying was in the armed services, not yet got their number dry. To have done so, however, would have led to even more duplication of the work already done by Josette Ray-Debove and Gilberte Gagnon, so I decided against it. I have, however, indicated when a particular word does not figure in the *Dictionnaire des Anglicismes*. This is, in general, a good guide to the fact that it is a relatively recent import. So, too, is the presence or absence in my index of the sign †, the one which indicates that the word figures in the 1992 edition of the *Petit Robert*, or the *Petit Larousse Illustré 1995*.

Readers will also notice that I have not followed the taxonomic system most frequently used when analysing language, which is that of analysing the role of the different parts of speech. Since 'le franglais' consists mainly of nouns, with only a scattering of adjectives, very few adverbs, and virtually no pronouns, prepositions, conjunctions, definite or indefinite articles, such an approach would merely have emphasised the point made in the Introduction: it is not a real language at all.

NOTES

1 See *Francophonie*, December 1994, p. 16. They are in fact dances popular in the 1920s.
2 *Forum for Modern Language Studies*, Vol. XVIII, no. 2, April 1987, pp. 169–83.
3 For further details on this phenomenon, see Professor Spence's article 'Les mots français en -ing' in *Le Français moderne*, Vol. 59, 1991, pp. 188–213.
4 It would be tedious to list all the cases where the Toubon gets it wrong on golf, though some indication is given in the entries on 'links' and 'rough' in IIc.
   Further indication of the inadequacies of the Toubon in this area can also be found in its entries on 'match play' and 'Stableford'. Match play is a competition in which you score by the number of holes won, lost, or halved, not by the total number

of strokes taken over nine or eighteen holes. The definition in the Toubon of the recommended 'affrontement direct', which is given in the index to the *dictionnaire des termes officiels de la langue française* as the term to be used as an acceptable substitute for 'match play', is 'partie dans laquelle s'affrontent deux adversaires ou deux équipes' (a game between two opponents or two teams). This could just as well apply to 'stroke play', in which the winner is the person who takes the smallest number of strokes, and not necessarily the one who wins the most holes.

It is not frivolous to quote this example, or to point out that the complexities of the Stableford method of scoring are not adequately rendered by 'partie par points', especially when the further definition of the term in the body of the Toubon contains no reference to the central role played in the Stableford scoring system by a competitor's handicap. It would certainly have been better if the authors of the Toubon had not ventured into the area of sports, which is one where they make themselves so vulnerable to the suggestion that they had not done their homework. If they can get it wrong on something so simple, there is a strong temptation to think that some of their entries on more difficult and important topics are not very accurate either.

a Business, Commerce and Politics

The asterisk * is a reminder that the word either does not normally exist in English or is used by the French in a different sense from the meaning it has in the United States or the United Kingdom. The dagger † placed after a word in the index indicates its presence either the *Petit Larousse Illustré 1995* or the *Petit Robert* (1992).

Arrangement n.m. Disliked by Étiemble, presumably because of its use to designate an arrangement between two people. This is not the meaning which it has had in French since the fourteenth century, which is that of the physical disposition of objects. The Toubon gives 'arrangeur' for 'arranger', in the sense of somebody who arranges a financial transaction. A letter in *Madame Figaro* for 15 November 1994 commented that 'l'attitude des commerçants est beaucoup plus arrangeante que par le passé' (the attitude of shopkeepers is much more accommodating than in the past).

Audit n.m. Although, as Jean-Pierre Colignon points out in *La cote des mots*, Volume 1 of the new *Dictionnaire de l'Académie française* does not accept this word, it is included in Joseph Hanse's *Nouveau dictionnaire des difficultés du français moderne*. M. Colignon comments on the advantage which 'audit' derives from its brevity over established expressions such as 'vérification comptable' or 'contrôle de gestion', and the word is in common use. Not in the Toubon.

Badge n.m. Although the Toubon omits the word 'badge', the word 'macaron' is becoming more frequent to describe what one wears to identify oneself to one's fellow attenders at a conference. The word can also mean a plastic card which enables the holder to pass through a security system, or to 'clock in' at work; hence the verb 'badger'. 'Étiquette' is still too closely associated with 'price tag'. The *Petit Robert* for 1992 associates the word 'badge' with humorous slogans of the 'Apple Pie Makes You Sterile' type.

Big bang n.m. This can have a different meaning from the political one given to it by Michel Rocard. On 6 October 1994, *L'Événement du jeudi* no. 518 published an article entitled 'Le big bang associatif actuel', in which it described how more and more 'Associations sans but lucratif' were being established every year. *L'Événement du jeudi* was worried about the lack of control exercised over such organisations, especially since many of them were being established 'en Provence-Alpes-Maritimes', a region which it rather nicely described as being 'connue pour son civisme aléatoire' (known for the intermittent nature of its civic spirit).[1]

Blue chips n.m. Jean-Pierre Colignon suggests that the traditional 'valeur de père de famille' is a more accurate term for a secure investment, and warns readers of *La cote des mots* against 'des glamour stock'.

Boat people n.m.p. First used in the late 1970s to describe the political refugees fleeing the communist régime in Vietnam, and applied in 1994 to the refugees arriving in Florida from Cuba. On 27 August 1994 Bernard-Henri Lévy enumerated in his weekly column in *Le Point*, no. 1145, the different ways in which communist régimes had ended:

> Le collapse foudroyant des Albanais. La catalepsie bulgare. La mort par overdose [see IId] des Serbes. On voyait même, depuis peu, une voie chinoise vers le néant, sur fond de frénésie commerçante et d'immobilité impériale. Or, voici qu'à cette série bien saturée, le vieux Fidel ajoute une variante inédite: ces milliers de boat people qui embarquent, chaque nuit, sur les radeaux de fortune. (The devastating collapse of the Albanians. The cataleptic trance

of the Bulgarians. The death by overdose of the Serbs.
Recently, there was even a Chinese pathway towards noth-
ingness, against a background of commercial frenzy and
imperial immobility. And now, old Fidel has added a
previously unknown version to this over-saturated series:
these thousands of boat people taking ship every night on
home-made rafts.)

The word does not figure in the Toubon, and could be
translated only by a periphrase such as 'des réfugiés politiques
qui fuient par bateau'. In her regular column entitled 'La vie
des mots' Isabelle Armitage commented in the February 1995
number of the *French Review*, the journal of the American
Association of Teachers of French, on the pronunciation 'baut-
pipels', heard on French television.

I have found no other examples of the use of the word
'collapse', used here in the sense of 'effondrement', but the
latinism 'collapsus' is frequent in a medical context and is
occasionally used metaphorically.

Boom n.m. An article in *Le Point* for 20 August 1994, no.
1144, commented that French industrialists knew that their
present industrial capacity was not strong enough to 'faire
face à un boom de la demande'. The normal word – the
Toubon recommends 'boum' – is 'la reprise économique', and
Le Point illustrated the permanence of one particular French
idiom when it asked:

> Combien de temps encore la reprise économique, la vraie,
> jouera-t-elle les Arlésiennes?

The joke in Alphonse Daudet's 1871 play, *L'Arlésienne*, later
set to music by Bizet, is that the coach for Arles never arrives.
The *Petit Robert* insists upon the transitory and unstable nature
of 'un boom'.

Boss n.m. Frequently used as 'patron', perhaps because of
the pun in the phrase 'quand le big boss nous fait bosser'
(when the big boss makes us work hard). On 30 December
1993, *L'Express* no. 2216 reported the arrest of Toto Riena

le boss de la mafia, qui a transformé la Sicile en stand [see IId] de tir (the boss of the mafia, who has turned Sicily into a shooting gallery).

See also 'foot business' in IIc.

Boycott n.m. In French since 1881, only a year after his neighbours in County Mayo refused to have any dealings with the unfortunate Captain Boycott. Also in the form 'boycottage' and the verb 'boycotter'. After the first round of the legislative elections of 1993, *Le Monde* for 23 March pointed out that Le Pen's National Front obtained 12.52 per cent of the votes cast

> malgré le boycott médiatique et la pauvreté des moyens d'information (in spite of being boycotted by the media and the shortage of opportunities to put across its message).

Brain-trust* n.m. A spelling given as the sole form in the *Dictionnaire des Anglicismes*, and included in the *Petit Robert*, as well as in Jean-Pierre Colignon's *La cote des mots*, instead of the more usual form in England of 'Brains Trust'; not in the Toubon. The activity described in the Toubon as 'brain-storming' is 'remue-méninges', in the sense of the collective racking of brains in a group session to find a new idea or the solution to a problem. 'Brainstorming' is absent from the 1990 Chambers, which restricts itself to 'brainstorm' in the sense of 'a sudden disturbance of the mind, a sudden inspiration'.

Briefing n.m., **briefer** v. and **debriefer** v. Although these terms are universally criticised, the Toubon does not mention them, any more than does the 1989 *dictionnaire des néologismes officiels* or the 1993 *dictionnaire des termes officiels*. In Michèle Fitoussi's *Le ras-le-bol des SuperWomen* (Calmann-Lévy, Paris, 1987), the successful 'executivewoman', working in advertising, often has 'des staffs de créatifs à briefer' (staffs of creative writers to brief). One could say 'mettre au courant'.

There is no obvious alternative to 'debriefer'. Someone who has mastered a brief has 'une bonne connaissance de son dossier'. On 3 March 1994, *The New York Times* reported a spokesman for the French Foreign Office as saying 'ce briefing est off the record'.

Bristol n.m. A visiting card. In a little dig at the extreme formality of Edouard Balladur's speech and life-style, *Le Nouvel Observateur* no. 1575 for 26 March 1995 reproduced what was said to be 'un Bristol' sent to his supporters:

> Monsieur Edouard Balladur, Premier Minister de France, est heureux d'inviter M. X à voter pour lui les dimanches 23 avril et 7 mai, 1995 à partir de 8 heures. Tenue correcte exigée. (Monsieur Edouard Balladur, Prime Minister of France, is happy to invite M. X to vote for him on 23 April and 7 May 1995 from eight o'clock onwards. Dress formal.)

Bulldozer n.m. The Toubon recommends 'bouteur', without mentioning the other form suggested by the official 'Comité d'Étude des termes techniques', and reported in the *Dictionnaire des Anglicismes*, of 'boutoir à lame' or simply 'boutoir'. Commenting on Étiemble's suggestion of 'bouledoseur', Josette Rey-Debove and Gilberte Gagnon point out that it sounds as if it could mean 'doseur de boules', somebody who doses bowls, an odd profession but a conceivable one. You could dose them by putting on an excessive bias, though this would not matter much in the game of 'boules' as played in France. Or, since you can 'doser l'ironie', measure your irony according to the person you are talking to, you could limit the number of bowls available.

Jacques Chirac is often described as 'un bulldozer en politique' (see the entry 'battling' in IIc), and deserves his reputation for getting things done. The moment you drive into the Département de la Corrèze, which he has represented since 1967, you notice an improvement in the quality of the roads. French electors expect their *député* to use his position in Paris to get things for them. See below, 'recordman'.

Business n.m. Very frequent, often in a derogatory sense. An article in *France Soir* for 5 August 1994 entitled 'Quand les barbus [bearded ones] font du business' described how the

Front Islamique du Salut (Islamic Salvation Front) ran a shop in Paris. *Libération* for 12 December 1994, parodied one of the best-known French carols by writing 'Il est né le divin enfant / Sonnez marchands, résonnez business' (The Christ Child is born / Ring out merchants, ring out business).

In *Le Point*, no. 1072, 3 April 1993, Jean-Sébastien Stilli, reporting from the USA, wrote in a more neutral and informative tone:

> Dans les années à venir, si les entreprises ne sont pas responsables socialement, elles ne sont plus dans le business. (In the years to come, if firms show no social responsibility, they are no longer in business.)

Businessman n.m. The *Dictionnaire des Anglicismes* dates its first use in French as 1871, and describes the plural *businessmen* as 'encombrant' (awkward). It quotes from Antoine de Saint-Exupéry's 1943 fairy-tale *Le Petit Prince*:

> La quatrième planète était celle du businessman. Cet homme était si occupé qu'il ne leva même pas la tête à l'arrivée du petit prince. (The fourth planet was that of the businessman. He was so busy that he did not even look up when the little prince arrived.)

This is a characteristic example of the dislike for the world of commerce which Saint-Exupéry shared with most twentieth-century writers.

Le Nouvel Observateur no. 1536 for 14 April 1994 described how Gerd Müller was 'un businessman averti' (streetwise businessman; the Collins-Robert gives 'fûté' for streetwise, the Oxford-Hachette 'dégourdi'), who had 'déposé son logo, son appellation, dans toute l'Europe' (patented his logo throughout Europe). The word 'appellation' immediately evokes 'appellation contrôlée', the legal guarantee by the 'office national du vin' that the grapes from which a wine is made were grown in a specific area. Müller offered firms the opportunity of embarrassing people who owed them money by having them followed in the street by a large man dressed as a white rabbit.

Neither 'business' nor 'businessman' is in the Toubon; perhaps because 'homme d'affaires' is so obvious; perhaps because the word is now fully accepted as French. In *Le ras-le-bol des Super Women*, Michèle Fitoussi talks happily – or, rather, unhappily – about 'une businesswoman', just as she talks about 'une careerwoman'.

Bye bye Interjection frequently used as an alternative to the equally jocular 'ciao', as well as by de Gaulle in one of his conversations with Alain Peyrefitte on the Algerian problem in 1959. Acknowledging that France could not bring the standard of living of the Arab population of Algeria up to that of the European settlers, de Gaulle said:

> Alors, puisque nous ne pouvons leur offrir l'égalité, il vaut mieux leur donner la liberté! *Bye bye*, vous nous coûtez trop cher. (So, since we can't offer them equality, we'd better give them liberty. Bye bye, you cost us too much money.)

See Peyrefitte, *C'était de Gaulle*, Fayard, Paris, 1994, p. 55. See also below, 'self-government'.

Campus n.m. In French since the 1920s, as a consequence of the need to place new universities outside towns. But as the *Dictionnaire des Anglicismes* remarks:

> la vie de campus est unanimement considérée par les étudiants français comme inconfortable et ennuyeuse. Ajoutons encore que le Français n'a pas, comme l'Américain, le respect de la nature, et que le parc est rapidement transformé en terrain vague. (Life on campus is unanimously considered boring and uncomfortable by French students. It should be added that the French do not, unlike the Americans, have a respect for nature, and the campus soon becomes a piece of waste ground.)

Cash n.m. In an interview in *Le Nouvel Observateur* no. 1556 for 1 September 1994, the former socialist Prime Minister Laurent Fabius explained why Edouard Balladur had decided to sell off Renault: 'il avait besoin de cash avant les élections' (he needed money before the elections). There is no immediate reason why 'cash' should not be replaced by 'argent'. The Toubon suggests 'comptant' or 'espèces' as in 'payer comptant' or 'en argent liquide', or the old-fashioned 'espèces sonnantes et trébuchantes'. 'Cash-flow problems' are 'des problèmes de trésorerie'.

See also 'fun' in IId.

Challenge n.m., also **challenger**. Used in a business and political context as well as in a sporting one. *Le Nouvel Observateur* publishes and advertises one of its own magazines under the title *Challenges*, a word which implies a support for a dynamic market economy (une vraie économie de marché) that might have surprised the more traditionally minded socialists who originally founded the magazine under the title *France-Observateur* in 1950, and remained faithful to it when it changed its name to *Le Nouvel Observateur* in 1974.

Like many other newspapers and magazines, *Le Point* no. 1126 described Jacques Delors as 'le challenger de Michel Rocard' (16 April 1994), a possible rival socialist candidate in the 1995 presidential election, before he announced on 11 December 1994 that he would not stand, and on 26 January 1995 Europe 1 spoke of 'le candidat favori Balladur, le challenger Chirac, et l'outsider, le candidat socialiste, que ce soit Jospin ou Emmanuelli' (Balladur the favourite, Chirac the challenger, and the outsider, the socialist candidate, whether Jospin or Emmanuelli). In a similar vein, France-Inter spoke on 3 April 1995 of how 'le spirit final' would see a competition between 'Chirac le favori, Balladeur le challenger et Jospin l'outsider'.

The Toubon suggests 'défi', as in Jean-Jacques Servan-Schreiber's 1976 *Le Défi américain* and his 1980 *Le Défi mondial*; or 'challenge' together with 'chalenger' (chalengeuse, n.f.), the change in spelling apparently being enough to satisfy the purists (see 'tackle' in the entry for 'foot' in IIc) and being authorised by an 'arrêté du sport' for 18 February 1988, published in the *Journal Officiel* for 6 March. The Toubon also recommends 'défieur' (défieuse, n.m.).

Checkpoint n.m. Not in the Toubon, and more surprisingly absent from the *Dictionnaire des Anglicismes*. The term 'point de vérification', suggested by the 1994 *dictionnaire des termes officiels de la langue français*, was not used by the French in the dramatic days of the Cold War. They, like everybody else, described the main crossing point between West Berlin and the Soviet-occupied part of the city as 'Checkpoint Charlie'. In *Le Nouvel Observateur* for 23 May 1993, no. 1480, a journalist described his visit to 'Arzamai-16', the centre of the Russian nuclear arms establishment, and noted

> 'le check-point', gardé par des militaires et des troupes spécialisées du KGB, comme à Berlin au temps du mur (the checkpoint guarded by soldier and specialised troops from the KGB as in Berlin at the time of the wall).

Clan n.m. Frequently used in a political sense: 'le clan Balladur', 'le clan Rocard'.

Clash n.m. In French since the 1960s, though given in the 1994 *Dictionnaire Hachette* as an americanism. Hard to find a French equivalent, and the Toubon doesn't try. A specific example of the way French syntax can remain quite uncontaminated by close contact with 'le franglais' was provided in an interview in *Paris-Match* in March 1993, in which the constitutional expert Thierry de Montbrial was asked: 'Doit-on s'attendre à des clashs entre Matignon et l'Elysée au cours d'une nouvelle cohabitation?' (Should one expect clashes between the Prime Minister's office and the President's palace during a new cohabitation?). 'S'attendre à', the French for expect, is a ticklish verb to handle: reflexive, conjugated with 'être', taking either an indirect object, or the subjunctive in a subordinate clause introduced by 'à ce que'.

De Montbrial enumerated three possible areas of conflict between François Mitterrand, who would remain President until 1995, and the new Prime Minister he would have to appoint from the conservative majority produced by the elections: NATO, which the French call OTAN (Organisation du Traité de l'Atlantique Nord); the GATT (the General

Agreement on Tariffs and on Trade), which all the French newspapers call 'Le GATT', but which the Toubon thinks should be 'Agétac' (Accord général sur les tariffs et le commerce); and the former Yugoslavia.

Club n.m. In French since 1702, and used especially in the revolutionary period in 'le club des Cordeliers', 'le club des Jacobins', etc. Now used mainly in a sporting context – 'le Sporting-Club de Paris'; see also 'goal' in IIc and 'junior' in IId – with 'cercle' taking on its social meaning. In Proust, Swann is referred to as 'un clubman', and was a member of the exclusive 'Jockey Club de Paris', founded by Lord Seymour in 1834 to encourage the breeding of racehorses. Still in existence. Women not admitted.

Collecter v. A long-established verb, going back to the eighteenth century. Used on France-Inter on 6 February 1995 when the results came in of 'les Primaires PS' (the Socialist primaries) which chose Lionel Jospin as candidate for the presidential election of 23 April and 7 May 1995: 'les résultats collectés donnent Jospin vainqueur' (the collected results give Jospin as the winner).

Commonwealth n.m. In one sense, no more a 'franglais' word than 'self-government' (see below), and as necessary a borrowing in French as 'ancien régime' or 'coup d'état' are in English. *Le Point* used the word to good effect on 12 November 1994, no. 1156, when it marked the fifth anniversary of the fall of the Berlin Wall by recalling that Gorbachev's hope had been to

> transformer en une bataille-éclair l'Empire en Commonwealth afin de réaliser un repli en bon ordre, afin de permettre au Parti de se sauver chez lui par une réforme économique assez radicale (change the Empire into a Commonwealth by a lightning campaign [note the absence of the term 'Blitzkrieg'] in order to carry out an orderly retreat so as to allow the Party to save itself at home [or to run away home?] by a fairly radical economic reform).

The French for the former USSR, known in English as the

Commonwealth of Independent States, is la Confédération des États Indépendants.

Consultant n.m. A term much used by radio and television commentators during the 1994 *Tour de France*, especially when they reported the views of Raymond Poulidor. The word is not, however, as Jean-Pierre Colignon points out in *La cote des mots*, a recent import. He quotes Boileau's *Art poétique* (1674) as using the word in the sense of somebody who receives advice:

> Ecoutez tout le monde, assidu consultant:
> Un fat quelquefois ouvre un avis important. (Listen to everyone, taking everyone's opinion. A fop can sometimes give useful advice.)

He also cites La Fontaine using it in the sense of somebody who *gives* advice:

> L'ambition, l'envie avec les consultants,
> Dans la succession entrent en même temps. (Ambition and envy with other consultants come along at the same time.)

M. Colignon suggests that the modern use of the word may stem from the impression that the older term 'conseilleur' (adviser) suggests someone who gives advice when you don't need it, but recommends 'conseiller-expert' as an acceptable substitute. The *Petit Robert* gives it both in the medical sense of a consultant, and – quoting Lacan – of somebody who is in the process of consulting a psychiatrist. A medical consultant is also known as 'un spécialiste'.

Coolie n.m. Claude Imbert, in *Le Point* for 15 May 1993, no. 1078, spoke of the need for Europe to protect itself

> contre des biens produits, à des coûts salariaux trente, quarante, cinquante, soixante fois inférieurs aux nôtres, par les nouveaux coolies de l'industrie mondiale (against goods produced at salaries which are thirty, forty, fifty, sixty times lower than ours, by the new coolies of world industry).

This was the only way, it argued, that the Welfare State, 'l'État-Providence', could be maintained, though Claude

Imbert insisted in the same issue, in what has become a characteristic italianism, that 'les largesses de la "mamma" étatique incitent les assurés sociaux à une irresponsabilitié d'assistés' (the generous hand-outs by the Welfare State encourage beneficiaries to adopt the irresponsibility of people in perpetual receipt of money they have not earned).

Design n.m. In French since the mid-1960s according to the dictionaries, but replaced in the Toubon by 'stylique' or 'conception'. This implicit banning of the word – the Toubon appeared several months before the 1 August decision by the Conseil Constitutionnel restricting the application of the new law to people directly employed by the state – attracted strong disapproval from Gérard Caron. In a letter to *L'Événement du jeudi* no. 496 on 5 May 1994, he complained that he was now practising what was designated as an illegal profession, in spite of the fact that he and his colleagues had asked for a French equivalent over twenty years ago and been told that none existed. 'Entre temps', he added, 'le design français a conquis le monde' (in the meantime French design has conquered the world).

In an interview on France-Inter on 15 January 1995, M. Caron was described as 'un designer', and again defended the use of the word, pointing out its Latin roots. The École nationale d'art de Nancy offers a 'Diplôme d'Études Supérieures' in 'Design et Qualité'.

Discount n.m. The Toubon suggests 'ristourne' (n.f.), or 'discompte' (n.m.), together with 'magasin discompte' for 'discount centre', and 'prix discompté' for 'discount price'. There is a shop in Nice called 'Le discounter du collant' (see 'body' in IId), and although the English term seems to be winning, Jean-Pierre Colignon reminds the readers of *La cote des mots* of the perfectly good French words which express the same idea: 'ventes au prix de gros' (wholesale price), 'rabais', 'remises', 'fortes réductions', etc. He also points out that 'discount' is what he calls a boomerang word, in the sense that the English borrowed the Middle French 'descompte', a deduction from the sum paid, and then gave it back to the French with an anglicised spelling.

The same happened to tennis. Originally, one said 'Tenez' (hold, get that) as one sent the ball. In Middle English, this became 'tenetz', and then 'tennis'; which the English exported as 'lawn tennis' in the late nineteenth century.

Dispatcher n.m. and v., **dispatching**†, n. If the Toubon and the established dictionaries are reliable guides, a 'faux ami' as well as an example of 'le franglais'. It does have the meaning of sending off mail, in which case the Toubon recommends 'ventiler' for the verb together with 'ventilation' for the noun 'dispatching'. But it is also used in the sense of allocating aeroplanes to a particular route and ensuring that they stick to it. In that case it should be replaced, according to the Toubon, by 'réguler', translated by the 1995 *Larousse* as 'to control'.

Again according to the Toubon, the noun 'dispatcher' should be translated as 'largueur', the person responsible for making sure that paratroops waiting to go through the hatch do in fact jump; presumably an adaptation of the expression 'larguer les amarres' (anchors away!). The activity of dispatching is then to be described as 'largage'.

Down adj. See below, 'up'.

Dumping n.m. Very frequent, and in French in its commercial sense since 1904, as well as in the term 'le dumping social', transferring industries to countries with lower wage costs. The Toubon gives 'dumper' in the sense of a dumping truck as 'motobasculeur', but presumably admits by its silence that the English term is admissible in an economic context. The 1993 *dictionnaire des termes officiels* translates 'to dump' as 'clicher', a technical term used in printing and translated by the 1993 *Larousse* as 'to plate' or 'to stereotype'.

Engineering n.m. The detailed entry in the *Dictionnaire des Anglicismes* leaves unsolved the mystery of why the French, who in 1749 established the first school of civil engineering, the *École Nationale des Ponts et Chaussées*, who have the equally prestigious *École Polytechnique*, founded in 1794, as well as the

École des Mines and the *École Centrale des Arts et Manufactures*, and who live in a country where engineers (les ingénieurs) enjoy the high salary and reputation which they deserve, have no generic term to designate the activity. 'L'ingénierie' (n.f.), recommended in the 1993 *dictionnaire des termes officiels*, is absent from the Toubon, and other terms such as 'l'art de l'ingénieur', 'ingénieurat' and 'ingénieurage' are not found outside the books or articles recommending them as substitutes for the English term.

Establishment n.m. A boo word, popularised in England in the 1950s by Henry Fairlie, borrowed by the French early enough to be criticised by Étiemble, who preferred 'les gens en place, les deux cents familles'[2] in *Parlez-vous franglais?*, and defined in the *Dictionnaire des Anglicismes* as 'groupe puissant de nantis, de gens en place qui défendent leurs intérêts et l'ordre établi' (a powerful group of well-off, well-established people, who defend their own interests and the established order).

In one of its articles on 'la nouvelle super-élite française', *Le Nouvel Observateur* for 3 November 1994, no. 1565, described André Rousselet, the director of the television chain Canal +, as possessing 'le codes de l'establishment politique, les manières du businessman, les goûts d'un gentleman' (the codes of the political establishment, the manners of the businessman, the tastes of the gentleman).

Jean-Marie Le Pen, anxious at one and the same time to be as French as possible and to present himself as the victim of a conspiracy by the French establishment to prevent him getting his message across, pronounces the word 'établissement' when interviewed on the radio. In *Le Monde* for 3 February 1995, however, he used the English term.

Euroleaders n.m.p. An article in *Le Point* for 1 October 1994, no. 1150, noted with surprise and disappointment that 'plus d'un tiers des Euroleaders, interrogés par le Sofres [Société Française d'Études par Sondages] ne connaissaient rien de nos grandes écoles' (more than a third of the Euroleaders, when asked by the Sofres, knew nothing about our 'grandes écoles'). See note 2; and below, 'leader'.

The prefix 'euro', in French as in English, lends itself to numerous neologisms: 'euro-tunnel', 'euro-chômage', 'euro-scepticisme'.

For more details on the *grandes écoles*, see also Thody and Evans, *Faux Amis and Key Words*.

Executive woman n.f., **executive women**, n.f.p. For the singular form see 'fitness' in IId. *Le Nouvel Observateur* for 3 November 1988, no. 1252, carried an article entitled 'Executive Women', with the subtitle 'Fini les faibles femmes, le business a besoin de gros bras. Même féminins' (The end of the weaker sex. Business needs strong arms. Even in women).

In a long review of what it called P. D. James's 'roman de science fiction', the 1993 *The Children of Men* (*Les fils de l'homme*), *Le Point* for 28 August 1993, no. 1093, described her as 'l'exemple type d'une *committee woman*'; the nearest the French can get to 'the Great and the Good'.

The religious associations of the title of P. D. James's novel *Devices and Desires* – 'We have followed too much the devices and desires of our own hearts' – are rendered into French by the title *Par action et omission*, with its echo of the other phrase from the General Confession: 'We have left undone those things we ought to have done and we have done those things we ought not to have done.'

Extra n.m. and adj. Slick, in Sartre's unintentionally anti-communist play *Les Mains sales* (1948; translated as *Dirty Hands* in the UK, *Red Gloves* in the USA), is an electrician by trade but 'fait un petit extra' by working as Hoederer's bodyguard. The *Dictionnaire des Anglicismes* says the adjective 'ne se dit en français que pour le champagne' (is used in French only for champagne), and 'extra-dry' is an official description. However, the *Petit Robert* for 1977 gives the example of 'des bonbons extra' (finest quality).

See also below, 'jackpot'; as well as 'shoot' in IId.

Far West n.m. On 2 February 1995, Bernard Guetta, in his 'Géopolitique', a broadcast which he gives at 08.20 each day on

France-Inter, described the breakdown of order in Russia as giving birth to 'un nouveau Far West'.

Fax n.m. According to the 1989 *dictionnaire des néologismes officiels*, 'un facsimile' is 'une télécopie'. Neither word figures in the Toubon. As a banking friend of mine said, 'Mais, mon cher ami, tout le monde dit "envoyer un fax" or "faxer quelqu'un"'. C'est tellement plus simple.' (But, my dear chap, everyone says 'send a fax' or 'fax somebody'. It's so much simpler.)

On 14 January 1995, Henriette Walter, commenting in the magazine *Libération* on how rapidly new words come into French, observed that 'faxer,' had rapidly replaced 'facser'. She also emphasised the volatility of popular language by recalling an incident in 1985 in which François Mitterrand pointed out that one no longer said 'branché' to express the idea of being up to date, but 'câblé'. She then went on to say that even in 1985, people who were really with it used 'bléca', the backslang form (*verlan* = language à l'envers, language the wrong way round) but that even this was now no longer fashionable.

Henriette Walter's contention that fashionable words and expressions can disappear with the same rapidity as they arrive is borne out by a remark on p. 50 of Volume I of Fraser MacKenzie's *Les Relations de la France et de l'Angleterre d'après le vocabulaire*: that most of the 800 English words noted by the German scholar Bachmann in the novels of Jules Verne were no longer in use by the end of the nineteenth century.

First adj. As used in Claude Imbert's leading article in *Le Point*, no. 1157, 19 November 1994: 'Le bas de laine *first!*' to point out that the newly elected, Republican-dominated Congress would think first of all of the economic interests of the United States.

Traditionally, mistrusting banks and investments on the Stock Exchange ('les valeurs cotées en Bourse'), the French kept their savings in gold coins in a woollen stocking (*bas de laine*) under the bed.

First lady n.f. On 5 January 1995, seeing the election of

Édouard Balladur as President as a certainty, *L'Événement du jeudi* no. 531 published an article with the headline 'First Lady de la République' anticipating, wrongly as it turned out, how Marie-Josèphe Balladur was about to succeed Danielle Mitterrand.

Flash bang adj. Stun grenades. As thrown by the unit of the GIGN (Groupe d'Intervention de la Gendarmerie Nationale) when they freed the hostages from the Air France Airbus A-300 on 26 December 1994. See 'cockpit' in IIb.

Forcing* n.m. An example of a false anglicism, comparable to 'le footing', 'un pressing' (dry-cleaner's), 'un lifting' (face-lift), 'un brushing', etc. The Toubon suggests 'pression' for 'forcing', which is quite near the meaning given to the word in the remark in *L'Humanité* for 7 November 1994 to the effect that Jean-François Hory, the president of the Mouvement des Radicaux de Gauche (MRG), which had now decided to call itself simply 'Radical',

> a fait le forcing, pendant trois jours, pour que 'Radical' présente un candidat pour l'élection présidentielle. En l'occurrence: Bernard Tapie. (put the pressure on for three days for 'Radical' to put forward a candidate for the presidential election. That is to say, Bernard Tapie.)

The word came into French in a sporting context in the early twentieth century, probably as an adjective in a term such as 'forcing play', but is nowadays more frequently used to describe the behaviour of politicians. When Charles Pasqua, the energetic Minister of the Interior, succeeded during the summer of 1994 in having the terrorist Carlos extradited from the Lebanon as well as having a number of Muslims living in France taken into custody as potential terrorists, *Le Nouvel Observateur* no. 1554 rather tartly asked on 18 August: 'Pourquoi tant de forcing dans la moiteur de l'août?' (Why put on so much pressure in the humidity of August?)

Gadget n.m. Used by Sartre in 1946 in his description of America in *Situations* III (Paris, Gallimard, 1946, p. 120), in his *Présentation* of the special number which *Le Temps Modernes* published on the USA that August. On sale in sex shops (see IId) but unmentioned in the Toubon. Also used in a more dismissive sense in an article in *Le Nouvel Observateur* no. 1569, 1 December 1994, describing how fed up French head teachers were: 'Pourquoi les proviseurs ont le cafard'. As the head of a *collège* – a school for 11- to 16-year-olds in the south, the Midi – put it:

> La réformite ambiante est un redoutable chronophage. Chaque année apporte un nouveau gadget. Ce fut tour à tour l'audiovisuel, l'aménagement du temps préscolaire, les projets d'actions éducatives (PAE) ou innovantes (PAI), l'informatique pour tous. (The current obsession with reforms eats up your time. Every year brings a new gimmick. One after the other, we have had audiovisual techniques, the planning of the correct use of time before classes, projects of educational or innovative action, computing for all.)

This reminder of how they can sometimes order things as badly in France as we do in the UK had to be given anonymously. As a civil servant, *un fonctionnaire*, the headmaster in question had to observe 'l'obligation de réserve' and not speak in his own name.

Gang n.m. *Le Nouvel Observateur* no. 1523 for 13 January 1994 gave the headline 'Moscou sous la loi des gangs' when talking about the power of 'la mafia russe'. The *Dictionnaire des Anglicismes* gives the form 'gangster' as occurring in 1925, but 'gang' not until 1946. It also quotes F. de Grand Combe's 1954 article 'De l'anglomanie en français' as protesting against the use of 'gang' instead of the French word 'bande', and 'gangster' for 'bandit'. 'Bande', however, can be used in a morally neutral or even favourable sense, as in Jacques Péret's 1950 novel *Bande à part*, while 'bandit' has Corsican association and 'gangster' American ones.

Garden-party n.m. Not in the Toubon, which restricts itself to recommending 'rez-de-jardin' for 'garden level'. *L'Événement du jeudi* no. 496 for 5 May 1994 described how cross were the 'magistrats' (juges d'instruction, magistrats du siège, procureurs de la République; see *Faux Amis and Key Words* for the meaning of these terms and a discussion of the wider meaning of the word 'magistrat' in French) at the social slights from which they had to suffer. Not only did they have no *grande École* such as the École Nationale d'Administration (ENA) or the l'École Polytechnique to train them, and therefore had to be content with the École Nationale de la Magistrature at Bordeaux. They were never invited, but my dear, never, to 'les garden-parties de l'Elysée'.

The word 'garden-party' had attracted an unfavourable comment from Étiemble, who deplored the fact that the École de Sciences Politiques, 'qui se pique de préparer les cadres du pays, ses administrateurs' (which prides itself on preparing the country's higher civil servants, its administrators) – traditionally, it is where one goes to prepare for 'le concours d'entrée à l'ENA' (ENA's competitive entrance exam) – should call its 'fête annuelle' 'une garden-party'.

The *Dictionnaire des Anglicismes* points out that the word arrived in France in the 1880s, in the wake of the anglomania which had already brought 'five o'clock' (see entry in IIb) and 'lawn tennis'. Josette Rey-Debove and Gilberte Gagnon comment that the custom reflects a taste for gardens which, even today, 'n'arrive pas à franchir la Manche' (can't manage to cross the Channel); any more, they add, than does the permission to walk on the grass.

Had Anthony Steen's bill to banish French words in English succeeded, 'fête' would have been an obvious target, especially since its pronunciation in Wodehouse's *Lord Emsworth and the girl friend* gives rise to such misunderstanding:

> 'Ern,' said Gladys, changing the subject, 'is wearin' 'air-oil today.'
> Lord Emsworth had already observed this and had, indeed, been moving to windward as she spoke.
> 'For the Feet,' explained Gladys.
> 'For the feet?' It seemed unusual.
> 'For the Feet in the park this afternoon.'
> 'Oh, you are going to the Fête?'

Gentleman-farmer n.m. The *Dictionnaire des Anglicismes* quotes

Chateaubriand as using the word in 1822, and comments that it retains its popularity in spite of its 'sonorités pénibles et discordantes' (= it is hard to pronounce).

Although the 1994 *Dictionnaire Hachette* gives the word in the sense of a man rich enough to live off the income derived from his lands, the Toubon does not mention the term. Its full implications are indeed virtually untranslatable into French, where 'un gentilhomme' has kept the sense of a nobleman, or somebody of gentle birth, and the primary meaning of 'un fermier' is a tenant farmer. Neither 'un riche propriétaire terrien', somebody who owns a lot of land but may well rent it out, nor 'un riche exploitant agricole', someone who farms either his own land or land which he rents from somebody else, has any social standing in French. Indeed, the phenomenon of the gentleman farmer, somebody who does farm, but probably has other sources of income, and who enjoys a certain social cachet, does not exist in the same form in France as it does in England – there is no American equivalent either – and the term is clearly being used by French journalists for snobbish reasons.[3]

Gimmick n.m. In 1986, an American girl called Fabienne, who had already become famous by travelling around Paris on a motor bike, dressed in black leather, in order to give English lessons, published a book called *Le Gimmick*. This contained a number of catch-phrases in English and American which successful French people ought to acquire. Useful and entertaining though both volumes of *Le Gimmick* remain, they nevertheless have the disadvantage of encouraging the illusion that language learning is largely a matter of the acquisition of vocabulary. It is not. It is far more a question of attaining a mastery of syntax.

On 5 May 1994, Odile Grand wrote in *L'Événement du jeudi* no. 496:

Dès qu'il a casé sa brosse à dents et son gobelet dans la salle à bains de Matignon, un Premier Ministre n'a qu'un rêve: trouver le gimmick (aucun équivalent français, pas même 'truc' or 'totem') qui grifferait son règne. (As soon as a

Prime Minister has installed his toothbrush and tooth glass at Matignon [the French equivalent of 10, Downing Street], he has only one dream: to find the gimmick [no French equivalent; and, indeed, the Toubon does not mention the word] which will leave its mark on his reign.)

For Balladur, according to Odile Grand, it was 'le face à face'; rather than actually doing anything.

Golden boy n.m. Oddly absent from Sarah Tulloch's *Oxford Dictionary of New Words* (1991), but current in conversation in France as well as in the United States and Britain in the 1980s. A boo or semi-boo word, as in the remark in *Le Point*, no. 1070, 20 March 1993, about Dr Garetta, head of the national blood transfusion service at the time of the 'affaire du sang contaminé', being

> un golden boy de laboratoire qui soldait des lots contaminés comme d'autres mettaient des junk bonds sur le marché (a golden boy who sold off contaminated supplies of blood in the same way as others put junk-bonds on the market).[4]

The magazine *Libération* for 14 January 1995 wrote that:

> Partout le modèle qui s'impose est celui du *golden boy*, la monaie d'échange est le billet vert, et l'horizon affiché le libre-échangisme du GATT. (The model which imposes itself everywhere is that of the golden boy, the exchange currency is the dollar, and the official horizon the free-trade philosophy of the GATT.)

The fact that I have not come across 'golden handshake' or 'golden parachute' does not mean that they would not be understood by French businessmen. The term already in use is 'pont d'or', literally a golden bridge.

Groggy adj. In *L'Événement du jeudi*, no. 514 for 8 September 1994, the headline 'Le passé de Mitterrand: les socialistes groggy' referred to the effect on socialist morale of the revelations in Pierre Péan's *Une jeunesse française* (Fayard, Paris, 1994) about Mitterrand's behaviour between 1940 and 1943.

Not only had he held office under Marshal Pétain, had his
photograph taken in his company, and accepted the award of
'la Francisque', the decoration given to those who had rendered service to 'la Révolution Nationale'. He had also made
no protest against the anti-Semitic laws which the Vichy
régime had taken the initiative in introducing in 1940 before
the Germans had even asked them to do so. In addition, he
had remained in friendly contact until 1986 with René Bos-
quet, who as 'secrétaire général de police de Vichy' had the
responsibility for deporting French Jews to the gas chambers.

Half-track n.m. Defined by the 1990 Chambers as 'a motor
vehicle with wheels in front and caterpillar tracks behind'. An
American term, popularised in France after 1944, and a
vehicle often mentioned under that name in accounts of the
Algerian war of 1954–62. Not in the Toubon, in spite of
the remark quoted in the *Dictionnaire des Anglicismes* from the
January 1964 issue of *Défense de la langue française*:

> après les *battle-dress*, les *half-track*, *close-combat*, *briefing*, etc.,
> on se demande quel langage parlera l'armée française dans
> quelques années (After *battle-dress*, *half-track*, *close combat*,
> *briefing*, etc., you wonder what language the French army
> will be speaking in a few years' time.

See also below, 'stick'.

Has been p.p. used as adj, and n.m. Absent from the
Toubon, even before the cartoon in *Le Monde* for 1 August
1994: 'Monsieur Toubon, on trouve que votre loi, c'est plutôt
has been.'
 The old Lincolnshire term 'a never-waser' has not so far
crossed the Channel.
 See also 'fitness' in IId.
 A relatively new French word which came to frequent
general usage in the 1970s was 'ringard' in the sense of old-
fashioned.

Holding n.f.; or occasionally m. Used since the 1930s in the
sense of a holding company and thus as an adjective used

substantivally as an abbreviation. A holding company is one that owns or controls a number of shares in a business without taking a direct part in its productive activities.

When the word 'holding' is being used in an aeronautical context, as when your plane is stacked in a holding pattern and waiting to land, the Toubon suggests 'attente', a word which it also recommends instead of the noun 'stand-by'.

In January 1994, a number of demonstrations were being held against what was interpreted in some quarters as the attempt by Balladur's government to strengthen the position of the Church in its relationship to the strictly secular system of national education established in 1881 and 1882 (L'Education nationale est obligatoire, gratuite, et laïque; National Education is compulsory, is free, and offers no religious instruction). An organisation called the Comité national d'action laïque, which played a major part in the protests, was described in L'Express no. 2219 for 20 January 1994 as 'une sorte de "holding spirituel" pour la laïcité' (a kind of spiritual 'holding company' for secularism).

Hold-up n.m. Purists recommend 'attaque à main armée', which has the disadvantage of being harder to use in a figurative sense, as in the headline in *L'Événement du jeudi* on 11 February 1993, no 432, 'Hold-up sur le Coran', describing the attempts being made to prevent Islam from being hijacked by militant extremists.

Le Monde for 24 February 1995 referred to 'le hold-up électoral de Bernard Tapie' when describing the way he was trying to use his earlier success in the European elections to influence the way people voted in the forthcoming presidential elections.

Hot money n.m. In *La cote des mots*, Jean-Pierre Colignon comments on the inadequacy of the officially recommended translation of 'capitaux flottants', on the grounds that this term does not render the atmosphere of financial crisis in which this type of money is moved around. He suggests 'capitaux fébriles' (feverish capital).

Iceberg n.m. The 1967 edition of the *Petit Robert* defines 'un iceberg' as a section which has detached itself from 'la ban- quise', a section of the polar ice field. The term is frequently used to describe the visible part of a larger object or phenom- enon of which the rest is hidden, as when Claude Imbert claimed in *Le Point* for March 26 1994, no. 1123, that the losses incurred by the *Crédit Lyonnais* – some 6.9 *milliard* new francs = 6.900 million new francs; £860 million) – were only 'la face visible de l'iceberg qui menace la République' (the visible part of the iceberg threatening the Republic). They were, in his view, merely a symbol of what he called 'le virus italien de notre vie publique' (the Italian virus of our public life). In a more flattering reference to French achievements, *Le Monde* for 15 August 1992 wrote of 'la Pyramide du Louvre' that it was merely 'la partie immergée de l'iceberg' – only an indication of the treasures underneath.

When, on 21 February 1995, the French government ex- pelled five CIA agents on the grounds of espionnage, their activities were equally described on France-Inter as 'la partie immergée l'iceberg', merely the visible part of an immense activity which generally remained hidden.

Image n.f. The impact of 'le franglais', like that of English in general, has only rarely changed the meaning of the words which the French themselves use in the normal course of business. Among the more famous 'faux amis' – words which have the same appearance in French and English but a different meaning – 'une demande' continues to mean 'a request' and not a demand, 'fastidieux' still means 'annoying' and not 'excessively choosy', and 'cet enfant a des végétations' means that the child is suffering from tonsillitis, not that he has grass growing out of him. There has nevertheless been an addition to the meaning of one of the most famous 'faux amis', the verb 'contrôler'. Whereas in the past this simply meant to 'check' or to 'verify', it is now increasingly taking on the additional meaning of 'to impose limits', and something similar is happening to 'image'. This is coming to be used in French as it is when one speaks in English of somebody's image of himself or herself, in the sense of their ideal self-image, a meaning not given in the French dictionaries. Thus in an interview with a psychiatrist in the March 1995 number of *20 ans*, the question is raised of how young girls who are having problems developing their femininity can 'se réconcilier avec leur image' (reconcile themselves with their image).

Changes of this kind are relatively rare for the same reason that changes in the syntax of a language are relatively rare, and can take place only over a long period of time. Just as the syntax of a language works because of the way the various terms are related to one another, so the meaning of individual words is determined by their place in the overall structure of the language. This, to use the same terms as Marcel Cohen in his *Histoire d'une langue: le français* (see Part I, Chapter 1, note 30) has a kind of water-tight quality so that the meaning of individual words is modified only gradually, whether in response to outside influence or as a result of changes in the society in which this language lives, moves and has its being. Indeed, it could be argued that new words are borrowed from other languages precisely because the relatively fixed meaning which existing words already have in the language whose structure gives them their meaning makes it difficult for them to be used to keep track of what is happening in a society experiencing rapid change. If that is the case, then the apparently large number of words borrowed from English and American by modern French is an indication, as Philippe Richert suggested in the debate in the French Senate on 12 April 1994 (see Part I, Chapter 3, note 10) that French society itself is perhaps not moving at a speed which enables it to keep up with what is happening in the modern world.

In adopted as an adjective and used as a collective noun. When, on 9 March 1995, *Le Nouvel Observateur* no. 1583 published a number of articles analysing what it called 'la France populiste', it argued that the way French people had voted on the Maastricht referendum of 1993 – a narrow majority for the 'yes' vote – did not correspond to a traditional left/right split, but 'à l'opposition entre les *in* et les *out*, entre ceux du dedans et ceux du dehors, entre les anciens et les modernes, entre ceux qui voient un avenir et ceux qui ne l'aperçoivent pas' (to an opposition between the ins and the outs, between the insiders and the outsiders, between the old and the new, between those who can see a future for themselves and those who can't). Significantly enough, Le Pen and Philippe de Villiers were both opposed to it; and Jacques Chirac was luke-warm. See also 'out' in IId.

Jackpot n.m. As *Le Nouvel Observateur*, 1551, 28 July 1994, explained in an article describing how, in order to obtain a McDonald's franchise, you have to show yourself capable of serving a hamburger within a minute and of clearing a table in ten seconds, the authorization could be very profitable, since

> le franchisé se retrouve parfois à la tête d'un jackpot, surtout s'il contrôle, comme à Lyon, plusieurs restaurants (the franchise holder sometimes finds himself in possession of a jackpot, especially if, as at Lyons, he controls several restaurants).

The normal abbreviation is 'McDo', used to describe the hamburger itself as well as the place where you buy it. The branch in the centre of Lille is highly recommended for its 'filet o fish'.

Jamboree n.m. The 1969 *Petit Robert* gives its origin as Hindustani, but its association with the Scouts movement justifies its inclusion as a 'franglais' word. It is used in French with the same ironic tone which it now has in English, as when *Le Point* for 3 September 1994, no. 1146, described 'les rencontres de Lorient' as 'le jamboree annuel du delorisme', the annual coming together of the supporters of Jacques Delors.

Job n.m. Attested in the *Dictionnaire des Anglicismes* as early as 1831, and often feminine in Canadian French. It has nevertheless been in French since the 1920s, tending to oust 'boulot' as a familiar term for 'emploi' as well as 'travail'. It is more particularly used in the sense of a temporary job, which is probably why it recurs frequently in *Talents*, a magazine founded in 1992 and specially addressed to 'ceux qui font des études supérieures', students in higher education, which publishes *Le Guide du Job-Trotter*.

In the February-March 1994 issue of *Talents*, in a series of special articles on 'les stages', periods of work experience, a cartoon showed a student telling his mother: 'J'ai trouvé un job.' She is leaning forward in amazement and saying:

> Quoi? Un Job? Avec un vrai patron, qui paye mal, qui engueule le personnel, et qui licencie? (What? A Job? With a real boss, who pays badly, shouts at the staff and gives them the sack?)

The nearest equivalents for job are 'un poste' and 'un emploi', with the word 'métier', implying skill and training, as when *France-Soir* for 5 August 1994, under the headline

> Happy Birthday à la Queen Mumm (pardon, M. Toubon)

praised the work she did for the monarchy by writing 'la Queen Mumm a du métier'. In spite of the inability of French printers to spell English terms (see below, 'last but not least'), *France Soir* nevertheless got her age right – ninety-four – in wishing 'Happy Birthday' to 'la plus célèbre granny d'Angleterre'.

Joint venture n.m. 'Coentreprise' for the Toubon. 'Entreprise commune' is more elegant; and more meaningful.

Kidnapping n.m. Together with the verb 'kidnapper', and the noun 'kidnapper' or kidnappeur', all terms familiar to the French since the kidnapping and murder of the Lindbergh baby in 1932. Used in a political sense in *Le Monde* on 18 January 1991 to say of Saddam Hussein's invasion of Kuwait that

> en août dernier, il a pensé que le kidnapping d'un État souverain passerait inaperçu et que l'URSS se ferait, comme dans le passé, son complice. (Last August, he thought that the kidnapping of a sovereign state would pass unnoticed and that the USSR would, as in the past, act as his accomplice.)

Label n.m. The Toubon lists it twice on the same page of the index, suggesting 'étiquette' in each case.

The body of the text then recommends the use of the word 'étiquette' in the sense of the English 'source' in a context either of the use of computers in education or of computer technology; as well as in that of 'code traditionnel de bonne conduite sur un terrain de golf' (i.e. not talking while your opponent drives or puts; not stepping over his line; moving off the green before marking up the score card, etc).

The Toubon does not, however, mention 'étiquette', as an alternative to the sense which 'label' has in terms such as 'label rouge', the red label denoting food which is guaranteed to have been produced in a particular area, or when 'le label NF' refers to 'les Normes Françaises', official French standards. An article in *Le Point* for 20 August 1994, no. 1144, pointed out that

> la qualité des jambons blancs Label rouge était désormais inférieur à celui des marques sans label. (The quality of the cooked hams with the red label was now lower than that of the unlabelled brands.)

Last but not least adj. phrase. The *Dictionnaire des Anglicismes* quotes the phrase as being used in an 1892 guide to George-town, Guyana, and comments that the Anglomania of the late nineteenth century gave the expression a certain popularity 'dans un usage légèrement snob' (in a slightly snobbish usage).

In 1993, a version of the term was used in no. 452 of *National Hebdo*, the newspaper of Le Pen's National Front, in a discussion of the blowing up of the ship *Greenpeace* in Wellington Harbour, New Zealand, on 11 July 1985. The article enumerated the people in France who must have known – senior officers in the army, the Prime Minister, and '"last but not least", le Président de la République lui-même'.

The impact of the phrase was slightly diminished by being printed as 'lost but not least'.

Leader n.m. and adj. Widely used in a political sense, and accepted by one of the best-known and most traditionally minded French dictionaries, the Littre, in 1875. The suggestion in the Toubon of 'séquence de tête' does not refer to the political context, which is not mentioned, but to a leader or leader sequence in molecular genetics. Michèle Fitoussi, in *Le ras-le-bol des SuperWomen*, gives the form 'leaderesse'. On 7 February 1995, in an advertisement encouraging listeners to buy shares in the forthcoming privatisation of SEITA (Service d'Exploitation Industrielle des Tabacs et des Allumettes), a government monopoly since 1925, France-Inter described it as 'une entreprise leader en Europe'.

As if to anticipate his own remark in *Le côté de Guermantes* about the word 'smoking', in the sense of a dinner jacket, Proust has one of the characters in *À l'ombre des jeunes filles en fleurs*, say:

> j'ai obtenu qu'il fasse désormais le *leader article* dans *le Figaro*. Ce sera tout à fait *the right man in the right place*. (I have arranged for him to write the leading article in the *Figaro* from now on. It will be absolutely the right man in the right place.)

See also the entry on 'right man in the right place' in IId.

The Toubon does not mention the generally accepted French term of 'éditorial' for the English editorial.

Leadership n.m. When, in July 1994, the United Kingdom vetoed the suggestion that Jean-Luc Dehaene should be President of the European Commission, and Germany was quick to approve the suggested alternative of Jacques Santer, *Le Monde* for 18 July argued that it was not a good idea to allow Germany to take the initiative in this way since 'ce serait lui reconnaître un leadership dans la politique européenne' (it would grant her a leadership in European politics) which would prevent France from playing her role.

It is probably the difficulty of finding a satisfactory equivalent for 'leadership' which explains why the Toubon does not even mention the word. When the *Dictionnaire des Anglicismes* quotes the suggestions 'primauté, conduite, direction' from an article in *Vie et langage* for December 1959, and 'commandement, suprématie, hégémonie, domination' from the review *Défense de la langue française* for April 1963, it is as though one were trying to find an English equivalent to 'ancien régime', 'coup d'état', or 'raison d'état'.

Lifting* n.m. 'Face-lift' in a figurative as well as a literal sense. When the Labour Party leader John Smith died, *Le Monde* commented on 17 May 1994:

> La droite et la gauche du parti n'ont pas encore accompli ce travail de synthèse, ce 'lifting' indispensable consistant à proposer aux Britanniques un projet de société à la fois moderne et solidaire. (The right and the left of the party have not yet managed to reach a synthesis, and carry out the face-lift essential if they are to put before the British people a vision of society which is modern and which also involves the sharing of privileges and responsibilities.)

In a discussion of the repairs needed to the Centre Pompidou, *Le Monde* for 11 November 1994 spoke of 'l'indispensable lifting'.

Face-lifts are clearly popular in France. On 1 September 1994, *Le Nouvel Observateur* no. 1556 published a letter pointing out that an earlier article 'Beauté, les femmes sont-elles devenues folles?' (Beauty: are women mad?) was mistaken in saying that there was a waiting list at the hôpital Boucicault for all operations involving 'la chirurgie esthétique' (aesthetic surgery). The three-year wait applied only to 'des liftings'.

'Un lifter' is a special kind of comb, for back-combing the hair.

Listing* n.m. The Toubon suggests 'listage'.

On 30 July 1994, *Le Point* no. 1141 described how, when its imaginary Monsieur X rings his daughter on arriving at his office,

> le numéro et la durée de la conversation seront repertoriés dans le listing téléphonique personnalisé de la société. (The

number and length of the conversation will be recorded in the personalised telephone records of the firm.)

Not unreasonable, if he is using the office phone for a private call.

Lobby n.m., **lobbyste**, n.m. or f., **lobbying**, v. The *Dictionnaire des Anglicismes*, which dates the use of the first noun in French from the 1950s, notes how misleading it would be to use the literal French equivalent of 'antichambre'. 'Faire antichambre' evokes the idea of hanging around outside the great man's door in the hope that he might agree to see you. 'Un lobby' has more power, though generally one which is seen as unfortunate, as when Jean-François Kahn argued in *L'Événement du jeudi*, on 3 November 1993, no. 436, that the followers of Jacques Chirac were not real Gaullists since they had replaced the original ideals of the movement by 'l'hypertrophie d'un pouvoir ultra-parisien et l'omniprésence des lobbies les plus corporatistes, et, donc, les plus archaïques. Le contraire même de l'état gaullien' (an overdeveloped, Parisian-based power, together with the inescapable presence of the most corporatist – i.e. those that seek to promote only the interests of their own members – and, consequently, those which are most archaic. The very opposite, that is, of the kind of state inspired by Gaullism.)

An alternative French term is 'groupe de pression', but it should be noted that the growth in importance of lobbying in Brussels has given the English term an increased prestige in France as a recognised profession.

'Un lobbyste' is someone who lobbies people. The activity is known as 'le lobbying'.

Lock-out n.m. Sufficiently part of French to figure in the 1967 *Petit Robert*. Like the word *Streik* in German, it is an anglicism which is instructive about the ability of the English to be first in the field in labour disputes. One also finds the verb 'lock-outer'.

Look n.m. Not mentioned in the Toubon. But *Le Monde*

wrote of Edouard Balladur, on 31 March 1993, shortly after François Mitterrand had appointed him Prime Minister, that

> changer son look pour satisfaire aux contraintes des médias, il n'en est pas question (he would never change his image to fit in with the needs of the media).

He probably did not need to try, since *L'Express* for 19 January 1995 no. 2271, described him as having 'le look du rassembleur'.

Talents for February–March 1994 gave sensible good advice to students seeking employment: 'Si votre look est d'un naturel hors-normes, il vous faudra donc l'assagir' (If your look is outrageously eccentric, you had better tone it down). See also IId.

The verb 'relooker', as in the remark in *L'Humanité* for 1 August 1994 that 'Le Conseil Constitutionnel a relooké le loi Toubon' (the Conseil Constitutionnel has given another look to the loi Toubon), is used in spite of the existence of a very well-established verb, the virtual homophone, 'reluquer': to look at closely, to ogle, to have one's eye on. One needs to have a very practised ear to distinguish between the two verbs.

Loser n.m. On 2 February 1995, in a rather unfortunate phrase, Jack Lang described Lionel Jospin, just before the latter's selection by the party members as their candidate for the presidential election, as 'un loser, un recordman des échecs électoraux'. See above, 'collecter'.

Lyncher v., **lynchage** n.m. Not in the *Dictionnaire des Anglicismes*, and seen as sufficiently French to be in the 1967 *Petit Robert*. When, however, *L'Événement du jeudi* for 21 April 1994 no. 494 described Cyril Collard (see 'Be Yourself' in IId) as having been 'victime d'un incroyable lynchage médiatique' 'unbelievably lynched in the media', the word gave the impression of being used in a more extended sense than its American original.

Mailing* For the Toubon, 'publipostage'; a word rarely seen. *La Voix du Nord* for 4 August 1994 wrote how un mailing a été réalisé auprès des entreprises, afin d'annoncer l'envoi d'un questionnaire sur le tri et l'élimination des déchets (a mailing had been carried out to tell firms that they were going to receive a questionnaire about how they sorted out and disposed of their waste materials).

It was M. le Préfet Poubelle, immortalised by the name for a dustbin in French, who in 1884 first required the inhabitants of Paris to use what are known in the USA as ash cans. For another example of words for things derived from names of people, see 'Chatterton' in IIb. As late as the 1970s, 'un Bendix' was a common term for the starting motor of a car, presumably after the inventor as well.

The same issue of *La Voix du Nord* used a *fait divers* (small news item) about the smell created by the importation of chicken droppings across the border between Belgium and northern France to have a little dig at the French passion for legislating on linguistic matters. M. Victor Gramont was reported as saying that no charge was made for the droppings themselves, and one only paid the cost of transport, which was 70 francs (£8; $11) a ton. The newspaper pointed out that

> puisqu'on ne peut plus parler d'importation, sauf dérogation (since you now had to have special exemption to use the word import)

the activities which had provoked the headline 'Pour aller aux Moëres, suivez l'odeur' (To get to Moëres, follow the smell) had to be referred to as 'des échanges intra-communautaires'.

Maintenance n.f. Considered until 1973 as an incorrect term for 'entretien', in the sense of running repairs. Now accepted, and given as correct French for the English 'maintenance', in the sense of major repairs, in the Toubon.

Management, manager n.m. One should say 'gestion scientifique des entreprises', but few people do. *Le Point* for 23 April 1993, no. 1075, referred to Karen Brady as 'le manager de Birmingham City', although the normal word in a sporting context is 'l'entraîneur'. Were the manager to be a woman – which is as unlikely in France as it is in Britain – she would probably not be referred to as 'une entraîneuse'. That is the term for a hostess in a bar who leads you on to buy very expensive drinks.

'Manager' is occasionally used as a verb, as when *L'Express* for 20 January 1994, no. 2219 described how 'Martine, divorcée pressée' (a divorcee constantly in a hurry) has to

> gérer seule l'éducation de ses trois enfants (de 15 à 3 ans), tout en manageant la société qu'elle a créée il y a trois ans (take it upon herself to organise the education of her three children, aged from 3 to 15, while at the same time managing the company she set up three years ago).

The existence of two verbs for comparable activities is clearly useful here, though 'gérer' is the one more normally used in a commercial context, as in 'une saine gestion' for 'sound management'. 'Le managament' also tends to be used for activities which are halfway between 'la gestion', the day-to-day running of a business, and 'la direction', with its connotations of strategic planning.

'Ménager' has the different meaning of to use sparingly, as in 'ménager ses forces', or to deal carefully with, or keep on the right side of, as when de Gaulle writes in his *Mémoires* that during the 1920s 'Londres ménageait Berlin pour que Paris eût besoin d'elle (London kept on the right side of Berlin so that Paris would need British help).

Michèle Fitoussi (see above, 'briefing') uses the word in the sense of organise when she writes of how 'la supermamman' (her spelling) has to 'manager un nombre quasi incalculable d'activités culturelles et sociales' (organise an almost incalculable number of cultural and social activities) for her children.

Marketing* n.m. In French since the 1950s. The *Dictionnaire des Anglicismes* quotes *Le Figaro* for 21 April 1967 as reporting that the word was condemned by the Académie Française, which recommended, as does the Toubon, 'commercialisation'. But the meaning is not the same, and marketing is sufficiently well established to give the verb *marketer*, spontaneously used in conversation at a farmhouse near Puygiron in August 1994. See also 'light' in IIb.

In its discussion of 'les labels' (see above) *Le Point* for 20 August 1994, no. 1144, commented that

> l'imagination des gens du marketing est sans limites. Ils inventent des labels tels que 'délicieusement rural' et 'boeuf verte prairie'. (There are no limits to the imagination of people in marketing. They invent labels such as 'deliciously rural' and 'green meadow beef'.)

When, on 22 February 1995, *L'Événement du jeudi* wrote about 'le "lesbian chic" de certain top models, qui ne cachent pas leur goût très marketing pour les personnes du sexe' (the 'lesbian chic' of some top models, who do not hide their very marketable taste for persons of the same sex), it presumably meant that they thought that to proclaim this kind of taste improved their image.

Meeting n.m. Used by Voltaire in 1734, to talk of 'les meetings des églises non-conformistes' (meetings of the Nonconformist churches). Frequently used instead of 'réunion' for a political meeting, as when *Le Nouvel Observateur*, no. 1477, wrote on 25 February 1993 that

> une heure avant le meeting, Laurent Fabius dîne avec Rocard, à Montlouis, sans que celui-ci lui parle de son Big Bang (an hour before the meeting, Fabius dined with Rocard at Montlouis, without the latter saying a word about his Big Bang speech).

See also below, 'staff'.

'Un grand meeting sportif' is quite frequent, though Tony Mayer, in *La vie anglaise*, speaks appreciatively of the atmosphere at 'les grandes rencontres Leeds-Manchester United' (the great clashes between Leeds and Manchester United).

Commenting on the term 'big crunch' – see Raymond Barre's comment on Michel Rocard's 'big bang' in Part I – *L'Événement du jeudi* explained that this would take place in 100,000 million years time, when the universe imploded back into itself, 'à l'occasion d'un grand meeting des étoiles' (on the occasion of a great gathering of stars).

Melting-pot n.m. Used by André Siegfried in 1927 in his *Les États-Unis d'aujourd'hui* to describe what was then, before the cult of ethnic authenticity, a central feature of American culture. Its absence from the Toubon can be explained partly by the fact that it is not a recent borrowing and also by the impossibility of finding a convenient French equivalent, in spite of the role played by the *école communale* in absorbing Belgian, Polish and Italian immigrants in the 1930s, 1940s and 1950s. Much of the quarrel about 'le voile islamique' (the chuddar) is linked to the fact that 'l'école de la République' (a state school) will not be able to continue to play this role if pupils are allowed to identify themselves as belonging to a particular religion by what they wear. My friend Jacques Magnet, Président de Chambre at the Cour des Comptes, tells me that when he went to the *lycée* in Rouanne in the 1940s, he was told not to wear a crucifix in class.

On 20 October 1994 in no. 2258 of *L'Express*, Roger Faur-oux, 'Directeur de l'École Normale Supérieure', contrasted the isolation of students at the university, as well as the relative isolation of the university from the rest of French society, with the much more favourable position of students at one of the *grandes écoles*. At *Normal Sup*, 'créée par la Convention le 9 brumaire An III' (30 October 1794), in contrast, as he pointed out,

> la coexistence entre littéraires et scientifiques – le fait de vivre, pendant quatre ans, avec des mathématiciens, des philosophes, des linguistes, des physiciens – constitue un melting-pot particulièrement stimulant (the coexistence between students of science and students of literature – the fact of living, for four years, with mathematicians, philosophers, linguists, physicists – provides a particularly stimulating melting-pot).

Merchandising n.m. 'Marchandisage' for the 1993 *diction-naire des termes nouveaux*, and for the Toubon, which gives the word twice, together with 'présentoir' as an alternative to 'marchandiseur' for 'mechandiser'. In *Talents* for February-March 1994, a series of articles on 'les stages' (periods of work experience; not a word for which there is a direct equivalent in English), students were advised that

> un mois dans un supermarché vous familiarisera avec le merchandising (a month in a supermarket will familiarise you with merchandising).

Must n.m. Not in the *Dictionnaire des Anglicismes*, or in the Toubon, but noted in the 1986 *Petit Larousse Illustré*.

In the summer of 1994, *Le Provençal* had a series of advertisements in which the furnishing firm Fly described itself as 'le must pour être in'. There are numerous advertisements for 'les must' in *Vendredi Samedi Dimanche* and elsewhere, especially for 'les must de Cartier' (a brand name).

In its 'Enquête sur la super-élite française' for 3 November 1988 (see below, 'up'), *Le Nouvel Observateur*, no. 1252, described one of the most prestigious of the Grands Corps de l'État, L'Inspection des Finances, as 'la voie royale. Le must' for anyone wishing to enter the élite. See also note 2 to 'establishment' above.

No man's land n.m. Adopted by the French during the 1914–18 war as a necessary term, and never seriously contested. There is no equivalent, and Michèle Fitoussi's description (see 'briefing', above) of the 'no woman's land' between the hard-pressed 'executive woman' and 'la très, très chère Augusta (Marie-Josée, Edwige . . .)' who looks after the house and children in her absence puts the problem in a nutshell.

Off-shore adj. 'Extraterritorial' for the Toubon. On 6 July 1994, *Le Monde* commented on the number of financial scandals involving well-known politicians ('les affaires' Carignon, Longuet, Tapie and others) and said that France was becoming like Italy. What characterised this state of affairs was

> un mélange de capitalisme à la française – où de grands groupes se sont construits sous l'aile protectrice de l'État et du politique non sans confusion des genres – et la spéculation acharnée et enjouée des années 80 – où se croisent délits d'initiés et recours aux paradis fiscaux et sociétés *off-shore* (a mixture of capitalism French style – in which major

groups build themselves up under the protective wing of the state and of politics, not without a some confusion as to what is precisely what – and the fierce, wild speculation of the 1980s – with a mixture of insider dealing and the use of tax havens and off-shore companies).

Off the record adj. 'Micro coupé' (microphone off) 'ce que l'on ne reproduit pas' (not to be repeated) according to the Toubory. See above, 'briefing'.

Pack n.m. The Toubon recommends 'paquet', both when talking about rugby and when the word is used in to describe information sent in a pack through E-mail. See also the entry in IIb.

Like other sporting terms, such as 'performance' (see below), 'pack' is also used in a political context, as when *Le Point*, no. 1072, for 3 April 1993, spoke of 'Édouard Balladur et son pack de fidèles'. It would sound derogatory, in this sentence, to replace 'pack' by 'paquet'.

Packaging n.m. In its account of a exhibition on 'l'emballage' held at the Cité des Sciences at La Villette, *Le Nouvel Observateur* for 24 November 1994, no. 1567, actually wrote 'D'ailleurs, on ne parle plus d'emballage: on dit *packaging*'.

Patchwork n.m. Quite a widely used word. Since 'mosaïque' implies a pattern, there is no real equivalent. *Le Nouvel Observateur* for 12 May 1994, no. 1540, described the intentions of the Education Minister, François Bayrou, as

un patchwork de propositions dans lesquelles on chercherait en vain les réponses aux questions essentielles: le bac pour 80 pour cent, la violence à l'école, le collège est-il une école primaire supérieure ou un pré-lycée' (a patchwork of propositions in which one looks in vain for replies to the essential questions of violence at school, or how 80 per cent of 18-year-olds are going to get the baccalauréat, whether comprehensive schools are a continuation of primary school or a step leading to the lycée).[5]

Pattern n.m. The Toubon suggests 'forme' or 'motif', the former in the context of artificial intelligence, the second, presumably, in that of a pattern in the carpet.

Performance n.f., **performant**, adj. Two of the words which, as Ian Pickup observes in his 'Anglicisms in the French Sporting Press',[6] began by being used mainly in a sporting context but now have a very much wider application. The *Dictionnaire des Anglicismes* gives three pages of examples, and also gives the adjective 'performatif' as the accepted translation, in a philosophical context, of 'performative' in the sense given to it by J. L. Austin in his 1962 *How to Do Things with Words* (Clarendon Press, Oxford). As when I say 'I call this child James', I use language to carry out an act which cannot be as neatly or as accurately performed in any other way.

One would have to translate 'performant' as 'high performance' as in 'une machine performante', a high-performance engine. The Toubon limits itself to suggesting 'performeur' or 'performeuse' for 'performer', and it is for once correct to take an omission from the *Dictionnaire des termes officiels de la langue française* as a reliable guide as to the non-existence of a word borrowed from the English: I have not come across 'performer' as a first-conjugation verb.

'Performance' and 'performant', however, although also unmentioned in the Toubon, are very frequent, especially in a political or economic context: 'l'économie allemande est très performante' is a standard comment in the French press, and when François Mitterrand told a press conference in March 1994 that France would not carry out any more nuclear tests, *L'Express* commented: 'Saluons la performance' (A splendid performance) and admired, on May 19, 1994, no. 2227, the way he had implicitly committed his successor. The article was entitled, with a touch of irony, 'Jupiter et la foudre' (Jupiter and the lightning [in the sense of lightning bolts]).

When, on June 12, 1995, Jacques Chirac took the opportunity of his first news conference as President to announce that France would resume nuclear testing at Muroa later in the year, and did so on the eve of his first visit to Washington as President, his gesture was widely interpreted, in France itself as well as in the United States and in New Zealand, as a return to traditional Gaullism, with all its deliberate defiance of 'les Anglo-Saxons', especially the Americans, its cult of French nationalism and its indifference to public opinion in the Antipodes and elsewhere.

Planning* n.m. Used more in the sense of a timetable or systematic organisation of one's time than in that of economic planning, where the recommended 'planification' is more frequent. *Nice Matin* for 5 May 1993, under the headline 'Elles ont du punch [see below] les pionnières de l'association Arielle' (the pioneers of the Arielle association are full of energy), reported how a group of parents had created 'une crèche parentale', in the sense of one where they, the parents, took turns to be on duty. It was only, the article pointed out, 'grâce à un planning rigoureux' (thanks to a rigorous timetable) that they could guarantee to be there on time.

The *Dictionnaire des Anglicismes* points to the frequency with which the word was used, from the 1950s onwards, in the sense of family planning. Until the repeal in 1967 of the law of 1920 forbidding the advertisement or sale of 'des préservatifs' (contraceptive devices) – 'la capote' (sheath, condom); 'la pillule' (the pill); 'le diaphragme' (Dutch cap); 'le stérilet' (the coil) – this was difficult to do except by the careful observation of the menstrual cycle or by the practice of *coitus interruptus* (see the entry *créature* in Thody and Evans, *Faux Amis and Key Words*). See also 'safe sex' in IId.

Punch n.m., **puncheur** n.m. Like 'performance' (see above), and like 'punch' itself in the entry above on 'planning', both terms illustrate two tendencies shared by other 'franglais' words: although used originally in the world of sport, they are found equally if not more often in other domains; they are even more frequently used in French in a sense which they do not always have in Britain or the United States. *L'Express* n. 2212 for 3 December 1993 described Philippe Séguin, the right-wing politician who had campaigned for the 'no' note in the Maastricht referendum, as un puncheur qui rêve d'incarner un jour l'alternative néo-gaulliste au néo-pompidolisme du trop sage Balladur (a puncher who dreams of one day incarnating a neo-Gaullist alternative to the neo-Pompidolianism of the over-sensible M. Balladur).

Racket n.m. *L'Yonne Républicaine* for 5 August 1994 reported Anne Vailleux, 'baba cool' (see IId) preparing to leave for Thailand, as saying 'quand on part en Asie, il faut prévoir 25 pour cent de son budget pour le racket' (when you go to Asia, put aside a quarter of your money for paying the racket money). One also finds the verb 'racketter', often in the sense of demanding money with menaces.

Raid n.m. Used in the sense of an air-raid by Proust, especially in the evocation in *Le Temps retrouvé* of 'des raids des gothas':

la duchesse de Guermantes superbe en chemise de nuit, le duc de Guermantes inénarrable en pyjama rose et peignoir de bain (the Duchesse de Guermantes superb in her night-gown and the Duke hilariously comic in pink pyjamas and a bathrobe).

The word is also used – again in a sense which it does not have in English – to describe the long-distance flights aimed at testing both men and machines carried out by Antoine de Saint-Exupéry, or more generally in the sense of an expedition. Frequent nowadays in the sense of an aggressive take-over bid, hence – presumably – the recommendation in the Toubon of 'attaquant', an adversary from whose grasp one might be saved by a 'white knight' (Toubon: chevalier blanc). The Toubon does not give the noun 'raid'. The linguistic calque of 'frappe aérienne' for 'air strike' occurs frequently in modern French.

Raider n.m. In the commercial sense of the author of a hostile take-over bid. The Toubon suggests 'attaquant'; Jean-Pierre Colignon wonders whether 'pillard', as in 'robber barons', 'des barons pillards'; 'prédateur', with the suggestion of predatory animals; or 'maraudeur' or 'pilferer' might not suit the case better.

Recordman* n.m. Another example (cf. above 'performance' and 'punch') of an anglicism taken from the realm of sport and used in a wider context. *Le Nouvel Observateur* for 3 November 1988, no. 1252, mentioned how Robert Hersant, the man whose group produces 22 per cent of the newspapers printed in the provinces and 30 per cent of the Paris dailies, described as a

> spécialiste du rachat de journaux en perdition, recordman du découvert bancaire et champion toutes catégories du mépris pour les syndicats et les journalistes (a specialist in buying up newspapers on the point of bankruptcy, a record holder of overdrafts and open champion in contempt for trade unions and journalists),

was trying to change his 'look' (see above) by moving the right-wing *Le Figaro* closer to the centre, and livening up the news programmes on his television channel La Cinq. Just as Jacques Chirac enjoys the reputation of being 'un bulldozer' (see above) in politics so Hersant was described as 'un bull-dozer du journalisme'.

A news item on Europe 1 for 11 January 1995, describing how the government had decided not to introduce a new motoring offence known as 'le délit de grande vitesse' (excessively high speed), spoke of how France was 'le recordman de l'Europe' in having some 9,000 fatal road accidents a year as against under 5,000 for the UK. The September 1994 number of *France*, 'the Quarterly Magazine for Francophiles', reproduced the figures recently published by Eagle Star. The UK had 1.5 deaths a year per 10,000 motor vehicles, France 3.6. The UK had 7.6 deaths a year per 100,000 inhabitants; France 17.3.

See also the entry 'tennisman' in IId and 'loser' above.

Saquer* v. To sack. Already in the *Petit Larousse Illustré* for 1986, and used in *Le Nouvel Observateur*, no. 1568, for 24 November 1994, to describe how Françoise Giroud was 'saquée' by the *Journal du Dimanche* for criticising the publication by *Paris-Match* of the photographs of François Mitterrand's illegitimate daughter, Mazarine.

She later appealed against the dismissal and was awarded substantial damages.

Score n.m. In French since the 1920s in a sporting context, and found in a political context, as 'un score électoral', as well as a financial one, as when *Le Monde* for 14 November 1994 reported that 'le CAC 40 a enregistré un score positif de 0.85 pour cent' (the French Stock Exchange went up by 0.85 per cent). The acronym ('sigle') CAC stands for 'cotation assistée en continu', the equivalent of the Dow-Jones or the Footsie. Both France-Inter and Europe 1 give the CAC 40 every day just before 1300 hours, but rarely mention it in later bulletins. Most commentators accept that 'score' can replace 'la marque'; with only the Toubon forgetting that 'marque' has the primary meaning of brand, as in 'la publicité de marque', brand advertising.

It would also be tricky to substitute 'marque' in the comment in *Le Point for 30 April 1994 no. 1128*, on the revelation that the average East German drinks 150 litres of beer a year, the equivalent of 10 litres of alcohol:

> un score qui détrône la France au hit-parade [see entry in IId] mondial des buveurs' (a score which unseats France from the top position in the world-wide hit-parade of drinkers).

The Académie Française and the Toubon recommend 'la marque', and 'marquer un but' is more frequent than 'scorer', which exists but sounds odd.

See also 'hit parade' in IId.

Self-government n.m. Confirmation of the fact that de Gaulle never had any intention of implementing the policy of 'L'Algérie Française' after his return to power in 1958 came with the publication of Alain Peyrefitte's *C'était de Gaulle* (Fayard, Paris, 1994), of which extracts appeared in *Le Point* for 15 October 1994, no. 1152, under the title 'Ainsi parlait de Gaulle'. After having described 'l'autodétermination' as 'un piège à cons' (booby-trap), he explained how the French had gone about colonisation in the wrong way from the very beginning:

> Nous avons fondé notre colonisation, depuis les débuts, sur le principe de l'assimilation. On a prétendu faire des nègres de bons Français. On leur a fait réciter: 'Nos ancêtres les Gaulois': ce n'était pas très malin. Voilà pourquoi la décolonisation est tellement plus difficile pour nous que pour les Anglais. Eux, ils ont toujours admis les différences de race et de culture. Ils ont organisé le *self-government*. Il leur suffit de distendre les liens pour que ça fonctionne (We based our colonisation, from the beginning, on the idea of assimilation. We tried to transform Negroes into good French people. We made them recite 'Our ancestors the Gauls'. It wasn't very clever. That is why decolonisation is so much more difficult for us than for the English. They always recognised differences of race and culture. They organised *self-government*. All they needed to do was to loosen the links and it worked.)[7]

An alternative explanation for the contrast lies in the fact that the French had the misfortune to establish 'une colonie de peuplement' in Algeria, where there were too many Arabs and Berbers for them to be massacred or driven from their lands with the same relative ease as the Native Americans in North America, the Aborigines in Australia, or the Maoris in New Zealand. The British never established Roman-style colonies in the Raj, or anywhere in Africa except Kenya and Rhodesia. When the time came, they could therefore remove their soldiers, merchants and administrators quite easily, something which the French had much more difficulty in doing with the million or so *pieds noirs* in Algeria.

The Toubon does not mention 'self-government', and limits itself to recommending 'autoconstruction' for 'self-help housing', which is perhaps not quite the same thing. The *Dictionnaire des Anglicismes* offers the reminder that 'self-government' was used in Flaubert's readable book, the 1880 *Dictionnaire des idées reçues*: 'AMERIQUE. Bel exemple d'injustice: c'est Colomb qui la découvrit et elle tient son nom d'Améric Vespucci. – Faire une tirade sur le self-government.'

(AMERICA. Fine example of injustice. Columbus discovered it and it gets its name from Amerigo Vespucci. – Write a tirade on self-government.)

See below, 'standard'.

Self-made-man n.m. When the word first came into France in the 1870s, an article quoted in the *Dictionnaire des Anglicismes*, 'L'anglomanie dans le français', whose publication under that title in 1878 is another indication that 'la lutte contre le franglais' (the struggle against franglais) predates Jacques Toubon, pointed out that the English had two words for the French 'parvenu': 'self-made-man' and 'upstart'. One could also say 'fils de ses oeuvres'; or, if a woman, one could echo what the Marquise de Merteuil tells the Vicomte de Valmont in letter 81 of Laclos's 1782 *Les Liaisons dangereuses*:

> je dis mes principes et je le dis à dessein: car ils ne sont pas, comme ceux des autres femmes, donnés au hasard, reçus sans examen et suivis par habitude, ils sont les fruits de mes profondes réflexions; je les ai créés, et je puis dire que je suis mon ouvrage. (I say my principles and I say so deliberately. For they are not, like those of other women, given by chance, accepted without thought, and followed by habit. They are the fruit of my deep reflections. I created them, and I can say that I am my own work.

Le Point no. 1125, for 9 April 1994, commented that

> comme Berlusconi et Ross Perrot, Bernard Tapie incarne une nouvelle race de *self-made-men* musclés à l'exceptionnel charisme télévisuel (like Berlusconi and Ross Perrot, Bernard Tapie is the incarnation of a new race of self-made-men, tough-looking characters who come over very well on the telly).

Unfortunately, like Madame de Merteuil, Bernard Tapie has since come something of a cropper.

I have not come across the term 'struggle-for-lifer' which my friend and mentor Philip Ouston assured me in the blissful summer of 1949 was frequent in the French press of the 1890s, but Michèle Fitoussi (see above, 'briefing') has 'self-made-woman'.

Self-scanning n.m. In an article entitled 'Jusqu'où ira l'automisation?' in *Le Nouvel Observateur* for 1 December 1994, no. 1569, the director of the large 'Carrefour' chain, René Brillet, talked about the possibility of checking the bar code yourself to find out how much the object cost but added that the instrument used, 'le self-scanner', was not quite 'au point', (ready to be used) since the customer was much slower using it than 'la caissière' (salesperson).

Shadow Cabinet n.m. Rare enough to be absent from the *Dictionnaire des Anglicismes* as well as from the Toubon, but used by *L'Action Française* on 20 May 1993 to describe some of the members of the Parti Républicain, a right-wing party offering its support to Valéry Giscard d'Estaing inside the framework of the Union pour la Démocratie Française, the political grouping of which he was the head but which has now been overshadowed by Jacques Chirac's more aggressive Rassemblement pour la République. According to *L'Action Française*, François Léotard, Gérard Longuet and others 'étaient censés former une sorte de "shadow cabinet"' (were believed to have formed a sort of Shadow Cabinet) able to act as an alternative government if Edouard Balladur got into difficulty.

The form 'contre-gouvernement' is also used, as in 'cabinet fantôme', but the French political system is not sufficiently bipolarised to adopt the British custom of an alternative team ready immediately to take over. The fact that the *députés* sit in a semicircle, and not with government and opposition facing one another, also makes any adoption of Westminster customs difficult, and there is no equivalent to the Whips. *Le Monde* normally translates Whips as 'chefs de file', but the decision of the government to use article 49.3 of the Constitution to make the passage of a particular bill a question of confidence is not normally preceded by consultation among the *députés* who officially belong to the party or parties in government. This is partly because the constitution of the

Fifth Republic also enables the government to count all absten-
tions in a vote of confidence as being votes in its favour, so it
doesn't really need to bother. The fact that most governments
are still coalitions, and that the Prime Minister is appointed
by the President, also makes it difficult for a particular leader
to present himself as the potential head of the next
administration.

From a linguistic point of view, the infrequency with which
anglicisms such as 'Whip' or 'Shadow Cabinet' occur in the
French press illustrates two obvious points about loan words:
they have to be understood; and there has to be a need for
them. Just as few readers of the English press understand
enough about French politics to grasp the significance of
'l'article 49.3', so few French people know enough about
British politics to understand the finer points of party discipline
at Westminster. There is therefore no point in journalists
trying to show off by talking about 'Whipping' or the role of
the 1922 Committee. Neither is there any need for the introduction of such terms as a convenient form of shorthand to
describe events in which most people are not very interested.

Shocking adj. Claude Imbert, commenting in *Le Point* for 19
November 1994, no. 1157, on the American decision to sus-
pend its embargo on arms shipments to Bosnia, wrote:

> Un coup de canif dans le contrat si évident que même la
> Grande Bretagne elle-même le trouve *shocking*. So blatant a
> breaking of ranks that even Great Britain finds it shocking.)

The change of idiom hides the fact that 'un coup de canif
dans le contrat' generally refers to an isolated act of adultery
i.e. one that puts a tear in the marriage contract. Another
example, like 'bas de laine' in the entry 'first' above, which
illustrates the peaceful coexistence between 'franglais' words
and traditional idioms and cultural references.

The word 'shocking' is often used ironically, especially
when the English behave with less than their traditional
puritanism in sexual matters, a custom which goes back at
least to Victor Hugo. See the entry 'hobby' in IIc.

Shopping n.m. A good example of a 'franglais' word which is open to criticism on the grounds that it quite unnecessarily takes the place of 'faire les courses'. 'Le shopping cathodique' is seeing an article advertised on television, ringing in and buying it. Like 'parking' (see IIb), 'shopping' also represents another aspect of 'le franglais': the tendency to use what are in fact gerunds in English, or gerunds used adjectivally (shopping precinct), as though they were nouns.

The Fimotel in Lille advertises itself being 'très agréable pour les affaires, le shopping et le tourisme'; and the waiter, having ascertained that I was not a Belgian, recommended the Auchan supermarché at Villeneuve as being 'très bien pour le shopping'.

Show room n.m. Frequently seen on the walls of the Paris Métro in 1995, especially for shops selling double glazing. Jean-Pierre Colignon suggests the longer form of 'magasin d'exposition et de démonstration'.

Shunter* v. Normally used as a technical term in electricity, with the meaning of 'to by-pass'. However, in its account on 2 April 1994 of how Jean-Yves Haberer was finally obliged to resign as director of the Crédit Lyonnais, after leaving it in debt to the equivalent of £36 ($50) million, no. 1124 of *Le Point* asked what the members of the *conseil d'administration* (Board of Directors) had been doing, and continued:

Quant à ceux qui plaident aujourd'hui que leur ministre les 'shuntait' en traitant directement avec Haberer, personne ne les empêchait de démissionner (as for those who now claim that their minister by-passed them by dealing directly with Haberer, nobody prevented them from resigning).

Skimming* n.m. Although not included in Sarah Tulloch's *Oxford Dictionary of New Words* (1991), the term is given the meaning in Jean-Pierre Coligon's *La cote des mots* of a commercial practice which consists of launching a product which is virtually identical to those already on sale, but at a higher price; thus hoping to attract a richer clientèle by the greater prestige associated with cost. The manufacturer then gradually brings down the price and takes business from his competitors.

Skinhead n.m. Like 'hooligan', an English word which everybody knows, in the same way as they used to know 'gentleman'. It was a group of young men most frequently described in the French media as 'des skinheads', and only rarely as 'des crânes rasés', who had been following a parade of Le Pen supporters on 1 May 1995 when they left it to throw a Moroccan into the Seine, where he drowned. The wearing of hair which is either very short or very long by contemporary standards as a sign of social dissent offers another example of the semiology of everyday life. It does not matter whether the hair is over-long or over-short, and the argument that short hair offers an advantage in close combat because your opponent cannot grab it is not convincing. In many cultures, long hair is the sign of membership of a warrior caste, and hair only an inch or two long is the sign in western society of a high degree of social conformity. It is the fact of the departure from the norm which is important, the defiance of the accepted grammar of communication and the establishment of a new convention. See entry on 'hit parade' in IId.

Slogan n.m. Originally a Scottish war cry. Now used widely both in politics and advertising.

Sniper n.m. A relatively new word in French, much used to describe the conflict in the former Yugoslavia. A letter in *L'Événement du jeudi* no. 496 for 5 May 1994 asked indignantly what was wrong with the word 'affûteur', which the *Nouveau Larousse universel* uses to describe 'un tireur à l'affût', and the Toubon suggests 'tireur isolé'. An equally good word is 'franc-tireur'.

Sparring partner n.m. A cartoon described in the 'Revue de Presse' on France-Inter on Sunday 27 November depicted Jacques Delors,

en combat de boxe, sur le bord du ring, poussé par ses

sparring partners Henri Emmanuelli, Michel Rocard, Laurent Fabius à entrer en combat contre Jacques Chirac (in boxing shorts and singlet, on the side of the ring, being pushed forward by his sparring partners . . .).

It is not, in point of fact, a boxer's sparring partners who stand behind him as he goes into the ring, but his seconds, 'des soigneurs'. The word was used in a more correct manner on Europe 1 for 1 May 1995, when it was announced that 'avant le duel télévisé, Jacques Chirac et Lionel Jospin se sont rodés avec des sparring partners' (before their television debate, Jacques Chirac and Lionel Jospin each had a warm-up with their sparring partners).

Another, franglais-free cartoon evoking Delors' continued delay in declaring himself as the socialist candidate for the 1995 presidential election showed him as a reluctant bridegroom being pushed towards the bed in which Marianne lay awaiting him with open arms: 'Allons, Jacques, fais ton devoir.'

Sponsor n.m., **sponsoring** n.m., **sponsoriser** v. The recommended 'parrain', 'parrainage' and 'parrainer' are slow in catching on, as is the term 'commanditaire'; perhaps because the godfather association is too strong in the first, both in the Christian sense and in the French title of the Marlon Brando film, and because 'un commanditaire' has for a long time been somebody who commissions work to be done.

Staff n.m. In French since the 1960s, in spite of the possibility of talking about 'le personnel' for one's colleagues, or 'l'état-major' for the people with whom one shares decision-making. Originally used in a medical context, now frequent in a political one, as when *Le Nouvel Observateur*, no. 1477, 25 February 1993, reported that after Rocard's 'Big Bang' speech on 17 February 1993 there reigned 'la stupeur et la colère' at the 'petit déjeuner hebdomadaire du staff fabiusien' (anger and amazement at the weekly breakfast meeting of the staff of Laurent Fabius).

Fabius, who succeeded Pierre Mauroy as Prime Minister in July 1984, after the failure of the Keynesian 'politique de la relance' which the Socialists had been elected to put into practice, is in fact quite a middle-of-the road Socialist of the type to whom Rocard's 'Big Bang' might have appealed. What annoyed him was that he had not been consulted (see above, 'meeting'), and saw Rocard as carrying out the modern French equivalent of Disraeli 'catching the Whigs bathing and running away with their clothes'.

Standard n.m. The most frequent meaning of 'telephone exchange' is itself, according to Josette Rey-Debove and Gilberte Gagnon, an anglicism. As a substitute for the more correct 'niveau', in the expression 'standard of living' for 'niveau de vie', the word 'standard' was used by de Gaulle in 1959 (see above, 'self-government') to offer the main reason why the French should get out of Algeria:

> Si l'Algérie restait française, on devrait asssurer aux Alge- 'riens le même standard de vie qu'aux Français, ce qui est hors de portée. (If Algeria remained French, we should have to provide the Algerians with the same standard of living as the French, which we can't do.)

The Toubon limits itself to 'indice normalisé' for 'standardised index', a usage justified by the most frequently used French word for standard, 'une norme'.

Stick* Toubon recommends 'groupe de saut' for what *France-Observateur*, on 27 April 1961, in an article on the Algerian war, describes as 'un stick de parachutistes'. The word is also used for a lipstick.

Stock options n.m.p. Not in the Toubon, though the 1989 *dictionnaire des néologismes officiels* gives 'plan d'option sur titres' for 'stock option plan'. In *Le Nouvel Observateur*, no. 1557 for 8 September 1994, Claude Bébéar, head of AXA, the fourth largest insurance group in Europe, spoke disparagingly of his 'stock options' as 'une fortune sur le papier' (a fortune on paper). His remark that he thought salaries of heads of firms should be published, as he said they were in the UK, implied that this did not happen in France. He revealed his salary as 10 million francs a year (£1,200,000; $2 million).

Stop and go twin verbs forming a composite noun. Not in the *Dictionnaire des Anglicismes* or in the Toubon, which nevertheless offers another puzzle to linguists by giving 'excédent de pertes' for 'stop loss', a term apparently used in the insurance world for certain techniques of reinsurance.

Le Nouvel Observateur, no. 1477 commented on 25 February 1993:

> en trente ans de *stop and go*, la Grande-Bretagne connaît tous les risques que fait courir une dévaluation. En 1961, la livre valait 12 marks. Aujourd'hui, elle n'en pèse que 2,3! Et pourtant, jamais l'industrie anglaise n'a réussi à damer le pion à ses concurrents germains. (In thirty years of stop and go, Great Britain has experienced all the risks associated with devaluation. In 1961, the pound was worth 12 marks. Nowadays, it is worth only 2.3. And yet, in spite of this, British industry has never succeeded in stealing a march over its German competitors.)

Stress n.m., **stressant** adj., **stressé** p.p. All self-respecting French people suffer from it, and Martine Aubry, Jacques Delors's daughter, told *France Soir* on 25 March 1993, when she was Ministre du Travail, 'pour moi, c'est le stress permanent' (I'm permanently under stress). However, an article in *L'Expansion*, no. 483, October, 1994, described how 'les dirigeants stressés et pressés' (under pressure and in a hurry) could forget their troubles for a while 'autour d'un plat bien mijoté' (over a well-prepared meal) in some of the more expensive restaurants in Paris and the provinces.

The Toubon does not mention the word, perhaps an indication that it has become thoroughly and respectably French.

Michèle Fitoussi has her 'SuperWoman' say 'sans stress, je m'ennuie' (without stress, I'm bored).

See also 'gag' in IIc.

Success story n.m. In the same issue, no. 1125, 9 April

1994, in which it described him as a 'self-made-man' (see above), *Le Point* also wrote that Bernard Tapie was not too unhappy about the various accusations of commercial malpractice brought against him, and that

> il s'offre même le luxe de considérer que l'épreuve judiciaire le lave de l'imputation d'un 'success story' qui ne collerait pas aux rigueurs des années 90 (he allows himself the luxury of thinking that the legal trials awaiting him would free him from the imputation of being a 'success story' which would be out of keeping with the rigours of the 1990s).

Suffragette n.f. Originally a pseudo-French formation (cf. 'usherette' or 'drum majorette') used to designate the English feminists of the late nineteenth and early twentieth centuries. The word then came into France, where feminism was slower to catch on, but never quite replaced 'feministe'. While all Frenchmen over twenty-five got the vote in 1848, women had to wait until de Gaulle gave it to them in 1945. One reason was that French socialists were afraid that women might vote for right-wing politicians who reminded them of their fathers.

Supertanker n.m. In an article on the preparation of the French budget – as open an operation as in the United States, and shrouded in none of the secrecy associated with Westminster – *Le Point*, no. 1149 observed on 24 September 1994 that

> L'État est, en fait, un supertanker qui ne peut freiner que sur une très longue distance – et recule à grand-peine (the state is in fact a supertanker which needs a very long distance to come to a halt and can go backwards only with the greatest difficulty).

Surfer* v. To surfboard. But another sporting term which turns up in a political sense, as in what sounded like an obituary for the ecology movement, after its early successes, in *Le Monde* for 30 March 1994:

> surfant sur cette vague verte, les écologistes français remportent quelques succès spectaculaires, puis de déchirent

sans accrocher un seul siège à l'Assemblée (riding the crest of this green wave, the French ecologists achieve one or two spectacular triumphs, and then tear themselves apart without winning a single seat in the Assemblée Nationale).

Le Point for 15 May 1993, no. 1078, created a rather poetic image of the newly appointed Prime Minister, Edouard Balladur, 'surfant sur l'état de grâce'. The 'honeymoon period' following an election is normally rendered by 'l'état de grâce'.

Suspense n.m. In French since the early 1900s. Not in the Toubon, though the *Dictionnaire des Anglicismes* quotes Simone de Beauvoir as combining it with a nicely placed imperfect of the subjunctive: 'J'insistai pour que Sartre introduisît dans son récit un peu du suspense qui nous plaisait dans les romans policiers' (I insisted that Sartre introduced into his story [*Les chemins de la liberté/The Paths to Freedom*] a little of the suspense which we liked in detective stories). A necessary piece of advice after *La Nausée*.

On Saturday 11 November, 1994 the day before Jacques Delors promised he would say whether or not he was going to be a candidate for the presidency, the 'Revue de Presse' on France-Inter used the word 'suspense' six times in as many minutes.

Tandem n.m. In the sense of a bicycle made for two, used in French since the 1890s, following its use for a horse-drawn carriage for two people in the 1830s. Indissociably linked in French popular memory with the summer of 1936, when the decision of the Front Populaire to require all employers to give their workers two weeks' paid holiday – 'les congés payés' –led to the publication in the newspapers of photographs of people leaving Paris on bicycles and tandems.

Like other sporting terms ('challenger', 'surfer'), 'tandem' can be used in a political context, as in the mention in *L'Express* for 27 January 1994, no. 2220, of 'le tandem Balladur-Chirac', the hope that one of the two main conservative contenders for the presidency might, if elected, appoint the other one Prime Minister. Cf. below, 'ticket'.

Téléshopping n.m. *Le Point* no. 1153 for 22 October 1994 used this word as well as the more authetically French 'téléachat' to describe the activity of ringing up to order goods you have seen advertised on the telly. The television channel M6 has what it calls a 'Home Shopping Service'.

Test n.m., **tester** v. The noun has been used in French in a scientific sense since the 1920s, and in a pseudo-scientific one to describe the intelligence tests invented by Alfred Binet (1857–1911) since 1895. The Toubon lists twelve uses of the word in the English sense of a test.

The French verb 'tester' also means to make a will. In *L'ancien régime et la révolution* (1856), de Tocqueville illustrated his thesis that the strengthening of the state by Napoleon after 1799 was merely the *ancien régime* writ large by pointing out that 'la limitation du droit de tester' already existed under Louis XIV. In France, the law still requires citizens to divide their money equally among all their children, and prevents them from leaving the lot to the Battersea Dogs Home or the Distressed Gentlefolk Aid Association (which has recently – and regrettably – changed its name to Home Life).

Think tank n.m. In its discussion in no. 1252 of 'la nouvelle super-élite française', *Le Nouvel Observateur* for 3 November 1988 described the Fondation Saint-Simon, established in 1982, as an organisation

> qui se conforme de plus en plus au modèle des *think tanks*, ces laboratoires d'idées américains dont les enquêtes et les analyses s'adressent aussi bien au décideur pressé qu'à l'étudiant ou au citoyen désireux de s'informer (which is becoming more and more like a think tank, one of those American ideas laboratories whose enquiries and analyses are aimed just as much at the decision-maker in a hurry as at students and ordinary citizens in search of information).

The fact that *Le Nouvel Observateur* italicised the word and then explained what it meant suggests that the term is seen as a new expression, and it is neither in the Toubon nor in the *Dictionnaire des Anglicismes*. The Saint-Simon in question is not the irascible duke (1675–1755) whose *Mémoires* criticised Louis XIV for neglecting the old aristocracy in favour of the new men of the rising middle class, but his great-nephew, one of the founders of French socialism, Count Henri de Saint-Simon (1760–1825). His view that society should be run by scientists and businessmen anticipates the philosophy attributed to 'la nouvelle super-élite'. The fact that Napoleon III was described as 'Saint-Simon in jackboots' heightens the parallel, more obvious when de Gaulle was in power, between the Second Empire (1852–1870) and the Fifth Republic. Both régimes are based on a combination between a strong presidency and a society run by experts.

Ticket n.m. In French since the eighteenth century, and familiar in 'un ticket de métro', 'les tickets de rationnement' between 1940 and 1945, and 'le ticket modérateur', the balance to be paid by the patient for medical treatment dispensed under the 'sécurité sociale'.

The inverted commas suggest that it was clearly being used in an American political sense when *Le Point* no. 1149 for 24 September 1994 talked about 'Jean-Louis Debré, secrétaire général du RPR' (general secretary of the Rassemblement pour la République) who 'vient de relancer l'idée d'un "ticket" Chirac-Balladur et souhaite que les deux hommes se rencontrent' (has just relaunched the idea of a Chirac-Balladur ticket, and expressed the hope that the two men will meet).

Trader, trading n.m. The first word is used in the sense of someone buying and selling stocks and shares, 'des actions et des obligations', and the second for the activity. *Le Monde* for 7 May 1994, describing the various people who had invested in the Channel Tunnel (le Tunnel sous la Manche) wrote:

D'un côté, les traders, qui jouent sur les bonnes et les mauvaises nouvelles, et, pour l'avenir, sur les taux d'intérêt. Mais c'est aussi une valeur de père de famille, qui garde ses actions contre vents et marées et les transmettra à ses enfants. (On the one hand, there are the traders, who speculate on good and bad news items, and on interest

rates. But it is also a blue chip investment, something for
the family man who will keep his shares whatever happens
and hand them on to his children.)

Some children might prefer parents who put their money in
unit trusts (Am: Mutual Funds; des SICAV [Sociétés d'Inves-
tissement de Capitaux à Revenu Variable]), building societies,
government loans (des bons de l'état), gold, or, even the
traditional 'bas de laine' (woollen stocking under the mat-
tress). When the Channel Tunnel shares were issued, they cost
35 francs. In May 1989, the price had risen to 129; only to go
down to 33 in 1994. *Le Monde* gave the 'seuil de rentabilité'
(break-even point) as 1998, and the first date at which divi-
dends (des dividendes, n.m.p.) might be paid as the year
2000. Originally, 62 per cent of the capital came from France,
25 per cent from the UK, 2.8 per cent from Belgium, 1.5 per
cent from the USA and 8.7 per cent from the Far East. In
1994, it had not yet proved necessary to require the taxpayer
(le contribuable) to finance the project. The French for an
estimate is 'un devis', and to go over the estimate, 'dépasser le
devis'.

Trust n.m., and **truster**, v. The noun has been in French since
the 1880s, often in a derogatory sense, as when the French
Communist Party described *Le Monde*, on the publication of
its first number on 19 December 1944 as 'un journal des trusts
protégé par le gouvernement' (a newspaper dominated by
trusts and protected by the government).

The verb 'truster' can have the same sense in French as
'accaparer', to create a monopoly in, as when *Le Monde* for 3
March 1994, in an article marking the two-hundredth anniversary of the founding of the École Polytechnique, described it
as having given birth to

> une société secrète, forte de 15,000 'anciens', trustant les
> plus hauts postes de l'administration et des entreprises,
> gérant les carrières – dit-on – comme on joue au jeu de go
> (a secret society, with some 15,000 old boys as members,
> with a monopoly over the top posts in the civil service and

private business, managing careers, it is said, in the same way that you play Go).

For a confirmation of this view modified by the recognition of the comparable role played by the École Nationale d'Administration, see note 2 below.

It may have been the requirements of English law which led to the noun 'trustee' being used in its English sense when a folder advertising a series of lectures on French politics to be given in London under the auspices of the Alliance Française in the spring of 1995 described one of the lecturers, Bernard Marx, as 'trustee de l'AF de Londres' a trustee of the London branch. 'To trust somebody' is 'avoir confiance en quelqu'un, faire confiance à quelqu'un'.

To translate the noun 'trust', the Toubon suggests 'fiducie', n.f.

Up adj. (also **down**). On 3 November 1988, *Le Nouvel Observateur*, no. 1252, in its enquiry into what it called 'la nouvelle super-élite française', described those who were 'up' as the industrialists and businessmen who had been to one of the 'grandes écoles' (see above, 'must' and 'establishment'), and those who were 'down' as 'les cercles mondains' (fashionable society), adding that

> la super-élite est plus Dîners du siècle que Jockey-Club. Plus Roland-Garros que polo de Bagatelle. Pour un week-end à la campagne, elle ira à Canisy, sorte de Club Med très bien fréquenté à 300 francs (seulement) la journée, plutôt que chez la princesse de Guermantes. (The super-élite goes more to the Dîners du siècle than to the Jockey Club, more to watch tennis at Roland Garros than polo at Bagatelle. It will spends its weekends at Canisy, a kind of Club Med with a very good clientèle at (only) 300 francs a day, rather than with the Princesse de Guermantes.)

The references to Proust – Charles Swann, whose wife Odette made him put 'Mr' on his visiting cards, was a member of the Jockey Club, another aspect of her anglomania (in addition to her proclaimed desire that people should not think she is 'fishing for compliments') – are easier to identify than the other social markers.

Le Club Méditerranée was established in 1953 as a small organisation offering cheap holidays. In 1990, it had a market valuation, 'capitalisation boursière', on the Paris Stock Exchange of 6.4 *milliard* new francs, roughly £640 million. A figure of 300 francs (roughly £30 at the time) is not much. Les Dîners du siècle began to be held in the RAC club in Paris in 1986 and are limited to fifty guests, by invitation only. As in Proust, what is most interesting is to see who has not been invited.

Ted Hope, to whose memory this book is dedicated (see Ch. 1, note 13), told me that in the Navy, in which he was awarded the DSC during the Second World War, boxes of ammunition frequently arrived with the label: 'To avoid confusion, top is labelled bottom throughout'.

A fuller version of the story explains the instructions in more detail:

> This box should be carried or stored upside-down. To avoid confusion, top is therefore labelled bottom.

Vouchers n.m.p. According to Jean-Pierre Colignon's *La cote des mots*, these are now included in the file of documents sent to people booking a holiday with an agency. He recommends anyone receiving them to keep all receipts and documentation, and also suggests that a more suitable word in French would be 'coupon' or 'bon d'échange'.

Welfare State n.m. In spite of the popularity and accuracy of the expression 'État-Providence', the English term is in use, as when Jacques Julliard wrote in *Le Nouvel Observateur*, no. 1477 on 25 February 1993, welcoming Michel Rocard's 'Big Bang', that

> l'écroulement du communisme oriental mais aussi l'épuisement du modèle social-démocrate (nationalisme plus welfare state) ont sonné le glas de l'expérience socialiste. (The collapse of communism in the east and the exhaustion of the model offered by social democracy – nationalism plus

the Welfare State – have marked the end of the socialist experiment.)

In 1989, the expression 'le welfare' was used in the sense of the Welfare State by a lecturer at the Institut des Etudes internationales in Paris, though without the negative connotations which it has in the United States.

Who's Who n.m. The actual title of the book telling you who is who in France is *Who's Who in France*. This may be for reasons of snobbery; or because *Qui est Qui en France* would be so obviously a linguistic calque from the English anyway.

NOTES
1 One of the major difference between the United Kingdom and the countries of continental Europe lies in the fact that 'charities', in the sense of the Royal Society for the Protection of Birds, the Missions to Seamen and the Distressed Gentlefolk Aid Association (Patron: Her Majesty the Queen Mother), enjoy a much more visible existence in the British Isles, where they derive most of their money from the freedom enjoyed by British citizens to leave their money as they think fit (see below, 'test, tester'). The place of charities, a word which has not made its way into French either as an anglicism or as an example of 'franglais', is taken by the 'Associations sans but lucratif', which have become sufficiently popular to create the expression 'la vie associative' for the various sporting, education and cultural activities which they organise. These organisations correspond, in the UK, to the 'Non Profit Making Companies Limited by Guarantee' and enjoy the same exemption from Corporation Tax (l'impôt sur les sociétés).
2 The term 'les deux cents familles' goes back at least to Edouard Daladier (1884–1970), and his reference at the Congrès radical-socialiste of 1934 to 'les deux cents familles maîtresses de l'économie et de la politique française' (the two hundred families which rule over the French economy and French politics). On 17 March 1994, *Le Nouvel Observateur* no. 1532 commented that 'c'est l'establishment en général que les jeunes récuseraient' (it is the establishment in general that young people are said to reject), and on 21 April in no. 1537 it described the controversial businessman Bernard Tapie as 'le voyou de charme opposé aux hypocrisies de l'establishment' (the charming rogue in conflict with the hypocrisies of the establishment). Jean-Marie Le Pen presents himself as the

great opponent of what he makes a point of pronouncing as 'l'établissement'.

See the entry in Thody and Evans, *Faux Amis and Key Words*, on 'les Grands Corps de l'État', which emphasises the role played by the *grandes écoles* in general, and by the École Nationale d'Administration (ENA) in particular, in forming the French political establishment, which is not quite the same as the Great and the Good in English. Edouard Balladur, Jacques Chirac and Jacques Delors are all former pupils of ENA. So, too, are Jacques Attali, Jean-Paul Chevènement, Claude Cheysson, Valéry Giscard d'Estaing, Lionel Jospin, Pierre Joxe, Alain Juppé, Michel Poniatowski, Michel Rocard, and . . . Jacques Toubon, Minister of Justice in the government formed by Alain Juppé after Jacques Chirac had appointed him Prime Minister in May 1995. (see below, 'up'). Edith Cresson, the first woman to be made Prime Minister in France, did not go to ENA; and she took the decision to move the school from Paris to Strasbourg. The word 'establishment' is not mentioned in the Toubon, or in the 1989 *dictionnaire des néologismes officiels*, or in the 1993 *dictionnaire des termes officiels*.

3 In a book which is now almost comically out of date, but which was a best-seller when it was published in the 'Que sais-je?' series in 1959, Tony Mayer uses the word in the correct additional sense of somebody who is socially acceptable, when he comments in *La vie anglaise*: 'Il suffit de beaucoup d'argent, d'un peu d'application – et de deux ou trois générations – pour transformer un nouveau riche en gentleman, mieux encore en gentleman farmer' (you need a lot of money, a little hard work – and two or three generations – to transform a nouveau riche into a gentleman, and better still a gentleman farmer).

It is a comment which recalls Matthew Arnold's remark that the public schools were not for sons of gentlemen but for fathers of gentlemen, and which echoes the theme of a novel published in 1902 by Paul Bourget entitled *L'Étape*. In it, Bourget argues not only that social stability is impossible without the help of the Catholic Church, but that nobody can expect to move from the peasantry into the upper classes in one generation. In his 1939 short story 'L'Enfance d'un chef' (The childhood of a leader), Sartre reminds his reader of this thesis by making his young fascist, Lucien Fleurier, explain his inability to get on with scholarship boys (les boursiers) by the fact that 'ils ont brûlé une étape' (missed out a necessary stage).

On 6 April 1993, after the French delegation had refused to use its veto in the debate on agriculture at the GATT conference, the

'Revue de Presse' on France-Inter quoted the editorial of *Le Quotidien de Paris*. It claimed that now that France was going to be allowed to export only 'les céréales cultivées par les gentleman-farmers dans la Beauce', 'les paysans français' were doomed to become 'des gardiens de la nature au RMI' (guardians of nature paid by the *Revenu Minimum d'Insertion*, a basic allowance paid to the unemployed while they were learning new skills to enable them to re-enter the workforce).

Le Point no. 1123 for 26 March 1994 acknowledged that 'les gentleman-farmers du bassin parisien' had a per capita income which was twenty times that of 'les petits éleveurs' (the small stockbreeders) of the Massif central. But it also pointed out that while, in 1954, France could scarcely feed itself, it now occupied second place after the United States as an exporter of agricultural produce.

On p. 157 of *Le Dico français-français*, in the section entitled 'Comment parler à Neuilly, Auteuil, Passy' (the three most fashion-able areas to the west of Paris; those living there are, according to M. Vandel, known as 'des Nap's'), Philippe Vandel explains that when a girl from there says 'Papa est exploitant agricole', you should interpret her as saying 'Nous vivons dans un manoir, au pied de nos terres' (We live in a manor, at the foot of our land); that he is, in other words, a gentleman farmer. But as the entry indicates, the French don't really have a word for it.

See also 'come-back' in IIc.

4 The reference is to one of the major scandals of the mid-1980s, the distribution of blood containing the AIDS (SIDA) virus to approximately 10,000 victims, including 1,300 haemophiliacs and other patients needing blood transfusions. The infected blood had been collected in prisons, with their traditionally high population of drug addicts and homosexuals, as well as from ordinary mem-bers of the public, and was not tested before being used. The fact that a large number of invalids had in fact been sentenced to an inevitable premature death gave rise to an understandable desire to find a culprit. Georgina Dufoix, Health Minister at the time, said that she felt 'responsable, mais non coupable' (responsible but not guilty), and there was talk of accusing the then Prime Minister, Laurent Fabius, of crimes ranging from criminal negli-gence to attempted poisoning. Dr Garetta, head of the National blood transfusion service, who does not seem to have made any money out of the affair, was sentenced to four years in prison. See 'safe sex' and 'relapse' in IId.

There was a strong feeling that he had been made to carry the can – 'que c'était lui le lampiste' – and an article by Theodore Stanger in *Newsweek*, reproduced in a special number of *Le Courrier international* for June 1994, argued that the French postponed the commercialisation of the Abbott test, developed in America and aimed at checking that the blood used in transfusions was free of the AIDS virus, until a comparable French test was available. The suggestion that it was thus French anti-Americanism which was the root cause for 'le scandale du sang contaminé' (the scandal of contaminated blood) had also been made by a French journalist, Pascal Bruckner in *Le Nouvel Observateur* no. 1536, for 14 April 1994, when he wrote:

> Si la France a atteint des records de contamination, ce n'est pas distraction ou négligence de nos dirigeants, c'est en raison d'un chauvinisme également partagé par la droite et par la gauche, et qui commandait de transfuser 'avant tout de bon sang français, des bons tests bien de chez nous, de préférence à des tests étrangers. (If France has a record number of cases of AIDS, this is not because of carelessness or negligence on behalf of the powers that be, but because of a chauvinism shared equally by left and right, and which required above all else the use of good French blood, and good, home-grown, French tests, rather than foreign products.)

This allegation was denied in an article in *Le Monde* for 22 September 1994, which argued that the only reason why the Abbott test was not used was that it was unreliable. *Le Monde* for 13 September reported that the long-running argument as to whether it was the Institut Pasteur or an American laboratory which had first identified the AIDS virus was finally settled to the advantage of the French, a decision apparently worth millions.

5 For pupils over sixteen. The *collège* takes pupils only up to the age of sixteen, so that one cannot take one's baccalauréat there.

6 *Modern Languages*, Vol. 69, no. 4, December 1988, pp. 218–24.

7 From an apparently legendary entry in a nineteenth-century French history book for schools, which began 'Nos ancêtres les Gaulois avaient les yeux bleus, la chevelure blonde, la stature fière (Our ancestors the Gauls had blue eyes, blond hair and a proud posture); or words to that effect. Unfortunately, although de Gaulle was clearly counting on everyone's ability to recognise the quotation, we have not been able to track it down. The English equivalent was making the African children attending the missionary schools in Ghana recite Wordsworth's 'Daffodils'.

See also the quotation from André Delacroix in Part I, Chapter 3.

b Food, drink and travel

The asterisk* is a reminder that the word either does not exist normally in English or is used by the French in a different sense from the meaning it has in the United States or the United Kingdom. The dagger † placed after a word in the index indicates its presence in either the 1995 *Petit Larousse Illustré* or the *Petit Robert* (1992).

Airbag n.m. An official trade name; but also 'sac gonflable', 'coussin gonflable de protection', 'coussin à air' or, for the Toubon, simply 'coussin gonflable'. On 10 October 1994, however, in a discussion on Europe 1 of the virtues of the new Volvo, the word used throughout was 'airbag', with the point being made by one of the contributors that 'au moment du crash [see below], on meurt étouffé. C'est plus propre' (at the moment of impact, you die of asphyxiation, it's cleaner).

At home n.m. Michèle Fitoussi, in *Le ras-le-bol des SuperWomen* (see 'briefing' in IIa), entitles one of her more disastrous chapters of accidents 'Week-end at home'. Odette Swann invites her guests to an 'at home'.

Autostop* n.m. 'Faire de l'autostop' is to go hitch-hiking, 'un autostoppeur/ese' somebody who does it. Not in the Toubon, although the *Dictionnaire des Anglicismes* quotes an article from *Vie et Langage* for April 1954 to the effect that '*auto-stop* n'est pas du français irréprochable' and prefers the French Canadian 'faire du pouce', a linguistic calque from 'to thumb a lift'.

Baby blues n.m. Michèle Fitoussi's 'SuperWoman' goes back to work 'en plein baby blues'. Another hapax legomenon for me, though no French dictionary suggests a translation. Her Nouveau Père (*sic*), who either was very much there at the birth, or else fainted and had to be carried out, also succumbs to 'le daddy blues'.

Baby-sitter n. generally f., and v., **baby sitting** n.m. In France since the 1960s. Josette Rey-Debove and Gilberte Gagnon explain the origins of the word in the United States by the fact that Americans 'se rendent volontiers visite le soir' (like to go and see one another in the evening) and rarely have domestic servants; in France – they are perhaps talking about an earlier period – people prefer to ask their parents or friends. They add: '*Baby-sitting* s'intègre mal au système français, et garde d'enfants convient aussi bien' (*Baby-sitting* does not fit into the French system and garde d'enfants is just as good). The term is nevertheless nowadays as fully part of French as 'au pair' is of English. The verb 'baby-sitter', though odd, is also in common use.

Barbecue n.m. Neither in the Toubon nor in the 1989 *dictionnaire des néologismes officiels*. The *Dictionnaire des Anglicismes* gives its first use, in 1913, by Apollinaire, as 'barbacue', which is perhaps closer to the Haitian original 'barbacoa', but does not avoid the involuntarily comic associations of its pronunciation as 'barbe-cul' (beard-arse).

The *Dictionnaire des Anglicismes* also observes that a barbecue offers 'une cuisine facile et amusante (*it's fun!*) pour un peuple pressé et qui a peu de traditions culinaires mais d'excellente viande de boeuf' (an easy and entertaining way of cooking for a people in a hurry [the Americans] who have few culinary traditions but excellent beef).

The menu in the Buffalo Grill restaurant chain translates 'Barbecue ribs' as 'travers de porc'.

Break* n.m. A shooting break. Professor Spence points out[1] in a reference to the *Oxford English Dictionary* that this word originally meant a four-wheeled carriage.

Brunch n.m. 'Grand déjeuner'.

Brushing* n.m. Blow dry. For the *Dictionnaire des Anglicismes*, the French terms *séchage-brossage* or *séchage à la brosse* 'n'ont qu'un succès d'estime' (only what, for absence of an English term, we have to call a 'succès d'estime').

Caddie* n.m. Not necessarily somebody who carries your golf bags, though the Toubon suggestion of 'cadet/ette' could mean that the word is occasionally used in this sense. It is a trade name for a supermarket trolley, and 'un caddie-boy', used in *Le Nouvel Observateur* for 1 December 1994, no. 1569, is the man who takes your purchases to the car.

The correct generic term for a supermarket trolley is 'un chariot'.

Cake* n.m. Generally designates a slice of fruit cake wrapped in cellophae and available across the counter at most cafés. One of the more expensive ways of avoiding starvation.

Camping n.m. A camp-site. Another English gerund which, like 'parking', the French use as a noun. Neither is mentioned in the Toubon. 'Un camping car' is what is known in the UK as a camper-van, and in the USA as an RV (recreational vehicle).

Car ferry n.m. 'Transbordeur', 'navire transbordeur'.

Carpool n.m. In a programme on France-Inter for 27 April 1994, a contributor to a phone-in programme who suggested that a possible solution to urban congestion lay in the adoption of American 'carpools' was rapidly called to order and told that she meant 'covoiturage', the word recommended in the Toubon. The loi Toubon was being debated at the time, and the Conseil Constitutionnel had not yet given its verdict.

Charter n.m. or adj. 'Un vol charter' is a charter flight. The Toubon gives 'affréter' for the verb 'to charter', but does not carry the logic of the language to the point of recommending 'avion affrété'.

Chatterton* n.m. Insulating tape. After the name of its inventor. Its full name in English used to be 'Chatterton's compound'.

Check-up n.m. In an article in *Francophonie* for December 1994, one of the journals published by the Association for Language Learning, Colin Asher quotes the following conversation between husband and wife from Luis Buñuel's 1974 film, *Le fantôme de la liberté*:

> *Wife* Tu devrais aller te faire un check-up. (You ought to go and have a check-up.)
>
> *Husband* Mais pourquoi un *check-up*? Il y a une expression en français qui signifie exactement la même chose: *examen général*. (But why do you say 'check-up'? There is a French expression which means exactly the same: 'General examination'.)
>
> *Wife* C'est trop long, *examen général*. Check-up, c'est beaucoup plus rapide. (But that's far too long, *check-up* is much quicker.)
>
> *Husband* Mais rien ne te presse. (But you're not in a hurry).

The word is not in the Toubon, but the *Dictionnaire des Anglicismes* quotes it as being used by Julien Green and Paul Morand, both in an American context. The French Canadian expression 'bilan de santé' is considered preferable in France itself to 'examen général'.

Chester n.m. The French for Cheshire cheese. For admirers of Proust, this is a term always associated with an incident in Part I of *Sodome et Gomorrhe* (*A la recherche du temps perdu*, Pléiade, Paris, 1954 Vol. II, p. 663; *Remembrance of Things Past*, translation by C. K. Scott-Moncrieff and Terence Martin, Chatto & Windus, London, 1981, Vol. II, p. 688) at which the Narrator is a guest at the reception given by the Duchesse de Montmorency for the Queen of England. As the royal party is moving towards the buffet, the Duc de Guermantes, the Queen on his arm, sees the Narrator from afar off, and makes the most welcoming gestures for him to join them, reassuring him by the warmth of his greeting 'que je pouvais m'approcher sans crainte, que je ne serais pas mangé tout cru à la place des sandwiches au chester' (that I need not be afraid to come closer, that I would not be eaten raw instead of the Cheshire cheese sandwiches). The Narrator, however, having learnt from his study of the semiology of everyday life just how great a gap can exist between the signs of apparent cordiality and the reality lying behind them, contents himself with a deep, silent, respectful bow.

Later, the Duchesse de Guermantes meets the Narrator's mother, and is full of compliments for her son's excellent manners, selecting for especial comment the elegance of his bow. She does not, however, Proust comments, mention its most important quality: its discretion, and the fact that it was not followed by any acceptance of the invitation to join the royal party.

The Duchess's compliments, the Narrator observes, were also a kind of warning for the future: if he wishes to remain socially acceptable, he will have to continue to read the signs correctly and realise that, for most of the time, an upwardly socially mobile commoner like himself can be granted only the outward signs of aristocratic friendship, which will be withdrawn if he attempts to enter the inner sanctum.

It is a lesson potentially appropriate to all societies, but especially useful to anyone from an English provincial university who happens to come into contact with senior members of the British Civil Service. Were such a person so naïve as to take up the invitation from someone in the Treasury or Foreign Office to 'make sure you drop in for lunch next time you're in Whitehall', his or her name will have even less chance than before of appearing on any future list of the Great and the Good.

Chewing gum n.m. Advertised in *Le Monde* for 9 June 1994, in a special number commemorating the Normandy landings, together with the reminder that the word had 'débarqué en France en 1914' (landed in France in 1914). 'Consultez plus souvent votre *Petit Robert*', advised *Le Monde*, 'et vous brillerez dans les dîners.' (Consult your *Petit Robert* more frequently, and you will shine at dinner parties.) An involuntary comment on why the word 'bore' is so hard to translate into French.

Clearance n.m. Should be 'clairance' for the Toubon. The word 'acabit' is the term more normally used to indicate the height of trucks able to pass under a bridge.

Clip n.m. Either an extract from a film or video, or a clip-on ear-ring, or the device for opening a carton of milk or fruit juice.

Cockpit n.m. The Toubon recommends 'poste de pilotage' or 'habitacle'. Neither word was used by the officer in charge of the special unit of the GIGN (Groupe d'Intervention de la Gendarmerie Nationale) which freed the hostages held prisoner on board Air France flight 260 at Marseilles airport on 26 December 1994. When interviewed on France-Inter, he spoke of 'des terroristes retranchés dans le cockpit' (terrorists who had barricaded themselves in the cockpit).

Cocktail n.m. Attested as early as 1836 in *L'Espion*, a translation of Fenimore Cooper's *The Spy*, and established well before its main vogue in the 1920s. Raymond Queneau, author of the 1959 comic novel *Zazie dans le métro*, liked to make fun of 'franglais' words by writing them as the French pronounced them: ouiquend, coquetèle, bloudjinze.

The permanence of the spelling 'cocktail' is attested by an article in *Le Point* for 6 August 1994, no. 1141, describing what it called 'la folie des cocktails miracle', the vogue for various mixtures of vitamins which were very popular in 1992 until the Inspection du Contrôle des Fraudes looked into what had become known as 'les smart drinks'. These included the quick pick-me-up known as 'Fast Blast', as well as 'le Party Pill' (a specific against hangovers, 'des gueules de bois'), and a tonic for late risers called 'Rise and Shine'.

According to *Le Point*, the French spend 1.5 per cent of their food budget on vitamin pills, a statistic which links up with Theodore Stanger's remark, in an article from *Newsweek* translated in the special June 1994 number of *Le Courrier*

International, to the effect that 'dans ce pays où il fait si bon vivre, une personne sur quatre est sous Valium' (in the country where life is so pleasant, one person in four is one Valium).

'Un cocktail' is also a cocktail party.

Connecter* v. Theoretically used only in a technical context. When Michèle Fitoussi's SuperWoman says she is 'connectée à l'actualité', she could just as well have said 'branchée', the more normal up-to-date term, and a possible translation for 'streetwise'.

Cookie n.m. 'sablé américain'. English children learning French used to be taught to translate 'biscuit' as 'petit four'.

Cosy n.m, **cosy-corner** n.m. An example of a false anglicism sufficiently well established to have become obsolete.

Crash n.m. **crasher** v. A crash (see above, 'airbag'), or to crash, as when the 'Revue de Presse' on France-Inter for 12 April 1994 reported that 'un avion français a crashé en Bosnie', and the same programme tried to encourage the French to drink less before driving by saying that cutting out apéritifs would save the equivalent in lives of 'quatre crashs de Jumbo jet'. On 11 August 1994, *La Dépêche du Midi* gave the headline 'En Corée, sept blessés dans le crash' (Seven people injured in the crash), and on August 13 *L'Indépendant de Perpignan* reported that 'le pilote d'un avion de tourisme se tue dans le crash' (the pilot of a light aircraft is killed in the crash).

The use of this word attracted understandably unfavourable comment from M. André Fanton in the debate in the *Assemblée Nationale* on 3 May 1994:

Des gens nous expliquent qu'il faut surtout employer des mots anglais car cela fait chic. Quand survient un accident d'avion, par exemple, on parle de 'crash', et l'on dit que l'avion 's'est crashé'. Et puisque toutes les chaînes de télé-'vision et tous les journaux emploient ce terme, les enfants croient qu'il faut écrire: 'Ne crashez pas dans le métro'

(*Sourires*). (People tell us that we must use English words above all because it is smart to do so. When an aeroplane accident takes place, for example, people talk about 'a crash' and say that the plane 'crashed'. And since all the television channels and all the newspapers use the expression, children think that you should write: 'Don't crash in the underground') (*Smiles*).[2]

The existence of this particular verb – especially in the form 'a crashé', when one would normally have expected at least the form 's'est crashé' given by M. Fanton – may stem not only from the snobbish use of English by French journalists, but also from the difficulty which some of them have with the reflexive verb 's'écraser'. The hero of Sapper's 1922 thriller *Bulldog Drummond* had the same problem, with his four years' service in France between 1914 and 1918 leading him to conduct the following conversation in Chapter 8 of the description of the first of his four rounds with Carl Petersen:

> '*Mais oui, Monsieur mon Colonel*', he remarked affably, when the gendarme paused for lack of breath, '*vous comprenez que notre machine avait crashé dans un field de turnipes. Nous avons lost notre direction. Nous sommes hittés dans l'estomac.*'

Drummond then tries to correct himself by saying

> '*dans un field de turnipes – non, des rognons*'

and refuses to accept Algy Longworth's observation that what he means is 'oignons'. The gendarme then reflects that

> Of course this large Englishman was mad; why otherwise should he spit in the kidneys?

> A gate-crasher is 'un resquilleur'.

Drink n.m. One of the more superfluous 'franglais' words. For its use see 'soft' in IId.

Drugstore n.m. There has been a drugstore at Saint-Germain-des-Prés since the early 1950s. It offers a wider choice of purchases than many of its American equivalents.

Duty free shop n.m. The Toubon recommends 'boutique hors-taxes'; and presumably, by implication, 'provisions hors-taxe' or 'achats hors-taxes'.

Entryphone n.m. The intercom system which enables your guests to tell you that they have arrived so that you can activate the mechanism which will unlock the main door to your apartment block.

The widespread installation of entryphones, especially in Paris and other large towns, marks an important change in the French way of life. Traditionally, it was the concierge who opened the door and kept a check on who came in and out. It is said that one of the reasons why the Germans had such difficulty in tracking down members of the resistance movement during the occupation was that they never managed to win over any concierges to their cause. When, on an early visit to France, I asked a Frenchwoman if she did not find it tiresome to have her comings and goings constantly watched over by the concierge, I received the spirited reply:

> Non, monsieur. J'aime savoir qui pourrait venir chez moi. On a raison de se méfier, surtout ici à Paris. (No. I like to know who might come and see me. You're right to be suspicious of people, especially here in Paris.)

For the central role in French life of the verb 'se méfier', to be suspicious, see the entries 'suspicious', 'Alsacien' and 'État civil' in *Faux Amis and Key Words* (Thody and Evans).

Fairplay* more often an adjective than a noun in French. The most difficult moment in the life of 'une careerwoman' (see IId) in France is, according to Michèle Fitoussi's *Le ras-le-bol des SuperWomen* (see 'briefing' in IIa), the day when she has to tell her boss she is pregnant:

> Et si, fair play tout de même, il vous félicite du bout des lèvres, ne croyez pas autant la partie gagnée: il y aura toujours un moment où ça grince. Le baby-boom [see IId] c'est d'abord, de son point de vue égoïste, un boom d'em-bêtements. (And if, playing the game none the less, he offers

you somewhat half-hearted congratulations, don't think you've won. There's always a moment when it becomes a spanner in the works. From his selfish point of view, the baby boom is above all a problem boom.)

French children protest against treatment which they see as unfair by saying 'ce n'est pas du jeu', but this was not the expression used by the commentator on France-Inter on the France-England rugby match on 3 February 1995. He accused the English of cheating, as well as of being favoured by the Scottish referee, and added: 'Nous sommes fairplay parce que nous sommes français' (We play fair because we are French).

Fast food n.m. Officially, 'restauration rapide' or 'prêt à manger'.

In a special issue studying reactionaries, no. 496, *L'Événement du jeudi* for 5 May 1994 quoted Antoine Waechter, the leader of Les Verts, the rival of Brice Lalonde's conservationist party Generation Ecologie, as denouncing 'la civilisation du fast food' for having made its way

jusque dans les paysages, avec ses hangars cosmopolites, ses pavillons préfabriqués et son tourisme de catalogue (right into the countryside, with its cosmopolitan sheds, its prefabricated houses and its catalogue-based tourism).

The term 'Fast Food' also refers to the eating house where the food is sold. *Le Monde* for 28 September wrote of the operation which had tidied up the Champs-Elysées:

il était temps d'intervenir: les trous se multipliaient, les arbres étaient malades, the voitures envahissaient les trottoirs, the poubelles débordaient, les fast foods proliféraient avec leurs cortèges d'emballages vides et d'enseignes lumineuses. (The time had come to do something: there were more and more holes in the road, the trees were dying, cars were invading the pavements, dustbins were overflowing, fast food stores were all over the place, with their accompanying processions of empty packages and neon signs.)

In Quentin Tarantino's 1994 film *Pulp Fiction*, Vincent

(played by John Travolta) astounds his partner in crime Jules (played by Samuel Jackson) by telling him that the existence in France of the metric system requires the French to call a quarter pounder 'un Royal Cheese', and that the French call a Big Mac 'le Big Mac'.

The verb 'fastfooder' means to eat in a fast food establishment.

Five o'clock tea n.m. One of the first examples of 'le franglais' to be noticed by early twentieth-century visitors to France, and a term sometimes made more conspicuous by the variant 'Five o'clock à toute heure', the equivalent of the English 'All-day breakfast'. In the tourist section of no. 1153 on 22 October 1994, *Le Point* spoke eloquently of the charms of Llandudno and wrote of one hotel:

> si le chef – anglais – pratique une nouvelle cuisine néo-française à la fois datée, empruntée et poussive, on se rattrape avec une cave splendide et un 'five o'clock tea' chaleureux. (If the chef – who is English – offers a neo-French *nouvelle cuisine* which is at one and the same time old-fashioned, artificial and slow in coming, there are consolations in a splendid cellar and a warmly served 'five o'clock tea'.)

If one assumes that the tea is also a hot meal, as well as being served in a very hospitable manner, it would seem that *Le Point* is talking about George Orwell's favourite meal, 'high tea'; as well as offering another illustration of Proust's remark about a dinner jacket being called 'un smoking'.

Flash n.m. In addition to its meaning of a brief news bulletin (see entry in IIc), the word also means a flashing light. As you drive down the A1 from Lille to Paris, you see the notice 'Flashs allumés = Danger' (Flashing lights = Danger).

Flipper* v. To feel depressed, as when Michèle Fitoussi's 'SuperWoman' writes of her relationship with her children, 'nous flippons, car nous avons toujours tout faux' (we feel down, since we always get it wrong).

The word can also mean to be taken aback, as when *Le Nouvel Observateur*, no. 1569, 1 December 1994, said after Jacques Delors's announcement that he would not stand for president:

> Les plus flippés sont des chiraquiens, qui s'interrogent: leur champion est-il éligible à l'Élysée? (Those most taken aback are the followers of Jacques Chirac, who are wondering if their champion is capable of getting himself elected to the Élysée palace.)

In the section of *Les mouvements de mode expliqués aux parents* devoted to 'les babas' (see IId), the authors explain how 'au sein de cet univers horrible, le Baba connaît une solution de survie: pour ne pas flipper, il sera cool' (within this horrible universe, the 'Baba' has one means of surviving: in order not to panic, he will be cool).

See also the adjective 'cool' and the noun 'flipper' in II.d.

Globe-trotter n.m. The July-August issue of the magazine *La Croissance* was devoted to 'les écrivains globe-trotter', and one is disappointed not to see the term mentioned in the Toubon, especially when the exquisitely French 'les écrivains dromomanes', recommended by H. J. G. Godin in *Les ressources lexicologiques de la langue française* (Blackwell, Oxford, 1960), is so conveniently to hand.

Hamburger n.m. Officially, either 'un sandwich américain' or 'un pain fourré de viande' (piece of bread stuffed with meat).

Home p.c.* n.m. A home personal computer, as advertised on Europe 1 on 12 December 1994.

Hovercraft n.m. The recommended form 'aéroglisseur' is beginning to catch on, as is 'navette' for shuttle, except for the trains carrying vehicles through the Channel Tunnel (see 'shuttle service' below).

Inner-cities n.m. or f. plural. When *Le Point* no. 1070 wrote on 20 March 1993 that

Les HLM [Habitations à Loyer Modéré] du gaullisme pressé sont devenues les 'inner cities' de la gauche Tapie (the cheap housing developments put up by the Gaullists in a hurry have become Tapie's 'inner cities')

it was talking about a social rather than geographical phenomenon. The highest incidence of social disaffection in France is among inhabitants of the large housing developments (officially, 'des centres urbains') built on the outskirts of large towns in the 1960s and 1970s. These are very different from the 'inner cities' of North America, for which the official term is 'les centres urbains'. See also 'rap' in IId.

Jet n.m. In 1976, a ministerial decree imposed 'avion à réaction'. A jumbo jet is 'un gros-porteur'.

'Jet set' occurs regularly in *Madame Figaro* and *Vendredi Samedi Dimanche*, and Michèle Fitoussi gives another example of the easy coexistence between 'franglais' words and some highly authentic colloquial French when she writes about

une de ces superbes blondes jet-set qui voguent de milliardaires en piscines (quoi qu'elles aussi, elles brassent dur pour se la couler douce) (one of those superb jet-set blondes who float from millionnaires to swimming pools (although they too have to swim hard to get the easy life).

Jogging n.m. Makes its appearance in French in 1974. *L'Express* for 19 January 1995, no. 2271, reported that Edouard Balladur 'ne fait pas de jogging', and the Toubon does not mention a practice which, as Wodehouse makes Gussie Fink-Nottle say of Roderick Spode's way of drinking soup, casts doubt over the view that man is nature's last word. See also 'gag' in IIc.

Jumbo jet n.m. 'Gros porteur'.

Kitsch n.m. Originally a German word borrowed by both the English and the French; perhaps the reason why it is not in the *Dictionnaire des Anglicismes*. An article called 'Standing' (see below) in *Le Point*, no. 1125, 9 April 1994, reviewing a book by Jean-Yves Jouannais entitled *Des nains, des jardins* [*Dwarfs and Gardens*], *claimed that*

> le kitsch, c'est la traduction de la bêtise des idées reçues dans le langage de la beauté et des émotions. (Kitsch is the translation of the stupidity of received ideas into the language of beauty and of the emotions.)

The term 'idées reçues' is a reference to Flaubert; see the last paragraph of 'self-government' in IIa. The reference on France-Inter on 13 May 1994 to 'un discours kitsch de monsieur Le Pen' (a kitsch speech by Monsieur Le Pen) may have meant that he was appealing to the 'petit bourgeois' sensibility which found satisfaction in what the article also called 'le luxe du pauvre'.

The article in *Le Point* also mentioned a house called DO MI CI LA DO RÉ (= domicile adoré).

Lad* n.m. An abbreviation of 'stable-lad'. Like 'groom', an alternative word for 'palefrenier' since the nineteenth century.

Lift* n.m. Used by Proust for the servant who works the lift – 'l'ascenseur' – at the Grand Hôtel at Combray. Probably no longer a word in use now that all lifts are automatic. But see 'goal' in IIc for a comparable usage.

Light adj. As applied to food, low in calories; as applied to prices, low. The shop 'Samy Lingerie', on the left as you walk down the Boulevard Saint Michel, offers underclothes 'à des prix super lights', and 'le choix à prix lights'. It must be very difficult, if you are teaching English in Paris, to persuade your pupils that adjectives in English are invariable.

'Light' is apparently a very common word in contemporary Spanish, where according to Phil Davison's article in *The Independent* for 1 January 1995 it is spelt either 'lait' or 'ligh', and used in a political context for 'la derecha light', the moderate right. The same happens in French, where *L'Événement du jeudi* for April 21 1994, no. 494 referred to 'le fascisme light' de M. Berlusconi, meaning that although he was right-wing, his political views were relatively mild, offering neither threats nor violence. The same issue stated that

> dans les années 80, pour encourager le public à consommer, le marketing [see IIa] a introduit le concept de 'light'. La consommation excessive alourdit. (In the 1980s, in order to encourage the public to consume, marketing introduced the concept of 'light'. Too much food makes you heavy.)

In 1973, the idea of food as a threat had already formed the subject-matter of a film entitled *La Grande Bouffe*, in which four highly successful men shut themselves away in a luxury villa in order to eat themselves to death.

A French word used to connote light, low-fat food is the past participle 'allégé'.

Loft n.m. The *Dictionnaire des Anglicismes* quotes a passage from G. de Dampierre's 1969 *Connaissance et technique du golf* describing the 'loft' to be obtained from the various irons and woods (officially, 'des fers et des bois').

Perhaps justifiably, Michèle Fitoussi uses the word to describe what is traditionally called 'un grenier', a word whose etymology evokes the part of a house in the country where one might in the past have stored grain. 'SuperWoman', however, lives in Paris, and would, as the 1993 Larousse French-English, English-French dictionary puts it, have 'dépensé beaucoup d'argent pour aménager les combles' (spent a lot of money on a loft conversion). There is no other word in French for what this operation would have produced except the 'franglais' term, a loft. In *Les mouvements de mode expliqués aux parents* (Obalk, Soral and Pasche), the young Basile, who is 'branché' (with it, streetwise) lives in 'un loft de 15 mètres carrés, rue de Montempoivre' (a 15-metre-square loft, rue de Montempoivre) in the newly fashionable 12th *arrondissement*, at Reuilly.

Lunch n.m. In Marcel Aymé's 1952 blackish comedy *La Tête des Autres*, the prosecuting attorney (procureur de la République), Bertolier, who has just managed to have a totally innocent man sentenced to death, says:

Pour préparer ce glorieux événement, j'ai fait préparer un lunch à la maison. (To celebrate the glorious occasion, I have had a lunch prepared at home.)

Like 'luncheon', which appears as early as 1840, it suggests a light meal, often after a wedding ceremony, and thus a contrast to the French habit of having the main meal at midday. 'A good lunch', in the sense of a fairly copious meal with plenty to drink, would be 'un très bon déjeuner'. There is something of the same distinction between the English 'a good trencherman' and the French 'une bonne fourchette' as there is in French between 'gourmand' and 'gourmet'.

Mixed grill n.m. Not in the Toubon – 'lunch' isn't there either – and more surprisingly absent from the *Dictionnaire des Anglicismes*.

In Part III of *Les Thibault* (1922–40), a family chronicle by Martin du Gard (1881–1958), the central character Antoine Thibault has an affair with a woman called Rachel. When they are dining together and he orders a mixed grill, she smiles, and later tells him why. One of her earlier lovers, a man called Hirsch, had used the term 'mixed grill' to describe the experience of being in bed in London with a prostitute ('fille à soldats'), her two sisters and younger brother.

Mixer n.m. The spelling of the French form 'mixeur' is very audible in the pronunciation, rhyming with 'fleur' and not, as in 'mixer', with 'flair'. There is no noun 'mélangeur' from the verb 'mélanger'; perhaps because the constituent elements of a 'mélange' remained separately identifiable, whereas if you put them through 'un mixer' they are all blended, merged together. 'Une mixture' is generally pejorative.

Open ticket n.m. 'Billet ouvert'.

Pack n.m. The expression normally used by rugby, in spite of the recommendation in the Toubon of 'paquet' though not in the sense of 'un pack de bière', a term frequently used in supermarkets. See also entry in IIa.

Le Point for 30 July 1994, no. 1141, used the term 'pack d'aération' to describe the air-conditioning process used in aeroplanes, explaining that while all the air used to be changed every three minutes, all of it drawn in from the outside and brought up to the appropriate temperature, half of it is now simply reconditioned. The worst effects are felt at the back of the aircraft, but can be mitigated by the intake of one litre of water every four hours. Air France has a better record than other airlines.

Parking* n.m. A car park. Not in the Toubon, but the approved term is 'parc de stationnement'. See above 'camping'.

Le Point for 7 January 1995, no. 1164, spoke of 'les stages parking pour les jeunes et les pré-retraites pour les personnes âgées' (periods of work experience in which you learn nothing for young people and early retirement for the old) as means of bringing down the employment figures. *L'Événement du jeudi* for 5 January, no. 531 offered a more genuinely French term when it talked about 'des stages bidon'. 'Bidon' is fake.

Piggyback traffic, rail-road transport n.m. For the Toubon, 'ferroutage'. The first of these terms does not figure in this sense in the 1990 Chambers.

Popcorn n.m. 'Maïs soufflé'.

Pressing* n.m. In addition to meaning a dry cleaner's (not mentioned in the Toubon but dating back to the 1930s), it is also used for pressure, as when 'le pressing acharné des Français' refers to their putting on the pressure – in, for example, a football match, rarely referred to as anything but 'un match de football' or 'de foot'. See 'forcing' in IIa.

Scanner n.m. The Toubon recommends 'un scanneur' for a scanner, and 'balayage' for scanning. French people describing their hospital experiences pronounce the first word to rhyme with the final syllable of France-Inter and not the second syllable of 'bonheur'.

'Balayage' has the particular disadvantage in a medical context of evoking 'le balayage des rues', sweeping the streets. It is used to evoke electronic operations.

Scooter n.m. A motorised scooter. A child's scooter is 'une trottinette'. Laws on who can drive motorised scooters are laxer in France than in England, as are also rules about noise emission. An article in *Le Monde* for 5 May 1994 stated that 'Le BW's 50 R, qui se conduit dès l'âge de 14 ans, n'est pas à proprement parler un modèle nouveau' (The BW 50 R, which can be driven by riders over 14, is not really a new model) and pointed out that it could legally be taken up on to the pavement (US sidewalk). *Le Point* for 13 August 1994, no. 1143, said that Peugeot was beating all production records with 800 'scooters' a day.

Scotch* n.m., and *scotcher*, v. Derived from the brand-name 'Scotch tape', Sellotape. 'Je vais scotcher ce paquet' (I'm going to put Sellotape round this packet). Also the drinks which may be ordered 'on the rocks' (avec des glaçons).

Self-service n.m. Generally referred to as 'un self'. Not in the Toubon, though the 1989 *dictionnaire des néologismes officiels* recommends 'restovite'. Not to be confused with 'un fast food', where you do not get the knives and forks which are available as you go along the counter in 'un self'.

Shuttle service n.m. The use of the term 'le shuttle' shows how far the French have come from an automatic ban on 'franglais' words; especially when one reflects on how few French words begin with 'sh'. The Toubon term for it is 'service de navette'. The word 'navetteur', recommended by the Toubon, is starting to be used in conversation in the sense of 'commuter', in the sense of 'celui qui fait la navette tous les jours entre sa maison et son lieu de travail' (somebody who goes to and fro between home and work every day). The term 'banlieusard', used earlier in the same sense, means only somebody who lives in the suburbs.

Side-car n.m. The 'revue de la presse régionale' in *France*

Journal, no. 12, October 1993, described the enterprising activities of Jean-Luc Dupont, who with five employees manufactured 10 per cent of the French production. It is not difficult to believe. The French for the rear seat on a motor bike is 'un tansad', after the name of the company which made them, and which also specialised in prams. The word also means a motor-cycle combination.

Spider* n.m. The *Dictionnaire des Anglicismes* does not offer any immediate explanation as to why the word 'spider' came to mean the dickey seat in an old-fashioned roadster. Perhaps it is because it also held the luggage, as a spider might hold a fly. The use of the word in this context apparently dates from the South Africa of 1879.

Squat n.m., **squattage** n.m., **squatter** v. The *Dictionnaire des Anglicismes* reports that the words were used in French in 1835 to talk about the occupation of land in America, and in 1861 in Australia, and on 1 February 1995 this earlier usage was referred to in no. 35 of *Le Réverbère: Périodique français de la précarité* (The Street Lamp: French periodical for the unemployed and temporarily employed; a magazine sold on the street and at 'des aires de repos' – service areas – on motorways) when it wrote:

> Oserait-on avancer le mot de 'liberté'? De celle que vivaient les premiers pioniers américains (dénommés squatters en France vers 1840) qui allaient s'établir sur des terres inoccupées. Celle de vivre un luxe inouï: entrer dans deux pièces vides et s'y installer. (Dare one speak of 'liberty'? Of the liberty enjoyed by the first American pioneers (called squatters in France round about 1840) who went and established themselves on empty lands. The liberty of experiencing an unheard-of luxury: that of going into two empty rooms and settling down in them.)

The use of the word in its predominantly urban sense reappeared in French in the 1950s, and became very common in the winter of 1994–5 when several groups of SDF ('sans domicile fixe', no fixed abode, the homeless) occupied buildings in Grenoble, Paris, Tours and elsewhere. At Tours, they took over what *L'Humanité* for 14 January 1995 described as 'un squat de luxe' in the form of an old people's home, 'une maison de retraite', with thirty-five rooms. Much was made in the press of 'un squat' in a block of flats and offices at 7, rue du Dragon, near Saint-Germain-des-Prés, and it was visited with approval by the now elderly but still fashionably bearded, media-conscious and progressive-minded cleric Abbé Pierre (see also 'gay' in IIb) and without apparent disapproval by Jacques Chirac, the mayor of Paris, who had already declared himself a candidate for the presidential election. Under a headline 'La légalité hors la loi' (Legality outside the law), *L'Humanité* wrote:

> La cour d'appel à Paris a ainsi justifié des squattages accomplis 'par nécessité'. Tout cela montre en fait que le droit au logement est devenu une exigence inépuisable. (The appeal court in Paris has thus justified squats carried out 'by necessity'. All this shows that the right to somewhere to live has become an inexhaustible demand.)

Monseigneur Gaillot, whose removal from his diocese at Évreux to a non-existent one in Madagascar on 13 January 1995, caused a great deal of comment, not all of it favourable, in the French press, was reported in *Le Réverbère* as saying that he had supported another 'squat de luxe' in the Avenue Coty, in the fashionable 16th *arrondissement* in Paris.

Stand by n.m. and adj. The Toubon gives the feminine 'attente' for the waiting period in which one stands by for something to happen, and also for a holding operation during which one waits for one's aeroplane to receive permission to take off. There seems to be no equivalent for 'stand by' passengers, in the sense of people who have not booked, unless this is what is meant by the mysterious 'go show' mentioned in the Toubon. However, *L'Événement du jeudi* for 5 January 1995, no. 531 when describing how the young waited for their elders to get out of the way, spoke of their tendency 'à taper carrément dans le dos des princes en stand by sur la roche Tarpéienne' (not to hesitate in giving a sharp tap on the back of the princes who stand waiting by the Tarpeian rock).

In an economic context, *L'Événement du jeudi* spoke in the same issue of how the International Monetary Fund was going to 'négocier avec la Russie un crédit en stand-by de 6 millions de dollars' (negotiate a standby credit of 6 million dollars with Russia).

Standing* n.m. Used in French almost exclusively to indicate position in society – 'un immeuble de standing', a high-class residential building – whereas in English the word has the additional connotations of respectability or reliability: 'a customer in good standing', 'I can guarantee his standing in the profession'. Up-market is 'haut de gamme', down-market, 'bas de gamme'.

Steamer n.m. Objected to by Étiemble (p. 308), but good enough for Mallarmé in *Brise Marine*:

> Steamer, balançant ta mâture,
> Lève l'ancre pour une exotique nature.

Steward n.m. As in English. Not in the Toubon. Although the word has been in French since 1825, one of the senators from Alsace, Henri Goetschy, did not know it. For when he complained in the meeting of the Sénat on 12 April 1994 about the fact that all the announcements on the aeroplanes belonging to Air France or Air Inter coming in to land at Mulhouse or Strasbourg were in French, when the two towns were only a few hundred metres from the German border, and thus in reach of a large number of potential German-speaking travellers capable of paying in really hard currency, he added:

> On ne me fera pas croire que, parmi les 2,000 hôtesses et leur *alter ego* masculins – je ne sais pas comment je dois les appeler – il n'y en ait pas une vingtaine qui soient capables de faire des annonces en allemand. (You can't expect me to believe that among the 2,000 or so air hostesses or their male equivalents – I don't know what I should call them – there aren't twenty or so capable of making announcements in German.)[3]

M. Goetschy was one of the few speakers in the debate either in the Sénat or in the Assemblée Nationale to mention languages other than English, and was scathing about the lack of teaching of regional languages in France.

The feminine 'stewardesse' has been replaced by 'hôtesse de l'air'.

Stop n.m. and **stopper** v., intransitive and transitive. In French since the nineteenth century, initially in a nautical context. Very frequent as a road sign. 'Une stoppeuse' is an invisible mender; or a female hitch-hiker.

On 14 December 1994, in its obituary article on Antoine Pinay (30 December 1891–13 December 1994) *La Croix* described how, during his period as 'Président du Conseil' (Prime Minister) in 1952, he

> il fait voter une loi d'amnistie fiscale, diminue le train de l'État, stoppe la course des prix et des salaires, et, surtout, fait son fameux emprunt au capital indexé sur l'or (introduces a fiscal amnesty, reduces public expenditure, puts a stop to the race between wages and prices, and, above all, launches his famous capital loan indexed on the price of gold).

Télérama 2038, 8 April 1994, reports Philippe Hermand, 'consultant [see IIa] linguiste' for companies inventing brand-names (noms de marque) as making a harsh but predictable comment on the attempt to halt the arrival of 'franglais' words:

> vouloir stopper des mots étrangers à l'heure où les satellites vont brasser des cultures en multipliant la diffusion de programmes venus des quatre coins de la planète relève de l'utopie. (To try to stop words arriving when communication satellites are going to mix up cultures by multiplying programmes coming from the four quarters of the globe is utopian.)

The verb 'stopper' is, in fact, sufficiently acclimatised to have been used by Jacques Habert, a senator representing

French citizens resident abroad, in the debate in the Sénat on 12 April 1994 (*Journal Officiel*, p. 971).

Surbooking* n.m. In a terrifying article entitled 'Big Bang dans le ciel russe', *L'Expansion*, no. 484, 10 October 1994, explained how 'une déréglementation sauvage' (sudden abolition of all controls) had led to a 3,000 per cent increase in prices on internal Russian airlines, as well as to 231 deaths since 1991. 'Le *surbooking* ou la surcharge des bagages sont mis en cause' (Blame is laid on overbooking or the loading of too much baggage). The official term is 'surréservation'.

A blackish but untranslatable pun in French advises: 'Empruntez un avion, il vous rendra un cercueil.' (Take a plane. It will give you back a coffin.) The verb 'emprunter' means both to borrow and to take a particular form of transport.

Tarmac n.m. On 25 December 1994 Europe 1 referred to the Islamic militants who had just hi-jacked the Air France AirBus as having 'jeté un cadavre sur le tarmac' (thrown a corpse on to the tarmac) at Algiers airport. The official term, not given in the Toubon, is 'une aire de manoeuvre'.

Tilt* n.m. Not banned by anybody, unknown to the 1977 *Petit Robert*, but translated as 'signal' in the 1995 *Larousse*, with the example 'ce mot a fait "tilt"' (the word rang a bell). It is the word which flashes up on a pinball machine (machine à sous) to show that the game is over, or that you have joggled the machine too much.

In *Le Nouvel Observateur* no. 1569 for 1 December 1994 an article on how everything in the Métro will soon be totally automatic explained:

> Le voyageur approche du tourniquet du métro, sort une petite boîte de sa poche, la met près de la borne. Tilt! Une lumière verte s'allume, le tourniquet se débloque, et le prix du transport est débité sur le compte du voyageur. (The passenger approaches the turnstile of the underground, takes a little box out of his pocket, and puts it next to the barrier. Bingo! A green light comes on, the

turnstile opens, and the transport cost is debited to the traveller's account.)

Toboggan n.m. Although no official publication gives the word, the *Dictionnaire des Anglicismes* quotes P. Pamart's 1974 *Les nouveaux mots dans le vent* as saying that the official word is 'autopont', a word that does not figure in any French dictionary. In an aeroplane, 'les toboggans' are the safety slides, and the word is also used of a slide down into the water in a swimming pool.

Top Quite a frequent adjective; also used as a noun, as when the commentator on France-Inter commented on 2 February 1995 'les rugbymen sont au top physique' (in top form). There is a magazine called *Top Santé*; and when, on 18 May 1995, François Mitterrand, officially handed over as President of the Republic to Jacques Chirac, the meeting at which he gave him the code for the French nuclear deterrent, 'la force de frappe', was described on France-Inter as being 'top secret'.

Top niveau n.m. *Le Point* for 7 January 1995, no. 1164, described 'le chocolat Bath Oliver' (Bath Oliver chocolate biscuits) as 'le top niveau de la gourmandise' (top level for gluttony) and reported that a famous City firm had saved £20,000 a year by ceasing to offer them at tea and coffee breaks. See also 'top model' in IId.

Tracking* n.m. In the sense of using a tractor to tow an aeroplane into position, the Toubon gives 'tractage'.

Train ferry n.m. 'Transbordeur', 'navire transbordeur'.

Travel store n.m. On 4 April 1995 a large shop was opened in Paris, near the Champs Elysées, called 'Travelstore'. It offered everything you needed for going on holiday; including, presumably, 'des vouchers' (see IIa).

Trench* n.m., **trench coat** n.m. Popularised in French during the 1914–18 war as the garment worn by British officers. Fell out of fashion until the mid-1970s, to be replaced by the more prosaic 'imperméable'.

The popularity of the garment was revived by a clever campaign for Burberrys with the slogan 'My Burberry is rich', an echo of the phrase 'My tailor is rich', the traditional equivalent of 'La plume de ma tante est dans le jardin' as the first sentence taught to learners of English. When the loi Toubon was first discussed in the press, the headline in *Libération* for 24 February 1994 was 'Toubon: My French Is Rich'.

Tweed n.m., and also adj. The description in *Talents* for February-March 1994 said *The Avengers* (*Chapeau melon et bottes de cuir*) contained 'action assaisonnée [flavoured with] d'humour tweed'. The term for the type of cloth has been in French since the nineteenth century, but the use of it as an adjective is too recent to appear in any dictionary.

The past participle in the description in *Le Nouvel Observateur* no. 1538 for 28 April 1994 of the former manager of the Sex Pistols as 'cravaté, tweedé et soigneusement permanenté' (with tie, tweeds and carefully waved hair) was followed by his reported remark that 'le rock anglais, c'est le blues américain plus l'existentialisme', a comment which may have owed something to the fact that he was being interviewed in Saint-Germain-des-Prés. See 'acid jazz' and 'country' in IId.

The headline of the article on *Chapeau melon et bottes de cuir* presented it as 'le must british' (see 'must' and 'shocking' in IIa, 'british' in IIc) and described Steed and Emma as 'le couple pur british le plus extravagant, le plus kitsch [see above] et le plus smart jamais vu'. The use of the term 'british', like that of 'shocking', is ironic.

Week-end n.m. In French since 1906 and accepted even by Étiemble. The spelling 'ouiquende' never caught on, and the expression 'la semaine anglaise', to designate either a five-day week or a week in which one left work at lunchtime on Saturday, has now virtually disappeared.

One of the results of the institution in 1881 and 1882 of a system of state education which was wholly secular (laïque) was the decision to hold no classes on a Thursday. This has now been changed to Wednesday, designated as the day on which children are free to attend the form of religious education chosen for them by their parents. This has had three main consequences: an increase every Wednesday in reported juvenile offences; the holding of most university lectures on a Wednesday so that students who are already teachers may attend classes which will enable them to improve their qualifications; the persistence of Saturday morning school, now being phased out in response to parental pressure.

Women's lib n.m. Unmentioned in the Toubon and banned by nobody. The *Dictionnaire des Anglicismes* gives it as occurring in French in 1974, some twenty-five years after the principal theses of 'le mouvement pour la libération de la femme' had been put forward by Simone de Beauvoir in *Le deuxième sexe*.

The term rarely occurs in a French context, and is used mainly to talk about the USA, sometimes with approval, as when *L'Express* for 25 March 1974 pointed out that the introduction of laws on equality of opportunity had enabled men to penetrate previously feminine bastions such as the American Telephone and Telegraph Company, sometimes more disparagingly, as when *National Hebdo*, the newspaper of M. Le Pen's Front National, talked in no. 452 for 1993 about one of the early effects of the Clinton presidency:

> Les Américains voulaient Monsieur et ils ont eu Madame et les copines de Madame. Et non pas n'importe qui: les superpétroleuses du 'Women's lib'. C'est dire qu'à la Maison Blanche, les mâles commencent à raser les murs. (The Americans wanted Clinton, and they got Hillary and Hillary's buddies. And not just anyone: the 'superpétroleuses'[4] of Women's lib. Which is to say that at the White House, the men are starting to hug the walls.)

NOTES

1 In his article '*Faux amis* and *Faux anglicismes*: Problems of Classification and Definition', in *Forum for Modern Language Studies*, Vol. XVIII, no. 2, April 1987, pp. 169–83.

2 The new word 'crasher' (to crash) is a homophone for the existing word 'cracher' (to spit). For M. Fanton's comment, see *Journal Officiel*, p. 1405, see above, Chapter 1, note 21.

3 *Journal Officiel*, p. 960.

4 Literally, throwers of petrol bombs. In the Commune of March–May 1871, the more enthusiastic women supporters of the movement are said to have thrown petrol bombs at the police and public buildings.

c   *The arts, the media and sport*

The asterisk * is a reminder that the word either does not normally exist in English or is used by the French in a different sense from the meaning it has in the United States or the United Kingdom. The dagger † placed after a word in the index indicates its presence in either the 1995 *Petit Larousse Illustré* or the *Petit Robert* (1992).

Background n.m. Sufficiently used to have the Toubon suggest 'arrière-plan', though without any indication of context or reference to a ministerial decree.

Baffle* n.m. An audio-speaker or baffle-board. The Toubon recommends 'enceinte acoustique'.

Basket n.m. The game of basket-ball. 'Il joue au basket' (he plays basket-ball). See also 'baskets' in IId.

Battling Jacquot adj. A term frequently used to describe Jacques Chirac during the campaign leading to the presidential elections of April–May 1995. On 23 February 1995, *L'Événement du jeudi* no. 537 described a meeting held at the Porte de Versailles at which 'Battling Jacquot fend soudain la foule à 18–30 heures pétantes' (Battling Jack suddenly strides through the crowd at 6.30 exactly) and wrote of his 'entrée surprise effectuée par la porte des lavatories'[1] (surprise entry through the doorway of the lavatories).

The article went on to say that 'sur cet aspect militaire du show [see below], Serge Lama l'a généreusement briefé [see entry in IIa]'. (He had been generously briefed on the military aspect of the show by Serge Lama.)

According to the same article, which somehow gave the impression that Jacques Chirac was not the favourite politician of *L'Événement du jeudi*, he was also introduced by Guy Drut, 'éternel espoir du music-hall, jadis hurdler de haut niveau, aujourd'hui reconverti en dresseur de caniches' (the eternal hope of the music-hall, formerly a top-class hurdler, now exercising the profession of a trainer of small dogs).

In an article in the *Spectator* for 25 March 1995, James Naughtie described how M. Chirac strode across France 'with a deliberately Gaullist arrogance, to the unlikely strains of Jimi Hendrix'; an odd choice of music for a man in favour of the imposition of strict quotas on non-French songs played on the French radio, a view unsupported by his daughter.

Best of n.m. On 8 April 1994, *Télérama*, no. 2308, under the title 'Savez-vous parler télé?', gave a list of 'franglais' expressions used to discuss French television. 'Florilège', n.m., was suggested as the best translation of 'best of'. Olivier Cachin (see below, 'Take your time') said that he would use 'best of' when talking of the Stones, but 'anthologie' if discussing poetry. It was a term selected for a disapproving mention by Marc Lauriol in the debate in the Sénat on 12 April 1994 (*Journal Officiel*, p. 957), together with 'franchising', 'marketing', 'sponsoring', 'mailing', 'management,' 'casting', 'cool', 'show' and 'brushing', which were described as 'multiplying at an accelerating speed' (qui pullulent à une vitesse accélérée). However, M. Lauriol continued, it was rather dangerous to pass laws on the subject, especially since words of such obviously Anglo-Saxon origin as 'sandwich', 'bifteck' (*sic*), 'hit-parade', 'corner' and 'penalty' had now become so indisputably French; see below the entry on 'timing', together with its reference to Mme Seligman's comments in the Sénat debate of 12 April 1994.

Best-seller n.m. The expression does not figure in the Toubon, and the *Dictionnaire des Anglicismes* points out that the recommended 'succès de librairie' is 'plus long, comme le sont toujours les traductions françaises des composés anglais' (longer, as French translations of English composite nouns always are). Josette Rey-Debove and Gilberte Gagnon comment that the term 'best-seller' embodies what they describe as the essentially American notion that 'ce qui plaît à tous ne peut être qu'excellent' (what pleases everybody cannot fail to be excellent), and contrast it with the idea that

> Certains écrivains qui ont une haute idée de leur talent et de leur mission s'inquiètent lorsque leur tirage augmente. (Some writers who have a high idea of their talent and their mission start to worry when their sales increase.)

Such writers clearly do not accept Dr Johnson's view that 'no man but a blockhead ever wrote, except for money'.

The invaluable *Quid*, published every year by Robert Laffont, describes itself very accurately on its cover as 'le best-seller des incollables' (the best-seller for people who can't be caught out; i.e. by tricky questions, such as when the word 'chewing gum' (see IIb) was first used in French).

Black-out n.m.; alternative spelling *blackout*. The *Dictionnaire des Anglicismes* points out that it is used in its original sense mainly to evoke the Great Britain of the Second World War, and suggests 'couvre-feu' as a suitable alternative. The figurative sense is much more frequent; France-Inter used it on 26 December 1994 when talking about 'le black-out des toutes les informations en provenance d'Algérie' (a black-out on all news coming from Algeria) after the hi-jacking by Islamic fundamentalists of the Air France Airbus. The Toubon suggests 'occultation' or 'silence radio', leaving it to the reader of the *Dictionnaire des Anglicismes* to discover that the second term, recommended by the *Journal Officiel* on 12 August 1976, refers to an aeroplane or ship not using its radio equipment in order to hide its position from the enemy. When someone of whose background little is known comes into prominence, there is talk of 'un blackout sur ses origines'.

Bluff n.m., **bluffer** v., **bluffeur** n.m. In use in French since the 1840s as a term in cards, and admitted by R. le Bidois in *Les mots trompeurs ou le Délire verbal* (Hachette, Paris, 1970) as 'un de ces anglicismes qu'on peut admettre' (one of the anglicisms which can be accepted). There is, indeed, no French equivalent, and the French also use the word in a rather wider sense than it generally has in English. In the title of a study of the novels of the *Série Noire*, *La Fin d'un bluff* (Gallimard, Paris, 1952), Pierre Boileau and Thomas Narcéjac use the word in the sense we now give to 'scam': that of trickery and deceit. The verb is also used in this sense.

Box office n.m. *Le Point* has a regular column called 'Box office'. On 15 October 1994 no. 1152 reported that 'la "gumpomania" franchit allègrement l'Atlantique pour gagner la France' (Gumpomania has cheerfully crossed the Atlantic and reached France), and that some 115,000 Parisians had already been to see Tom Hanks in *Forrest Gump*. More than 600,000 French people had, however, also been to see the film based on Balzac's *Le colonel Chabert*.

British adj. 'Il est très british' used to mean that he carried an umbrella, smoked a pipe and said little. When, however, Serge Gainsbourg described Oscar Wilde, in *Le Monde* for 27 February 1995, as 'Gentleman, voyou et poète "très british"', he obviously meant something else; though precisely what is not clear.

See also 'out' in IId.

Cameraman* n.m. Officially, 'cadreur'. A camera, in the sense of one to carry around with you, is 'un appareil photographique'. 'Une caméra' is for films, and a 'caméscope' for making home videos.

Cartoon n.m. The normal word is 'dessin', but since this does not necessarily mean 'dessin humouristique', somebody whose face is easily caricatured is described as having 'un visage de cartoon'.

It used to be said of Antoine Pinay (see 'stopper' in IIb), who was very frequently caricatured, that 'il a une tête d'électeur', he looks like an elector. However, he was less easily taken in than this remark implied, and maintained sufficient popularity in 'la France profonde' – the French equivalent to middle America – for it to be rumoured that one reason why de Gaulle insisted on changing the constitution in 1962 so that the President of the Fifth Republic was elected by universal suffrage was his suspicion that the 'notables' (local worthies) who made up the electoral college which had originally chosen him in 1958, could not be relied on not to prefer M. Pinay in 1965.

Casting n.m. Recent enough not to be in the *Dictionnaire des Anglicismes*, but frequent enough for the Toubon to suggest 'distribution artistique'. This was not, however, the term used when the credits came up on the screen after the 1994 film *La reine Margot*, which was 'Casting France'.

On France-Inter for 17 March 1995, Yvon Levaï explained the fact that Edouard Balladur had lost the commanding lead in the public opinion polls which he had enjoyed before even saying that he would be a candidate for the presidency by what he called 'une erreur de casting', comparing the Prime Minister to a baritone required to perform as a tenor. In France, 'les ténors de la politique' are speakers with a full mastery of rhetoric; like Jacques Chirac, who at the time was moving ahead in what Yvon Levaï called 'le show-biz politique'.

Catch* n.m. All-in wrestling. Originally, 'Catch as catch can'; the French found this impossible to pronounce and therefore shortened it, thus creating another English word which exists only in French (cf. 'le camping', 'le footing', 'pressing' and other words marked with an asterisk in the index as well as in the main body of the text).

The essay 'Le monde où l'on catche' in Roland Barthes's 1954 collection *Mythologies* explains why the official translation as 'lutte de combat' is inappropriate. As Barthes points out, all-in wrestling is essentially a spectator sport, not one which involves any genuine fighting. The wrestlers are pretending, and take it in turns to win. They are also using a conventional set of signs in order to communicate their supposed anger and frustration to the public, and in this respect Barthes's essay is the most accessible starting-point for a study of what is known as semiology, or the science of signs. We communicate by signs, not only in language, but also through dress and gesture. See 'boots' and 'baskets' in IId, and 'skinhead' in IIa.

'Franglais' words act as signs in two ways. Like all words, they derive their meaning from the structure of the language. As de Saussure, the founding father of semiology, argued in his *Cours de linguistique générale* in 1913, the connection between words and the objects or activities they designate is arbitrary. Although the different words 'un smoking' and 'a dinner jacket' refer to the same object, there is no natural connection between either of them and the garment they designate. The meaning is provided by the way they fit into the language. (See 'image' in IIa.)

However, 'franglais' words also work as signs of a second-order type. By talking about 'le casting' rather than 'la distribution', or 'le rewriting' rather than 'la révision de son texte', French journalists are trying to show that they are 'with it' and know where power is situated in modern society: 'chez les Anglo-Saxons'. They are, in English terms, behaving like upwardly mobile grammar school boys who are acquainted with the arguments about U and Non-U and would sooner be seen dead than heard referring to a napkin as a serviette.

CB n.f. Citizens' band radio, officially 'bande de fréquences banalisées'.

Choc n.m. Seen as an anglicism, and often spelt 'shock' in the nineteenth century. Now used in a medical sense as well as in the wider one of an unexpected blow or a violent surprise. On 3 April 1993, in no. 2174 of *L'Express*, Eric Conan commented in his review of Jean-Pierre Azéma's recently published *Vichy et les Français* on how long it had taken the French to realise what had happened between 1940 and 1944 and wrote of 'le choc décisif, venu de l'extérieur, du livre de Paxton' (the decisive shock, from abroad, caused by Paxton's book). Robert O. Paxton, an American historian, was the first to reveal, in his *La France de Vichy* (Paris, Éditions du Seuil, 1973) just how enthusiastically the Vichy government had collaborated with the Germans, especially in the persecution of the Jews.

See entries on 'groggy' in IIa and 'scoop' below.

Come-back n.m. On 13 May 1993, *L'Express* no. 2183 commented in a long article on Pamela Churchill that

> le Tout-Paris s'interroge et suppute les chances de réussite de son 'come-back' trente ans après. (The whole of Paris is asking itself and calculating the chances of her making a successful come-back thirty years on.)

It used one particular adjective in a reassuringly old-fashioned sense when it described her as 'la "gay divorcée" des années 50'.

Compact disc n.m. The Toubon suggests 'disque audio-numérique', 'mini-disque' and 'disque compact'; but without much effect on the advertising industry, which uses the word all the time. According to *Le Nouvel Observateur* for 28 April 1994, no. 1538, 'un CD' costs only five francs to produce, the same as a cassette.

Corner n.m. Although the *dictionnaire des termes officiels de la langue française* recommends 'tir de coin', 'coup de coin' and 'coup de pied de coin' in the place of the English footballing term, M. Toubon himself, in the debate in the Sénat of 13 April 1994, said that he could not see how the French could actually use the term 'coup de pied de coin' as part of their current vocabulary (*Journal Officiel*, p. 983).

Crash TV* n.m. Defined in *Télérama* no. 2308 on 8 April 1994 as 'une sorte d'Intervilles à l'américaine' ('Intervilles' is another term for *Jeux sans Frontières/It's a Knock-out*). According to *Télérama*, there are 150 American television stations putting on 'des programmes "crash" mêlant allégrement sexe, sport, violence et hard-rock' ('crash' programmes cheerfully mixing sex, sport, violence and hard rock).
See also 'crash' in IIb.

Cross n.m. Competitive cross-country running.

Dandy n.m. In French since the nineteenth century, popularised by Baudelaire, and used twelve times in *Le Monde* for 27 February 1995.

Databank n.m. 'Banque de données' is widely accepted in France.

Dogleghs* n.m.p. Although the authors of the guide to provincial golf courses in *Madame Figaro* for 12 November 1994 can't spell, what they call 'les dogleghs' are more recognisably a feature of the average course than the 'chiens de fusil' recommended by the Toubon. 'Être couché en chien de fusil' means to sleep with your legs drawn up or curled up against your body. The typical dog-leg hole involves a drive of some 200 yards, followed by an angled turn of 30 degrees or so, followed by the need to cover another some 250 yards before reaching the green.

Drive v., **driver** n.m. The Toubon suggests 'bois un' or 'masse' (presumably feminine) for the club. But everyone talks about 'un driver', because this is what one needs to 'réussir son drive' and what one uses to 'driver', to drive off from the tee. *Madame Figaro* has a regular page on golf, and on 19 November 1994 Patricia Meunier, who won the Ladies Open (l'Open d'Angleterre) in 1993 described how best to get out of 'un bunker' (un ensable, une fosse de sable): 'fermez un peu votre main droite sur votre grip' (close your right hand a little over your grip). Ms Meunier made no reference to either of the two words recommended by the Toubon: 'prise' and 'poignée'.

As a noun, 'driver' is also a jockey in a trotting race (des courses à trot attelé) popular in France and the United States but – unlike flat racing (courses sur du plat), fences (courses de haies) and steeple-chasing (le steeple) – virtually unknown in the United Kingdom.

Drive-in cinema n.m. Officially, 'un ciné parc'. They do exist, in the south of France, where the word is pronounced 'un draîve-in'.

Drop* n.m. A drop goal in rugby.

Émotionnel adj. Used in the English sense on the television chain France 2 on 19 February 1995 (cf. 'image' in IIa) of somebody easily moved and on the verge of losing control of themselves. Not yet used in the sense given in *Private Eye* to the term 'tired and emotional': drunk.

Euro-pudding* n.m. *Télérama* 2308 on 8 April 1994 translates as 'feuilleton européen' the equivalent of a European soap (opera), and instances the plot of a European co-production in which a young German au pair girl falls in love with her employer, a charming Italian journalist, who is already sleeping with an English female pianist on her international tour.

Fairways n.m.p. According to *Madame Figaro* for 12 November 1994, the ones at Saint-Étienne are particularly 'étroits et bordés de précipices ou de dunes' (narrow and bordered by deep chasms or dunes).

Fan n.m. or f. *Le Monde* for 31 March 1993 described Edouard Balladur's wife as 'une fan de Johnny Holliday'. One also finds the expression 'fan club'.

Finish n.m. Another sporting term frequently used in a political context – 'une course au finish entre Chirac et Balladur' (a closely run race between Chirac and Balladur which one of them must win) – and also, as in a quotation in the *Dictionnaire des Anglicismes* from an article on *Great Expectations* in *Les Nouvelles littéraires* in 1972, in a literary one:

> Entre Pip et ses supérieurs, ce sera un match au finish, par la force et la persuasion, et malgré ses efforts, il se trouvera contraint de rejoindre sa tribu, sa classe, son destin de bourgeois. (Between Pip and his superiors, it will be a fight to the finish, by force and persuasion, and in spite of his efforts, he will be compelled to join his tribe, his class, and his middle-class destiny.)

Flash* n.m. As in the news flash in *Le Monde* for 11 November 1971: 'A 9.40 mardi matin, un "flash" des agences de presse annonce: "Le général de Gaulle est mort"' (At 9.40, on Tuesday morning, a news flash from the press agencies announced: 'General de Gaulle is dead'). Followed by Georges Pompidou's 'La France est veuve' (France is now a widow).

See also the entry in IIb.

Flashback n.m. Étiemble quotes Sadoul's *Histoire du cinéma* as using the acceptable French 'retour en arrière'. If 'flashback' still seems to be winning, it is partly through snobbery and partly through the greater impression of speed and immediacy.

Flop n.m. The *Dictionnaire des Anglicismes* points out that since 'un four' already exists to describe a play that fails, 'on risque de voir s'installer "flop" pour l'échec au cinéma' (there is a risk of the word 'flop' establishing itself as the term for an unsuccessful film). As is shown by Giscard d'Estaing's comment about Rocard's 'Big Bang' quoted in the Introduction, the word is also used in a political context. The opposite of 'un flop' is 'un tabac': '*Quatre mariages et un enterrement a fait un tabac en France, comme partout ailleurs*' (*Four Weddings and a Funeral* was a great success in France, as everywhere else).

Foot* n.m. A very frequent abbreviation for football, and used to make another cultural reference when *France-Soir* for 27 June 1993 had the headline 'La foot connection' to an article about the financial problems of the Marseilles football club, l'Olympique de Marseille, owned and managed at the time by Bernard Tapie. On 9 February 1995, France-Inter used a similar construction when it spoke of 'la coke connection' when discussing drug smuggling.

Libération for 12 December 1994 described Eric Cantona as 'le de Gaulle du foot', in spite of the problems which he created for Alex Ferguson' 'le coach de Manchester', by his insistence on going in for 'le tacle', described by Ferguson as 'un geste qu'il ne maîtrise pas' (something he can't do). 'Le tacle' is the word officially recommended in the Toubon, together with 'tacler', 'tacleur' and 'tacleuse', an indication, like the suggested spelling of 'challenge' as 'chalenge' (see the entry in IIa), that the purists can sometimes by satisfied by a mere change of spelling. In rugby football to tackle is 'plaquer'.

See below, 'goal'.

Foot business* n.m. A disparaging term used by *L'Humanité* on 13 January 1995 in its account of the trial in Corsica of those responsible for putting up the temporary stand which collapsed on 5 May 1992, when the Sporting-Club de Bastia was playing l'Olympique de Marseille, killing seventeen people and injuring two thousand. *L'Humanité* also described the President of the Fédération Française de Football, Jean Fornet-Fayard, as 'le big boss du football français'. See 'boss' in IIa.

Footing* n.m. Odette Swann, *ci-devant* de Crécy, does a little 'footing' in the Bois de Boulogne, and the word has a late nineteenth-century air to it, being first attested, according to the *Dictionnaire des Anglicismes*, in 1895. Gilberte Gagnon and Josette Rey-Debove quote an article in *Le Nouvel Observateur* for 18 January 1971 suggesting that the word can also mean a place specially set aside for people to walk in.

Free style adj. and n.m. 'Le free style' is normally free-style jazz rather than swimming and the term 'le free jazz' was used in *Le Monde* for 6 April 1995. When Lucien Fleurier, Sartre's young fascist in the 1939 short story 'L'Enfance d'un chef' (Childhood of a leader), goes on a visit to England, he learns 'le overarm stroke'. It is not a term used in English swimming, and the description of it in the *Dictionnaire des Anglicismes* makes it sound very uncomfortable. You swim on your side, doing a swift scissor kick with your legs as you bring your arm out of the water and over your head.

Gag n.m. In the sense of a joke, appears in French as a result of the influence of the cinema in the 1920s. Since it was originally visual – 'les gags de Chaplin' – to translate it as 'une blague', which is essentially verbal, is misleading. The word was nevertheless used in a more general sense in an article in *France-Dimanche* on 24 August 1994 entitled '20 bonnes raisons de faire l'amour plus souvent' (20 good reasons for making love more often) by Yvonne Poncet, 'Diplômée de Psychologie, spécialiste de sexologie' (graduate in psychology, specialist in sexology).

In addition to being 'son jogging à lui, son aérobic à elle' (his jogging, her aerobics), and on condition that you did not try to do it too often 'quand on porte un pacemaker' (when you wear a pacemaker; see below), making love was 'le meilleur des anti-stress, plus efficace qu'une séance de stretching' (the best remedy against stress, more effective than a session in the gym). It could even, added Yvonne Poncet, give you better hair – 'non, ce n'est pas un gag' (and that's not a joke).

The Toubon does not mention 'pacemaker', but the 1995 *Petit Larousse* recommends 'stimulateur cardiaque'.

Goal n.m. Generally replaced by 'un but' as in 'La France a marqué deux buts' (France scored two goals), but also used to describe the goal-keeper, more correctly 'le gardien de but', as in 'Camus a joué goal pour le Racing-Universitaire d'Alger' (Camus kept goal for the Racing-Universitaire of Algiers). See above, 'foot', and below, 'golf', for a similar abbreviation, as well as 'lift' in IIb.

The French also talk about 'la goalaverage', pronounced as a single word with no tonic accent, so that it would rhyme with 'un homme d'un grand âge'. They calculate it in the same way as the English Premier League: take the number of goals conceded from the number of goals scored, and the team with the highest positive difference is placed above another with the same number of points.

Golf* n.m. 'Un golf' is a golf course, as when *Libération* magazine for 14 January 1995 asked its readers whether or not the news item was true which said that 'le golf de Saint-Martial-sur-Vézère n'a que 17 trous' (had only seventeen holes). It was false.

Greens n.m.p. 'Des cibles' (targets) to aim for as you go along 'les fairways' and around 'les dogleghs' (see above).

Guest-star n.f. In its review of Harold Becker's film *Malice*, *L'Événement du jeudi* no. 496 for 5 May 1994 commented that 'un tueur en série et une guest-star [Anne Bancroft] mi-alcoolique mi-sorcière viennent s'ajouter à une intrigue déjà franchement tirée par les cheveux' (a serial killer and a guest star who is half witch and half alcoholic add to a plot which is already highly improbable). Too recent to be in the *Dictionnaire des Anglicismes*, and not in the Toubon.

Hand-ball or **handball** n.m. When the French won the world championship on 21 May 1995, the presenter of the 'Revue de Presse' on France-Inter reported with some disappointment that the event had gone unnoticed by newspapers outside France. The word does not figure in the *Dictionnaire des Anglicismes*, and the *Petit Robert* for 1965 says that it is of Germanic origin. The *Petit Robert* also says that, it is like football, but played with the hands. See below, 'street-ball'.

Handicap n.m. As in the verb 'handicaper', used in the nineteenth century for horse-racing, and from the 1930s onwards in a wider sense. There was 'un Secrétaire d'État aux handicapés' in Balladur's government, Michel Gilibert, and the word is often used in a political context, as in the remark that 'le grand handicap de Balladur dans la course de l'Elysée fut la révélation de l'importance de son patrimoine' (the great handicap of Balladur in the contest for the presidency was the revelation of how rich he was).[2]

Happy End n.m. The *Dictionnaire des Anglicismes* gives it as entering French in 1947, and comments that although it is 'mal assimilable en français' it may stay as much a part of the language as 'deus ex machina'; or the 'Happy Few' to whom Stendhal dedicated his unfinished novel *Lucien Leuwen* in 1836.

The term was used in an extended sense when *L'Express* for 27 January 1994, no. 2220, wrote that 'il ne s'agira sans doute pas d'un happy end' (no question of a happy end) in the relationship between Jacques Chirac and Edouard Balladur.

Not in the Toubon; and there seems to be no French equivalent to the prediction once made to me by my colleague Penny Francis as we sat listening to the overture to *Il Trovatore*: 'Tears before bedtime again, I think.'

Heroic fantasy n.f. According to *L'Express* for 12 December 1994, a characteristic of a new type of 'science fiction', contained in the novels of Philip K. Dick. 'La fantasy est féminine', wrote the reviewer. 'Une princesse est aux prises avec ses démons, ses dragons, ses donjons.' (Fantasy is feminine. A princess is faced with demons, dragons, castle towers.)

Hobby n.m. In French since the 1830s, and never totally replaced by the official 'violon d'Ingres'. According to Josette Rey-Debove and Gilberte Gagnon, the word 'appartient en français au langage des gens cultivés' (belongs in French to the language of people with a certain culture), and is 'critiqué par les puristes français et canadiens' (criticised by purists in France and Canada).

The usefulness of having two words was illustrated by an article under the headline 'Hobby' in *Le Nouvel Observateur* for 17 March 1994, no. 1531 after the MP Stephen Milligan had been found hanged, wearing women's stockings, with an orange in his mouth and with a plastic bag over his head:

Cause du décès: auto-asphyxiation érotique. Un violon d'Ingres tout à fait respectable en lui-même, mais peu compatible avec le puritanisme. (Cause of death: erotic self-strangulation. A respectable enough hobby in itself, but hard to reconcile with puritanism.)

For other visions of England currently offered to the French see 'hit parade' in IId and 'hooligan' below. It is all very different from Gibbon's remark in his *Autobiography*:

I reached Paris on the 28th of January, 1763 ... Our opinions, our fashions, even our games, were adopted in France; a ray of national glory illuminated each individual,

and every Englishman was supposed to be born a patriot
and a philosopher.

Hooligan n.m. Sufficiently recent not to be in the *Dictionnaire
des Anglicismes*. Normally associated with football, and probably the most important word we have exported since 1945.
After the murder in 1993 of the three-year-old James Bulger
by two ten-year-old boys, *L'Événement du jeudi*, for 3 November
1993, no. 436, asked:

> Pourquoi le mufle des hooligans et les portraits-robots des
> tueurs de dix ans ont-ils supplanté, quant on songe à
> l'Angleterre, les végétariens en sandales et les robes pastel
> des filles de pasteur? (Why have the mugs of hooligans and
> the identikit photos of ten-year-old murderers replaced the
> vision which one used to have of England as the country of
> vegetarians in sandals and clergymen's daughters in pastel-
> coloured frocks?)

See also 'hobby' above.

Horse-ball* n.m. According to *Nice Matin* for 25 April 1993,
first played in Bordeaux in 1969. A mixture of basket-ball,
rugby and polo. Unmentioned in any dictionary.

Hurdler n. generally m. but could be f. See above, 'battling'.

Interview n.f.; *interviewer*, v. The English 'interview' can be
translated into French in three ways, according to the context:
'entrevue' is formal, as with one's superior; 'entretien', as well
as being a general conversation, is a job interview; and 'une
interview' is used only in the context of the media.

The *Dictionnaire des Anglicismes* gives the word 'interview' as
appearing in the nineteenth century, and comments that it is
now accepted even by purists. It is, in this respect, an example
of a 'franglais' word which is probably no longer seen as such,
and accepted as a useful addition to the language, clearly
having a different sense from 'entretien' and 'entrevue'.

The person conducting the interview is now, after a long
period in which one found mainly 'le journaliste', called

'l'intervieweur', or 'intervieweuse', though in *Les rencontres des jours* (Gallimard, Paris, 1995, p. 175) Claude Roy gives the spelling 'interviouver'.

Jingle n.m. The Toubon recommends 'sonal'. The word would sound odd in the headline in *Le Nouvel Observateur* for 11 August 1994, no. 1553: 'La guerre des ondes . . . Récit d'un combat au son des jingles' (the war of the waves . . . an account of a struggle to the sound of jingles), the introduction of an analysis of the competition for audiences between the different public and private radio stations (Radio France, Europe 1, Radio Monte Carlo, etc.).

Jockey. As in English. No French term. See the entry 'club' in IIa for the still exclusive 'Jockey Club de Paris'.

Juke-box n.m. No alternative suggested anywhere.

Karting* n.m. A track on which you can drive a hired go-kart, 'un kart'.
A sign frequently seen as you drive through France, and less easily misunderstood than 'ball-trap', a clay-pigeon shoot (see Thody and Evans, *Faux Amis and Key Words*). Like 'le camping', 'le footing' and 'le parking', another gerund used nominatively, and in a way which seems odd to the native speaker of English.

Kit n.m. The Toubon suggests either 'lot' or 'prêt-à-monter', the second word being obviously the sense in which the word 'kit' was used in no. 1556 of *Le Nouvel Observateur* for 1 September 1994 in its discussion of the breakdown of the family. Because of the frequency of divorce and remarriage, it) argued, 30 per cent of French children

> vont avoir aujourd'hui des parcours assez compliqués, à travers des familles recomposées en 'kit' (are going to have a rather complicated pattern of family life through families put together from a kit)

as they moved with their natural mother or father into a family which included a step-parent and step-siblings.

Links n.m. The guide to golf courses in *Madame Figaro* for 12 November 1994 says of the course at Evreux that it is 'vallonné et ondulé comme un links anglais' (hilly and goes up and down like a links in England).

Mixage n.m. A term used when describing the mixing and presentation of images on the television.

Mixer v. Originally found mainly in the vocabulary of the cinema to describe the mixing of the different elements of the sound-track, and now widely used in cooking. (See the entry in IIb.)

Modern style* n.m. What both the French and the English call 'art nouveau': a decorative style popular in the 1900s. In 1913, Proust described Odette Swann's 'salon' as being like 'un de ces dortoirs modèles qu'on présente dans les expositions "modern style" du mobilier' (one of those model dormitories presented in 'modern style' exhibitions of furniture). When, in 1951, in *Les Voix du silence*, André Malraux argued that

> le style roman n'est pas un modern style médiéval; et tout vrai style est la réduction à une perspective humaine du monde éternel qui nous entraîne dans une dérive d'astres selon un rythme mystérieux (Romanesque architecture is not a kind of medieval 'art nouveau'; and any true style is the reduction to a human scale of the eternal world which surrounds us and which carries us off in its mysterious rhythm in a flight of stars)

he meant that the architecture of transition from Norman to Gothic should be seen as an attempt by the artists of the time to make sense of their experience in their own terms, not as an slightly kitsch imitation of what other artists had done before them.

Mountain bike n.m. These threats to the ecology of the Lake District have now made their appearance in France, where they wreck the surface of mountains under the name of 'vélos tous terrains'.

Music-hall n.m. The *Dictionnaire des Anglicismes* points out that the term begins to replace that of 'café-chantant' or 'café-concert' from 1893 onwards. Proust reports M. Verdurin as committing the 'faux-pas' of going there 'en veston et en cravate noire de notaire de village' (in a black jacket and with the black tie of a village notary) rather than 'en smoking'. Tom Stoppard's translator, Guy Dumour, describes his plays as 'du music-hall littéraire de haut vol' (top-class literary music-hall).

Net n.m. Often used in tennis and table tennis instead of the perfectly good French word 'filet'; perhaps because the French say 'let' for 'a let', and the same confusion sometimes arises between the two words in France as it does in England.

New look adj. Not only a reference to the style to which Christian Dior gave what now seems so provocatively English a term in 1947. In its comment on the partial censuring of the loi Toubon by the Conseil Constitutionnel on 31 July 1994 the *Nouvelle République du Centre Ouest* commented that 'la langue de la république reste le français. Pas le franglais ou n'importe quel sabir *new look*.' (The language of the republic is French. Not le franglais or any old new look jargon.)

It is possible that the now very frequent 'franglais' word 'look' (see the entry in IIa) originally stemmed from 'new look'.

News n., m. or f., s. or p. Given in *Télérama* 2308 on 8 April 1994 as a word occasionally used instead of the French 'Informations' on the 'journal télévisé', together with the reminder that France can export its abbreviations and terminology as well: 'Suisses et Italiens disent TJ pour "téléjournal"' (the Swiss and Italians say TJ for 'téléjournal').

News magazines n.m.p. According to *Le Nouvel Observateur* for 3 November 1994, no. 1565, monthly reviews in France are giving way to 'les news magazines, moins austères et plus vite lus' (less austere and quicker to read).

While the same tendency brought about the demise of

Encounter, French weekly news magazines enjoy a much wider readership than The *Spectator* or the *New Statesman and Society*: *Paris-Match*, 875,000; *Figaro Magazine*, 640,000; *L'Express*, 555,000; *Le Nouvel Observateur*, 360,00; *Le Point*, 320,000.

Off* adj. If the comment on 5 May 1994 in the review in *Le Monde* of the film made of Daudet's *Les Lettres de mon moulin* – 'le rapport entre la voix *off* et l'image est constamment banal' (the relationship between the commentary and the pictures is constantly banal) – is anything to go by, this is what we call the 'voice-over'. 'Voice off' is normally 'la voix hors champ'.

'Off' is neither in the Toubon nor in the *Dictionnaire des Anglicismes*, which nevertheless gives 'off-off Broadway show' as coming into French in the 1970s. On 30 March 1994, Bertrand Poirot-Delpech wrote of how appreciated Ionesco was 'dans les salles *off* du monde entier' (in the 'off-Broadway' theatres of the whole world). 'Le théâtre off' is fringe theatre.

One-man-show n.m. The Toubon recommends 'spectacle solo', and only future usage will tell which term will win.

Open n.m. Open championship, as in 'le Open de Paris'; or 'l'Open de Roland Garros'.

Outsider n.m. Used of racehorses as early as 1857. Extended to other areas, and used in *Madame Figaro* for 12 November 1994 to describe Dave Stewart in his latest album *Greetings from the Gutter* as 'un outsider musclé'. See also 'challenger' in IIa.

According to the *Dictionnaire des Anglicismes*, the word was used to denote a social outsider by Jane Austen in 1800.

Pace-maker n.m. Not in the Toubon, but the 1994 Larousse gives 'stimulateur cardiaque'; or 'pacemaker'. See above, 'gag'.

Panel n.m. In French since the 1960s, but not in the Toubon. *Le Monde* for 29 December 1994 talked about 'un "panel" de Français sélectionnés par la SOFRES' (a panel of French

people selected by the Société Française d'Études par Sondages) to ask questions of Edouard Balladur.

Pin-up n.f. On 12 December 1994, reviewing a programme
on 'Le Décolleté' broadcast on Canal + the evening before,
Libération defined 'la pin-up' as 'la fille qu'on épingle' (the girl
you pin up on the wall), recommended her as the best kind of
'safe sex' (see entry in IId), and remarked that 'on plonge tel
le couch potato de base dans cette nuit de la pin-up' (you dive
like the basic couch potato into this evening of the pin-up).

It also commented of Betty Page, 'la queen de pin-up
sadomasochisme de bazar', and her mentor, Irving Claw,
that:

> elle accumule les covers, tourne trois navets produits par
> Claw, et disparaît en pleine gloire, laissant son Pygmalion
> devant une commission sénatoriale l'accusant de dévoyer la
> morale et les bonnes moeurs (she appeared on innumerable
> covers, made three appallingly bad films produced by Claw,
> and disappeared at the height of her fame leaving her
> Pygmalion facing a Senate Committee accusing him of
> corrupting public morals).

Piqueup* n.m. After Bertollier comes home triumphantly in
Marcel Aymé's 1952 play *La Tête des Autres* (see 'lunch' in
IIb), his mistress Juliette says: 'On fera marcher le piqueup.
Je danserai avec le héros du jour.' (We'll put the piqueup on.
I will dance with the hero of the hour.) Also spelt pick-up, the
term is now archaic, having been replaced by 'l'electrophone'
and 'la chaîne hi-fi'.

Pitch and put n.m. Advertised in *Madame Figaro* in November
1994 as next to the golf training centre – 'le centre d'entraînement' – at Saint-Étienne.

Playboy n.m. Familiar to the French since the 1960s through
Hugh Heffner's magazine, of which there is a French edition.
Two of the characters who recur in Jacques Faizant's cartoons
in *Le Point* are a very traditionally dressed elderly French

couple; on August 22 1994, no. 1144, they were discussing re-
incarnation. The husband announced his intention of coming
back as 'un playboy':

> multimilliardiare, beau comme un dieu, tenant le whisky
> comme pas un, tombeur de toutes les stars et capable, au
> lit, d'exploits incroyables. Ça, c'est moi dans une prochaine
> vie! Des brunes, des blondes, des auburn [*sic*], des multi-
> colores. (A multimillionaire, handsome as a Greek god,
> unrivalled as a whisky drinker, getting into bed with all the
> stars, and capable of unbelievable exploits there. That's me
> in the next life! Brunettes, blondes, redheads, girls with hair
> all colours of the rainbow.)

His wife listens sceptically before announcing her intention of
coming back as 'une play-girl'.

Practice* n.m. 'Un practice', according to *Madame Figaro* for
12 November 1994, is a practice ground for golf – just as 'un
self' is a self-service restaurant or 'un snack' a snack-bar.
Thanks to the European Community's 'set aside' policy, (la
mise en jachère), agricultural land is now being transformed
into golf courses. Golf is therefore becoming a cheaper and
more popular sport, and the driving range is now making its
appearance in France. It too is called 'un practice'.

Prime time n.m. Officially, 'heures de grande écoute'; but
used in the *Quid* in the reminder that French television stations
have to devote 15 per cent of their 'prime time' to programmes
produced in France, as well as 50 per cent of their total
broadcasting time to French products and 60 per cent to
European ones. In *Le Nouvel Observateur* for 8 September 1994,
no. 1557, Françoise Giroud talked about 'ce qui s'appelle en
anglais le *pre-prime-time* et en français la tranche horaire qui
précède le journal' (what in English is called 'pre-prime-time'
and in French the hour preceding the news).

In its 'Savez-vous parler télé?', *Télérama* 2308 on 8 April
1994 commented that

> Prime Time et access prime time (de 19 à 20 heures) sont

aux annonceurs publicitaires ce qu'est la rue de la Paix aux joueurs de Monopoly: rentable mais pas donné. (Prime time and access prime time (between seven and eight in the evening) are to advertisers what Mayfair and Park Lane are to players of Monopoly: profitable but not cheap).

In another context, the rue de la Paix is the equivalent of Bond Street or Fifth Avenue, a shopping street well known for the high price of the goods on sale. It was already being alleged, in the 1930s, that it was impossible to know what was on sale in the rue de la Paix unless you had a good knowledge of English.

An article in *Le Nouvel Observateur*, no. 1553, for 11 August 1994, made the interesting claim that since the French have a light breakfast, which they eat in the kitchen, they are the only people to listen to the radio in the morning, so that 'le prime time de 6 à 9 heures est une tranche publicitaire en or' (the prime time from 6 to 9 is an expensive and profitable period for advertisements).

While this article shows how long-lived in France is the vision of the English going into the breakfast room to spend an hour or so eating porridge, bacon and eggs or kedgeree, a more probable explanation is that the time when most people listen to the radio is, in both countries, when they are stuck in their car on their way to work.

Public address system n.m., also P. A. The 1989 *dictionnaire des néologismes officiels* recommends the widely used 'la sonorisation'.

Putting n.m. and **put**, v. The Toubon makes no suggestion for suitable French words to replace what *Madame Figaro* used on 19 November 1994, in its account of how Michael Wolseley manages 'les longs putts' when it is his turn to 'putter'.

Puzzle n.m. Normally a jigsaw puzzle. The word is frequently used in a figurative sense, as when *Le Nouvel Observateur*, no. 1252, for 3 November 1988, reviewed a new edition of Georges Lefebvre's 1934 classic *La Grande Peur de 1789* by describing how en reconstituant pièce à pièce ce puzzle aux mille morceaux (by putting together this thousand-piece jigsaw puzzle bit by bit)

he had shown how the generalised terror of famine and of an aristocratic counter-revolution which gripped the French countryside in 1789 had led to events such as the voluntary abolition, on 4 August 1789, by the aristocrats themselves, of their feudal rights.

Reality-show* n.m. Not in the Toubon, nor in the *Dictionnaire des Anglicismes*, nor in the 1991 *Oxford Dictionary of New Words*. But the 'Savez-vous parler télé?' in *Télérama* no. 2308 (8 April 1994) translates it into French as 'téléréalité' and defines it as the 'exploitation télévisuelle des petites misères de la vie' (presentation on the telly of life's minor miseries):

> Maman m'a abandonné dans un chenil, mon mari me trompe avec le pompiste. (Mother left me in a kennel, my husband is having an affair with the petrol pump attendant.)

In *Le Point* for 5 November 1994, no. 1155, when Catherine Péard commented on how all Mitterrand's secrets, unlike those of de Gaulle, 's'évaporent déjà dans le "reality show" ambiant' (are already dissolving into thin air in the media-dominated atmosphere) the word seems to take on something of the meaning of the English 'media event'.

Remake n.m. Not in the Toubon, but according to the *Dictionnaire des Anglicismes*, in French since 1946. Josette Rey-Debove and Gilberte Gagnon cite a number of suggested official replacements – 'copie', 'adaptation', 'révision', 'refonte', 'remaniement', 'reconstruction' – before quoting a remark by R. Jeanne and Charles Ford in *Le Vocabulaire du cinéma* to the effect that none of them quite fits the bill. This matches the enthusiastic review in *Le Nouvel Observateur* for 3 November 1988, no. 1252, of Marco Ferreri's proposed film of Plato's *Symposium*. Since this is known in French as *Le Banquet*, the reviewer offered the reassurance that it would not be 'un remake de *La Grande Bouffe*' (see 'light' in IIb).

The verb 'remaker' has not survived. 'Refaire' has replaced it.

The word was used in a historical and political context in *France-Observateur* for 10 August 1961 by Pierre Nora in his review of Robert Fossaert's recently published *L'avenir du capitalisme*. He asked:

> La France des luttes ouvrières et des révolutions sociales peut-elle devenir un *remake* de l'économie américaine, fondée sur la consommation de masse? (Can the France of working-class struggles and social revolutions become a remake of the American economy, based on mass consumption?)

Basically, the answer seems to be 'yes'. A news item on France-Inter on 5 January 1995 claimed that there were now, in France, 'plus d'actionnaires que d'ouvriers' (more shareholders than workers).

Remix n.m. One of the words used by Olivier Cachin on television (see below, 'take your time').

Rough* n.m. According to *Madame Figaro* for 13 November 1994, the fairways at Evreux are – as in other courses – 'bordés de roughs en hautes herbes' (the grass in the rough is very tall). It is unusual in English to use the plural to describe the rough on a golf course.

Rush n.m. As in 'le grand rush du week-end'. Also used in film-making, as in 'nous avons récupéré le rushs' (we found all the rushes). The Toubon recommends 'épreuve' in the latter sense, which is not the one in which *Le Point* for 27 August 1994, no. 1145, used it in its headline 'Chute française et rush américain', contrasting the fact that 75 per cent of the films seen in France during that month were American and only 12 per cent French.

Charlie Chaplin's *The Gold Rush* is *La ruée sur l'or*.

Scoop n.m. The Toubon recommends 'exclusivité' or 'primeur', and it would be possible to say 'Nous vous donnons cette information en exclusivité, (This is an exclusive news item) or 'Vous connaissez la nouvelle? Je vous la donne en primeur' (Have you heard the news? You can be the first to find out), especially since the *Petit Robert* quotes Sainte-Beuve: 'Elle prenait ainsi pour elle la primeur des conversations' (She was always the first to say something).

It is nevertheless hard to see how either word could replace 'scoop' in the wish expressed by Jean Planchais in his review of Eric Conan's and Henri Rousso's *Vichy ou les dérives de la mémoire* in *Le Monde* for 9 September 1994:

> Que cesse ce rituel infantile consistant à s'indigner tous les six mois parce qu'un scoop a révélé que les Français ou des Français ont collaboré avec le régime de Vichy. (Let us put an end to this infantile ritual which consists of expressing indignation every six months because a scoop has revealed that the French people – or some French people – has or have collaborated with the Vichy régime).

See also 'groggy' in IIa.

Script-girl n.f. In French since 1929. Singled out for disapproval by Étiemble, and the *Dictionnaire des Anglicismes* claims that the form recommended in the Toubon, 'scripte', is catching on. As far as *Le Point* for 29 October 1994 was concerned, it had not caught on enough to be used in the article in no. 1154 on Françoise Giroud, who began what turned out to be a very interesting career in journalism as co-founder of *L'Express* in 1953 and the first 'Secrétaire d'État à la condition féminine' in 1976, as well as being a successful essayist and novelist, by becoming 'script-girl de Jean Renoir'.

Set n.m. As in tennis, 'gagner par deux sets contre un' (to win by two sets to one).

Sex-symbol n.m. According to *L'Événement du jeudi* for 24 April 1994, no. 495, Sharon Stone

> est devenue un sex-symbol, elle pèse des millions de dollars, mais son ambition est de devenir aussi une bonne comédienne (has become a sex symbol, weighing millions of dollars, but her ambition is also to become a good actress).

The article added that 'en wasp blonde et glacée elle fait merveille' (she is marvellous as a cold, blonde Wasp); but did not say whether she did or did not commit the murder at the beginning of *Basic Instinct*, a film distributed under the same title in France.

Show n.m. Although the Toubon recommends 'spectacle solo' for 'one-man-show' (see above), it makes no mention of a word that has been in current use in French since the 1950s, as well as being used, as the *Dictionnaire des Anglicismes* points out, by Voltaire in 1773 in *Les Lois de Minos*:

> Puissent les tragédies n'être désormais ni une longue conversation partagée en cinq actes par des violons ni cet amas de spectacles grotesques, appelé par les Anglais *show* et par nous, la rareté, la curiosité. (Let tragedies cease to be either a long, shared conversation split up into five acts by violins, or a heap of grotesque horrors which the English call a *show* and to which we give the name of a rarity, a curiosity.)

The word is also known in modern France through 'le bebête-show', a satirical programme on television on the same lines as 'Spitting Image'. It was suggested to me by a Frenchman in 1991 that most French people derived their knowledge of politics principally from 'le bebête-show'.

L'Humanité for 16 January 1995 described the visit of Pope John Paul II to the Philippines as 'un show papal', and drew a contrast between his popularity with the two million people who came to listen to him there and the criticisms made of him in France for having moved the progressively-minded bishop of Évreux, Monseigneur Gaillot, to an extinct diocese in Mauritania.

The word is widely used in a political context, as when a student who was going to be just old enough to vote in the presidential election told an interviewer on France Inter on 25 February 1995 that he was going to do so 'pour protester contre le show médiatique' (to protest against the fact that it had become a media show). See also the entry 'battling Jacquot' above.

Show-business n.m. The *Dictionnaire des Anglicismes* gives it as appearing in French in the 1960s, especially in relationship with the music-hall. It also reveals a fact which the Toubon hides from its readers, namely that 'L'Administration française [Administration is even more frequently capitalised in France than Royal in the UK] préconise l'expression *industrie du spectacle* en remplacement de cet emprunt' (recommends 'industrie du spectacle' in place of this loan word). See also 'come-back', above and 'Be Yourself' in IId.

The abbreviation 'show-biz' is quite frequent, as when the review in *Le Nouvel Observateur*, no. 1252, for 3 November 1988 praised Gérard Depardieu's recently published *Lettres volées* (Stolen letters) – letters which he had written to various well-known people, including François Mitterrand, Catherine Deveuve and Isabelle Adjani, but never sent – as giving a better portrait of him than the one provided by 'ces biographes tordus que sont les commères du show-biz' (the weird biographers writing for the show-biz gossip columns). The letters confirmed that while Depardieu had indeed been 'un blouson noir' (juvenile semi-delinquent) in his youth, he was a good writer who gave a particularly good portrait of his poverty-stricken childhood. See also the entry 'casting' above.

Show view n.m. On 14 August 1994, the newspaper *Midi-Pyrénées* told its readers that

> vous n'avez qu'à tapoter sur le boîtier SHOW VIEW pour enregistrer vos programmes à la télé. (All you need to do to record your programmes on the telly is press the buttons on your SHOW VIEW).

Sitcom n.f. As in 'Savez-vous parler télé'. (See above, 'Reality-Show', 'Euro-pudding', etc.) A character in Jacques Faizant's cartoon in *Le Point* for 3 September 1994, no. 1146, expressed disapproval of 'des sitcoms' by talking about 'les rires enregistrés à l'avance pour indiquer à l'imbécile que je suis que c'est là qu'il faut rire' (pre-recorded laughter to tell fools like me that this is where you laugh).

Soaps n.m. Too recent to be in the *Dictionnaire des Anglicismes*, and translated as 'téléroman' in 'Savez-vous parler télé' in *Télérama* 2308 on 8 April 1994. The remark by Catherine Humboldt in *Le Nouvel Observateur* for 3 December 1989 no. 1308 that English television was much better than French because of 'les soaps virulents' (hard-hitting soap operas) showed an imperfect understanding of the word.

The programmes she praised, *Jewel in the Crown*, *Singing in the Rain* and what she called 'l'irrésistible et hilarant "Yes Minister"' (the irresistible and hilarious 'Yes, Minister') are not soaps in the true sense of the word, since they come to an end after a specified number of episodes. True soaps, as the article in *Télérama* pointed out, are 'étirables à l'infini' (can be stretched out to infinity); as is the case with *Coronation Street* or *Brookside*.

Speaker* n.m. A loudspeaker is 'un haut parleur', supplemented in a stereosystem by 'un baffle' (see above).

The Toubon has not had much success in replacing the term 'speaker de radio' (a news reader or an announcer on the radio) by 'un annonceur'. The term goes back a long way, for when in the summer of 1950, I tried to improve my spoken French by going on a hitch-hiking tour (see 'autostop' in IIb), its stilted hyper-correctness made people tell me: 'Vous parlez comme un speaker de radio.' One also finds the term 'speakerine'. The French equivalent of the Speaker in the House of Commons is 'le Président de la Chambre des députés'.

Spot* n.m. The Toubon recommends 'message publicitaire'. A false anglicism, though one which could be usefully taken back into English. *Le Point* for 20 August 1994, no. 1144, noted:

> on retient le nom de la marque dans 4 spots sur 7 quand ils sont diffusés dans une plage courte et seulement dans 5 spots sur 13 si la coupure publicitaire atteint six minutes. (A spectator remembers the name of the product in 4 advertisements out of 7 if they are broadcast in a short

break and only 5 out of 13 if the interruption lasts for six minutes.)

Sprinter n.m. and v. Frequently used of athletes and horses; not mentioned in the Toubon; according to the *Dictionnaire des Anglicismes*, in French since 1865. There seems to be no feminine form 'sprinteuse' or 'sprinteresse'. For 'sprint', see 'challenge' in IIa.

Star n.f. Not mentioned in the Toubon, but very frequent in the sense of 'étoile de cinéma' as well as in a sporting or in a political context, as when *Le Monde* for 31 March 1993 described Edouard Balladur as having been 'une star dans les milieux d'affaires' (a star in the business world) in spite of the fact that he had never been 'manager de l'année' (manager of the year) when in charge of the Société française des accumulateurs between 1980 and 1986. The word 'star' keeps its feminine form even when referring to a man, perhaps by analogy with 'étoile'.

The ability of anglicisms and 'franglais words' to coexist very happily with highly French expressions comes out in a remark in *Le Point*, no. 1150, for 1 October 1994, about the actress Geneviève Castile who had

accompli toute sa carrière dans l'obscure clarté de la Comédie Française, qui est au star-system ce que le Carmel est au Vatican (spent the whole of her career in the dark light of the Comédie Française, which is to the star system what a Carmelite convent is to the Vatican).

Any French person likely to be interested in the *Comédie Française* would immediately recognise the quotation from the opening line in Rodrigue's description in Act V of Corneille's 1636 *Le Cid* of the successful night-time attack against the Moorish invaders: 'Cette obscure clarté qui tombait des étoiles . . .' There is, the comment in *Le Point* implies, as much difference between the avoidance of publicity required of actresses in the Comédie Française and the Hollywood star system as there is between the austerity of the Carmelite order and the elaborate goings-on in Rome.

The profits of what is also known as 'La Maison de Molière' are divided into thirty-two shares, of which thirty are divided among 'les sociétaires', actresses and actors who have attained that status after eleven years as 'pensionnaires'. Although reformed in 1975, the system remains basically what it was when established by Napoleon during a spare half hour in Moscow on 15 October 1812.

Starlette n.f. *Libération* for 16 January 1995 described the Trotskyist politician Arlette Laguiller as 'la starlette de la classe ouvrière' (the starlet of the working class). She is a regular candidate at presidential elections, normally obtaining slightly under 1 per cent of the votes cast.

Starting-blocks n.m.p. Frequently used in a political context, as when Balladur was reported on Europe 1 for 2 February 1995 to be 'déjà dans les starting-blocks' (already in the starting-blocks) for the presidential race.

Stock-car n.m. In an article on Fun Radio and Skyrock for 9 March 1995, *Le Nouvel Observateur* no. 1583 said that the rules governing their behaviour were like those applied 'dans les courses de stock-cars' (in stock-car racing): 'Privés de freins, ayant pour unique consigne de ne pas se faire doubler, les animateurs pilotent la plupart du temps à la limite de l'adhesion intellectuelle' (with no brakes, and with the only rule that of not being overtaken, the presenters drive for most of the time in a way with which it is hard to agree).

Street-ball On 6 April 1995, *Le Monde* described how Edouard Balladur, 'en campagne dans les banlieues de Paris' (on campaign in the Paris suburbs) claimed to 'connaître les règles du street-ball' (know the rules for street-ball). It was an attempt to popularise his image (see 'bristol' in IIa) which was unconvincing on two grounds: the rules vary so much from place to place that they don't really exist; a French child as well brought up as Edouard would never have been allowed to play out with other children in the street, and so would never have learned to play street-ball at an early enough age to know whether it had rules or not. Ernest Renan commented that in order to write well about religion, you have to have believed and then stopped believing. The same thing is true about the ability to write well about popular fiction: you have to have read *Bulldog Drummond* at an age when you swallowed it whole to be able to analyse it in later life. To understand games, you have to have played them as a child; something which Camus did early, but Sartre only rather late (see the entry 'the right man in the right place' in IId).

There is also a difference here between Anglo-Saxon and French views on child-rearing. In Britain as in other English-speaking countries, parents attach great importance, when buying a house, to the presence in the neighbourhood of other children. They think it important for their offspring to learn what are rather grandly referred to as 'social skills' by playing with the other kids on the block. When, at a dinner in France, I explained how this had been a factor in my choice of a house, one of my fellow guests, a rather elegant lady, asked: 'Comment? Vous? Un professeur d'université, vous permettez que vos enfants aillent jouer dans la rue'? (What? You? A university professor? You let your children go out and play in the street?)

Sunlights* n.m.p. In French since the 1920s but not in the Toubon; or, for that matter, in the 1990 Chambers. The English equivalent would presumably be 'spotlight', unusable in this context because 'un spot' is used in the sense of an advertisement on the telly.

An unkind article about Princess Diana in *L'Événement de jeudi* no. 514 for 8 September 1994 claimed that 'la pauvrette s'étiole à l'écart des sunlights' (the poor wee thing wilts away far from the spotlights); had been consoling herself by telephoning a married man; and 'telle une toxico privée de son "fix", n'a réussi à "décrocher" qu'après un très cruel sévrage' (like a drug addict deprived of her fix, could ring off only after a cruel period of cold turkey).

Superstar n.f. In French since the 1970s, popularised by the show *Jesus Christ Superstar*. Used in a political sense when *Le*

Nouvel Observateur for 1 January 1976 described Jimmy Carter as 'une superstar de la politique mondiale', and *Libération* for 17 January 1995 commented disparagingly on how Alain Minc's right-wing *La France de l'an 2000* had been written by 'des superstars du grand patronat et de la très haute fonction publique' (superstars of major employers and the very top ranks of the civil service).

Supporter n.m. A football supporter. Officially the verb 'supporter' means to bear or endure, as in 'il supporte courageusement la douleur' (he bears pain bravely). However, it is frequently used in the English sense of 'to support', instead of the correct 'soutenir'. This may be because the noun 'souteneur' means a pimp, and the noun is both written and pronounced 'supporteur'.

An instructive example of this particular use of the verb 'supporter' occurred when the *présidente* of a successful branch of the Alliance Française in the West of England rose to thank me, with some reluctance, for a lecture I had just given on 'la querelle du "franglais"'. Fixing me with an eye which would have done credit to Bertie Wooster's Aunt Agatha, she said:

> Quant à moi, et à la différence de certains, je supporte entièrement la tentative de monsieur Toubon de purger la langue française de tous ces intrus. (As far as I am concerned, and unlike Some People, I am absolutely in favour of Monsieur Toubon's attempt to purge the French language of all these intruders.)

Another reminder of the anecdote about the Belgian brothel-keeper given earlier (p. 37).

Swing n.m., *swinguer*, v. As in boxing; also in music, especially in the 1940s. During the early years of the Occupation, when the Vichy government strove to revive a sense of traditional morality in France by what it called 'la Révolution Nationale', newspapers such as *Au Pilori*, *La Gerbe* and *Je Suis Partout* caricatured not only the Jews but also young men in what were known in England at the time as 'Oxford bags', and which in the 1960s came back to fashion in France as 'des pantalons à pattes d'éléphant', as belonging to the decadent 'génération "Swing"'.

Also used in golf. *Madame Figaro* for 12 November 1994 describes how, at Poitiers, 'on swingue de l'école primaire à la fac' (you practise your swing from the primary school to the university).

Take your time An injunction used on TF1 by the 'animateur' Christophe Dechavanne. *Télérama* no. 2038 on 8 April 1994 gave marks to five of the leading presenters on French television for the purity of their language, seen in terms of its freedom from 'franglais' words. Dechavanne was 'passable', with 26 'anglicismes' (*Télérama*'s word) an hour, as opposed to 156 for Olivier Cachin on Fax'O on M6, and only 2 ('live' and 'en charge de') for Daniel Bilalian on France 2. Bernard Pivot, the best-known name on French television for his book programme 'Apostrophes', had 24, using 'star' six times as well as 'peace and love', 'leader', 'juke-box' and 'baby boom'.

Talk-show n.m. 'Causerie' (n.f.) for the Toubon; 'téléparlote' for *Télérama* no. 2308 (8 April 1994). The French have not yet borrowed 'talkmaster' from the Germans for the man who directs the proceedings, who is normally called 'l'animateur'.

Tests matchs* n.m.p. Reporting that the 'Tournoi des cinq nations' in rugby (le rugby à quinze; rugby league is 'le rugby à treize), was now seen as out-of-date (not a widely accepted opinion), *Libération* for 12 December 1994 suggested the adoption of 'des tests matchs de pays à pays' (test matches between countries). The printer's error may create a word which enters as permanently into existence in French, as did 'brain-trust' in IIa.

Thriller n.m. On 9 April 1994, *Le Point* no. 1125 described the film which Philip Kaufman made of Milan Kundera's *The Unbearable Lightness of Being* (*L'insoutenable légèreté de l'être*) as 'un thriller de l'âme', and the use of 'le vieux Lyon' as a substitute for Prague 'très plausible'.

Timing n.m. Mentioned by Madame Françoise Seligman in the debate in the Sénat on 12 April 1994 (see note 6 to Chapter 2). Perhaps less an example of 'franglais' than a necessary loan word; the suggestions of 'calendrier' or 'minutage' made by the Toubon are limited in their application to the amount of time allowed for the completion of a project. A phrase such as 'his timing was excellent' when speaking of an actor is impossible to render except by a paraphrase; just as the term 'à propos' has no English equivalent. In a sporting context, the English term is used in French in the discussion of all ball games.

Trash adj. Not frequently used, being absent from the *Dictionnaire des Anglicismes* as well as from the Toubon. Used in *Le Point* for 5 November 1994, no. 1155, by Jean-Marie Colombani, *directeur* (chief editor) of *Le Monde*, to describe a paper called *Voici*.

Travelling* n.m. A travelling shot in the cinema. Not in the Toubon. The *Dictionnaire des Anglicismes* dates the entry of the term into French from 1921, quotes from an entry by R. Godiveau entitled 'Terminologie de l'Audio-Visuel' in *La Banque des mots*, no. 3, 1972, to the effect that it is 'un mot d'apparence anglaise forgé en France' (an English-looking word made up in France), and notes the failure of attempts to find a French equivalent.

Like 'camping', and 'parking', 'travelling' is another example of a gerund used adjectivally in English (camping ground, travelling shot) becoming a noun in French.

Tuner n.m. An advertisement on France-Inter on 10 October 1994 invited listeners to take part in a competition to win 'un radio avec tuner', a car radio with an automatic tuning device.

Underground n.m. Not in the sense of 'le métro à Londres', but in what the 1990 Chambers defines as being

characterised by avant-gardism and experimentation ... appealing to minority, anti-establishment tendencies.

The April–May 1994 number of *Talents*, 'pour ceux qui font des études supérieures', a magazine for students in higher education, described David Kronenberg, maker of the 1970s film *The Fly*, as 'le roi du gore underground' (the king of underground gore). There is no more a French word for what the *Encyclopedia universalis* suggests is characterised essentially by its style of production – relatively cheap, 16- or 8-millimetre films – than there is an English term for the *film noir*.

Walkman n.m. The officially recommended 'baladeur' is holding its own against what is in fact a Sony brand-name (marque déposée).

NOTES

1 The normal word is 'toilette', and there was an interesting exchange on the best term to use in the debate in the French Sénat on 13 April 1994 (*Journal Officiel*, p. 988; see above, Chapter 1, note 21):

> *M. Marc Lauriol*: Le Canada, comme vous le savez, est un pays bilingue. Au Parlement d'Ottawa, j'ai vu au coin d'un mur, avec une flèche, un indication *'toilet'*, en anglais et 'W.-C.' en français. (*Sourires.*) Nous en sommes là!
>
> D'ailleurs, je dois reconnaître qu'actuellement l'expression 'water-closet' est de moins en moins utilisée. De plus en plus, on va aux toilettes. (*Sourires.*)
>
> Au Sénat, par exemple, on va aux toilettes beaucoup plus qu'aux waters. Mais waters est quand même entré dans les moeurs, si j'ose dire . . . (*Rires.*)
>
> *M. Ivan Renar*: Attention aux accidents de chasse!

> (Canada, as you know, is a bilingual country. In the Ottawa parliament, I saw on the corner of a wall, with an arrow, the sign: 'Toilet', in English, and 'W.-C.' in French. (*Smiles.*) That is where we've got to!
>
> Besides, I must admit that nowadays the expression 'water-closet' is less and less used. More and more, people go to the toilets. (*Smiles.*)
>
> In the Senate, for example, people go to to the toilets much more than to the W.C. But waters [pronounced in French:

vaters] has become part of our customs, if I may be allowed the expression. (*Laughter.*)

M. Ivan Renar: Watch out when you pull the chain/Be careful of hunting accidents!

The French are fond of puns, and 'chasse' can mean either hunting (as in the proverb 'Qui va à la chasse, perd sa place' = huntsmen are easily cuckolded) or the chain to flush the lavatory.

For a further discussion of lavatories in France, see the entry 'loo/US john' in Thody and Evans, *Faux Amis and Key Words*.

2 In March 1995, the satirical weekly *Le Canard enchaîné* revealed that Edouard Balladur had made a capital gain of 2.5 million francs by selling stock options which he had acquired when he was general manager of a large computer firm, the GSI filiale d'Alcatel. Although he had acted throughout in a perfectly legal manner, the revelation did not do him much good in his campaign for the presidency. It did nevertheless lead to the publication in *Le Monde* for 21 March 1995 of details of the income, property and taxes paid of all the candidates; except for Jean-Marie Le Pen.

d *Youth, clothes and entertainment*

The asterisk * is a reminder that the word either does not normally exist in English or is used by the French in a different sense from the meaning it has in the United States or the United Kingdom. The dagger † placed after a word in the index indicates its presence in either the 1995 *Petit Larousse Illustré* or the *Petit Robert* (1992).

Acid jazz n.m. 'Jazz' has been in French since the 1920s, and was violently denounced by Georges Duhamel, in *Scènes de la vie future* (1930) as the 'triomphe de la sottise barbare' (triumph of barbarous idiocy). Duhamel's book was even more of an attack on America than *Parlez-vous franglais?*

In the 1930s, Sartre's and Simone de Beauvoir's liking for jazz was one of the ways in which they were seen as defying bourgeois conventions, and in 1938 Sartre used Sophie Tucker's rendering of 'Some of these Days' to illustrate the basic idea of *La Nausée*: that there is a difference between physical life on the one hand and musical tunes or mathematical formulae on the other. Nothing in nature is perfectly round; and even if you broke the record and destroyed all the sheet music, the song would still continue to exist.

'Acid jazz' is obviously jazz written under the influence of drugs. Virtually all pop music in France is American or English, and the April–May 1994 edition of *Talents*, the magazine for students in higher education, 'pour ceux qui font des études supérieures', had other English terms apart from 'acid jazz', 'folk-rock', and 'swing county' (p. 39). There was an advertisement for

> The Breeders: des mélodies vocales sucrées façon 'lollipop sixties' avec un zeste de Blondie et une rage guitariste à la

Pixies, le tout saupoudré de country. Le 23, 16 heures, avec Bad Brains, The Lemonheads, Pacualito and Les Thugs. (The Breeders: sugarized vocal melodies in the 60s manner, with a touch of Blondie and a Pixie-like guitar madness, with an over-all sprinkling of country music. On the 23rd, at four o'clock, Bad Brains, The Lemonheads, Pacualito and The Thugs.)

The same page had references to Counting Crows with their song 'August and Everything After'; to Therapy, 'un trio originaire d'Ulster qui réinvente un punk et un heavy metal britanniques que l'on croyait à jamais disparus' (a trio from Ulster, reinventing a British punk and heavy metal style which had been thought to have disappeared for ever), with their song 'Troublegum'; to Iggy Pop, 'avec les Rita Mitsouko et Cowboy Mouth'; and to Christine Lakeland, 'ex-complice du lézard J. J. Cale avec qui elle partage un goût prononcé pour le swing country version rocking chair' (former partner of the lizard J. J. Cale, with whom she shares a marked taste for swing country version rocking chair); together with mentions of 'regga', 'reggae' and 'rap'.

Terms of this kind recur in most magazines aimed at readers under twenty-five. See below, 'country', and 'Fun (for 'Fun radio').

Baba cool* n.f. An article in *Le Point* no. 1073 for 17 April 1993 pointed out how cheaply you could still buy land in certain parts of France, where a hectare (100 square metres; the size of Trafalgar Square) cost as little as 10,000 francs (£1,200; $2,000) as against 100,000 francs in Holland or 50,000 francs in the south-east of England. It then described how a Dutchman's explanation of why he had bought land in France revealed no 'nostalgie de baba cool' but a genuine attempt to farm efficiently.

The *Dictionnaire des Anglicismes* explains that the term originates from the Hindi baba, and was imported by the hippies of the 1960s. Although the 1960s expression 'cool chick' is no longer recognised by the young in America and Britain, Michèle Fitoussi's *Le ras-le-bol des SuperWomen* (see 'briefing' in

IIa) refers to an organisation called 'Mammans-Cool' which, like 'le Baby-Service', will come and look after your children in an emergency.

Baby-boom n.m. The sudden increase in the birth rate after 1945, attributed by Christiane Rochefort in her 1961 *Les petits enfants du siècle* (Grasset, Paris), though not by serious demographers, to the generosity of the *allocations familiales* (family allowances). Étiemble suggests the alternative of 'la forte natalité' (high birth rate), which doesn't give the idea of sudden increase.

Baby-boomer* n.m. On 25 February 1993 no. 1477 of *Le Nouvel Observateur* described people in their forties, 'les quadras', as 'les baby-boomers nostalgiques', and invited them to look back at France as it was before Mitterrand 'sans walkman, sans répondeur, sans fax' (with no Walkman, no automatic telephone answering machine and no fax).

Baby-foot* n.m. As played in most cafés in France. The official English translation is 'table football'.

Baskets* n.m.p. Rubber-soled shoes, worn when playing basket-ball. In a special series of articles on drug trafficking in France, no. 436 of *L'Événement du jeudi* on 3 November 1993 observed that 'les trois interpellés portent tous des baskets trois pointures au-dessus de leur taille' (the three young men arrested all wear shoes three sizes too big) – in order, it explained, to hide the drugs (*la came*) they were carrying.

Such footwear may, of course, merely have been a sign of social disaffection. In Chapter 2 of Tom Wolfe's *Bonfire of the Vanities*, the lawyer Lawrence Kramer tenses his muscles when three boys 'black, fifteen or sixteen years old, wearing big sneakers with enormous laces, untied but looped precisely in parallel lines' get into the same subway car.

See 'catch' in IIc, 'autostop' in IIb and, below, 'boots' and 'out' for other examples of the theory and practice of the semiology of everyday life.

When, on 8 September 1994, *L'Événement du jeudi* no. 514

described the future presidential candidate Jacques Chirac as being 'à l'aise dans ses baskets', it was using what has become a very frequent phrase to indicate relaxed self-confidence.

Be Yourself What is best described an imperative verb used nominally occurred in *L'Express* no. 2233 on 28 April 1994. Cyril Collard, maker of a cult film entitled *Nuits mauves*, had died recently, probably of AIDS (SIDA; see below, 'safe sex' and 'relapse'). In apparent ignorance of the fact that he was HIV-positive, he had made love to a seventeen-year-old girl without using a condom – 'un préservatif' – and infected her.

He belonged to what *L'Express* called 'un certain milieu, celui du show biz' (see 'show-business' in IIc), and had also been described by François Mitterrand as 'un exemple pour la jeunesse française' (an example for French youth), presumably for his work in the cinema. See also 'lyncher' in IIa.

When *L'Express* commented that 'le nouvel impératif (depuis les années 60) s'énonce en anglais, n'en déplaise à certains: "Be Yourself"' (the new commandment – since the 60s – is said in English, whatever some people may say: 'Be Yourself') the last part of the sentence was obviously a criticism of Jacques Toubon, whose bill was being discussed at the time in the National Assembly. Whether *L'Express* was also endorsing a kind of existentialist cult of authenticity, in which people were true to their sexual nature, whatever the consequences either to themselves or to other people, is less clear.

Black adj. As in English, although Philippe Bewitte, editor of the review *Hommes et Migrations*, which is frequently critical of what it sees as racialist tendencies in France, was reported in *Le Point* no. 1125 for 9 April 1994 as saying that he prefers the term 'nègre'. This was the word used by Jean Genet for the title for his 1960 play, *Les Nègres*, translated into English as *The Blacks*.

In its special series of articles on drug trafficking (see above, 'baskets', and below, 'dealer', etc.) *L'Événement du jeudi* no. 436 for November 3 1993 said that 'ceux qui approvisionnent [the suppliers] ne sont ni beurs[1] ni blacks' but regular members of the still largely Caucasian professional criminal classes (*le milieu*). Since French colonial administrators were not selected on athletic ability, it could not be said of the French Empire that it consisted of blacks governed by blues.

Blues n.m. In French since the 1920s, deriving from the Black American expression 'blue devils' for intense depression. There is also a term 'bluesman', accurately described by Josette Debove and Gilberte Gagnon as 'un faux anglicisme', and *Le Monde* for 6 April 1995 said of one musician that 'il commence comme sideman dans d'obscurs orchestres de blues' (he began as an accompanist in little-known bands playing blues).

Like other anglicisms and 'franglais' words, it can sit perfectly comfortably with characteristically French expressions, as when *L'Express* no. 2233 for 28 April 1994 described the result of an enquiry made by the sociologist Sabine Chalvon as 'une révélation du blues hexagonal', the word 'hexagonal' being the fashionable term to evoke France, based on the idea that the country has six sides (see the entry 'Hexagone' in Thody and Evans, *Faux Amis and Key Words*). Nobody, in the analysis made by Sabine Chalvon of the popularity – 'la cote' – of the different professions, came out very well, not even doctors. 'Au hit parade [see IIc] des bêtes noires', wrote *L'Express*, 'les promoteurs immobiliers viennent en tête' (top of the pops in the unpopularity stakes are property developers).

In an article about violence on the buses in north-east Paris, *Le Point* no. 1160 for 3 December 1994 said that 'les machinos ont le blues des banlieues' (the bus drivers have suburban blues) and described them as 'victimes de ce que le jargon du management [see IIa] nomme des facteurs de stress' (see IIa) (victims of what management jargon calls 'stress factors').

Body n.m. As a sign of a return to the bad old days, *Le Monde* for 21 March 1994 reported how prostitutes in Cuba 'montent la garde devant les hôtels en minijupe ou "body" flou' (parade in front of hotels in miniskirts or loose-fitting bodysuits). *Vendredi Samedi Dimanche* for 5 May 1994 had a photograph of a very handsome black youth clad in a tight-fitting garment advertising 'le body au masculin'.

Body-building n.m. *Nice Matin* for 25 April 1993 reported the quarter finals – 'quarts de finale' – as taking place in Menton, with Isabelle Schreider as 'first en catégorie fitness'. The finals, also due to take place at Menton, would include 'une démonstration de step et d'aérobic'. See below, 'fitness'.

Bogarter* v. According to both Obalk, Soral and Pasche, *Les mouvements de mode expliqués aux parents* and Robert Merle, *Dictionnaire du français branché*, to monopolise 'le joint' (the joint) when smoking hashish or pot, instead of passing it around. An allusion to Humphrey Bogart always smoking a cigarette.

Bomber* n.m. A bomber jacket, generally in black leather. According to an advertisement in *National Hebdo*, no. 452 (1993), a shop called Darkside 'habille le militant européen' (dresses the European militant). In a context such as this, 'européen' means the extreme right wing, as when the royalist newspaper *Rivarol* describes itself as a 'journal d'opposition nationale et européenne' (newspaper of national and European opposition).

Boots n.m.p. From a semiological point of view (see 'catch' in IIc), the clothes worn by the highly fashionable philosopher Bernard-Henri Lévy (see 'boat people' in IIa) when interviewed by *Madame Figaro* for 12 December 1994 – 'chemise blanche, pantalon gris perle, boots de cuir' (white shirt, pearl grey trousers, leather boots) – were as meaningful a statement as the open-necked shirt, with collar turned back outside the sports coat, as worn by F. R. Leavis, Wittgenstein, or Gilbert Ryle in the England of the 1930s and 1940s. Wittgenstein and Leavis were expressing their rejection of the formal clothes of the business bourgeoisie and declaring their openness to the new ideas and bracing winds of Cambridge; Ryle, who occasionally wore a tie, was emphasising that a good chap could just as easily have been a country gentleman as a linguistic philosopher. Lévy was underlining the fact that support for the Bosnians of Sarajevo was perfectly compatible with the latest Parisian fashions, and that the two were in fact inseparable.

When the group SHA-LA-LA-LEE made their triumphant

return to Tourcoing on 5 May 1994, *Sortir* described them as wearing 'des boots pointus', and it is not easy to find a French word for 'boots' in this context when what is meant are unisex fashion boots. 'Des bottines' are lace-up boots and not normally worn by men. 'Des bottes' are often heavy, as in 'des bottes de caoutchou' (Wellington boots). Étiemble suggests 'botillons', which doesn't sound quite right for a man.

Box* n.m. Two meanings which illustrate how English words can have a use in France different from the one they have at home: 'le box des accusés' for what we call the dock; as well as a lock-up garage in a block of flats or at some distance from your home.

Boxer* n.m. Not the man, which is 'boxeur', but boxer-shorts.

Boy-friend n.m. The remark in the *Dictionnaire des Anglicismes* to the effect that

> ce mot ne s'emploie guère, en français, que par référence aux moeurs américaines, différentes des nôtres (this word is scarcely used in French except in relation to American customs, which are different from ours)

implied that a French girl either slept with what was still known in 1980 as 'son petit ami' or kept men at arm's length. The idea evoked by the term 'boy-friend' – always hyphenated in French – of emotional commitment accompanied by a degree of heavy petting was seen as alien to what the French regarded as their more direct and honest approach to sex. The term popularised by Marcel Prévost in his 1894 novel *Les Demi-Vierges* has never been a compliment. See below, 'flirt'.

I have not come across the term 'significant other'. 'Mon ami(e)' can have a sexual sense in certain contexts, as does the feminine form 'compagne'. They also occur in a context where the English might use the term 'partner', or even 'common law wife' or 'common law husband'. As in the past, 'maîtresse' and 'amant' imply that at least one of the people involved is married to somebody else. 'Cohabitation' occurs when two people live together without being married, but it is also a political term, implying a left-wing President and a right-wing Prime Minister, or the other way round, and is widely applied by the French radio to the situation created in the United States by the congressional elections of November 1994, which required Bill Clinton to govern with a Republican majority in both the House and the Senate.

The administrative term for living together without being married is 'le concubinage', though it is more usual to say 'il (or elle) partage sa vie avec X ou Y' for people who are, as the Yorkshire term still has it in older speakers, 'living over the brush'. It was said with some horror of Simone de Beauvoir, in the 1930s, that 'elle vit en concubinage ouvert avec Jean-Paul Sartre' (she lives openly with Jean-Paul Sartre without being married to him) and they remained unmarried and unfaithful to each other until his death in 1980. The implications of 'an open marriage' are rendered by the obvious linguistic calque, 'un mariage ouvert'. In the past, it was said of a woman who 'fermait ses yeux sur les incartades de son mari' (closed her eyes to the goings-on of her husband) that 'elle connaissait l'usage de l'eau dans le vin' (she knew how to water the wine).

Le Point no. 1077 for 8 May 1993 told a story about the painter Francis Bacon which illustrated how the word 'boy-friend' can now used for what Balzac called 'les deux sexes et autres':

> Ayant aperçu dans une galérie une des oeuvres dérobées dans son atelier par un boy-friend d'un soir, le peintre la rachète – fort cher – sur-le-champ pour la détruire dans l'instant sur le trottoir. (Having seen in a gallery one of his own works stolen by a boy-friend of a one-night stand, he bought it back – for a lot of money – and destroyed it immediately on the pavement outside.)

On 17 March 1994, *Le Nouvel Observateur* no. 1531 reported that the latest CD by the Pet Shop Boys had sold 200,000 copies in France, and spoke in some detail about the song 'Can You Forgive Her', in which a girl criticised her 'boy-friend' for being bi-sexual. According to the analysis of the song in *Le Nouvel Observateur*, the fact that he could not fully admit the duality of his tastes meant that more blame should be attached to the boy than to the girl, with the boy being described as 'un Hamlet moitié-vanille, moitié-chocolat, dont la question serait "to bi or not to bi"' (a half-chocolate, half-vanilla Hamlet, who asks himself whether he should be bi- or not).

The French are fond of puns, and also assumed a comparable knowledge of Shakespeare when translating the title of the film *Doctor in the House* as *Toubib or Not Toubib*. 'Un toubib' is a slang word for a doctor, derived from the Arabic word for a magician or witch doctor.

Call girl n.f. *Vendredi Samedi Dimanche* for 5 May 1994 told the story of Jacqueline Berissi, 'Directrice de l'école maternelle Léon Frappié' (headmistress of a nursery school) at Neuilly-Plaisance, Seine Saint-Denis, who after having contracted the habit of transforming herself 'en call girl la nuit', ended up by organising 'un business discret' with a wide clientèle. Her work with the children was much appreciated by the parents, who were sorry to see her go.

Come-back n.m. In *Le Point* for 30 April 1994, no. 1128, shortly after Richard Nixon's death, Bernard-Henri Lévy described how he had once seen him drinking mint tea alone in a café in Marakesch, and was led to think of him as a mythical incarnation of

> l'Amérique qui use ses vedettes, les tue et n'aura jamais su, au fond, les mythifier de leur vivant. L'Amérique et ses has been définitifs. L'Amérique et le come-back impossible. L'Amérique et son warholisme spontané: six, dix minutes, ou dix jours – pas un de plus: pas de sursis: on y meurt dans l'oubli, ou d'un overdose de barbituriques, en sirotant un thé à la menthe sur la place Djemaa-el-Fna. (America which wears out its stars, and kills them without basically ever having been able to make them into myths when they were still alive. America and its impossible comeback. America and its spontaneous Warholisme: six, ten minutes,

or ten days – not a moment more: no reprieves: you die
forgotten, or of an overdose of barbiturates, sipping a mint
tea on the Place Djemaa-el-Fna.)

Cool adj. As in 'Baba cool' above. *Les mouvements de mode
expliqués aux parents* (Obalk, Soral and Pasche) explains that
'pour ne pas flipper [see entry in IIb], il sera cool' (so as not
to lose control, he will be laid back).

Country* n.f. In the sense of country music. In *Le Point* for
October 1994, no. 1153, Lyle Lovett, Julia Roberts's husband,
was reported as talking about

la chanson populaire, qui puiserait ses forces et son inspiration dans les racines des blues, du gospel, du folk et de la
country (the popular song, which is said to draw its strength
and inspiration in the roots of blues, gospel music, folk and
country).

See below, 'fun'; and above, 'acid jazz'.

In a sense, it would be as inappropriate to complain about
the omnipresence in French of American or English terms in
discussions of popular music as it would be to criticise the use
of expressions such as 'square leg' or 'silly mid-off' in a
commentary on a game of cricket which happened to be
played in France.

Crack n.m. Either the drug, or an expert in sport or in any
other field. When, in 1953, I revealed to a family who had
invited me to dinner in the working-class 18th *arrondissement*
that I was 'lecteur anglais' at the Sorbonne, one of my fellow
guests exclaimed: 'Ah, mais vous êtes un crack, alors' (You
must be a real expert then).

Deal, dealer n.m. and v. To sell drugs; somebody who does
so. *L'Événement du jeudi*'s articles on drugs (no. 436, 3 November 1993, see above, 'black', 'baskets') pointed out that in the
Zone d'Urbanisation Prioritaire (priority housing zone) at Amiens
'on deale a 100F minimum les trois grammes de haschich, soit
33,000F le prix de vente d'un kilo qu'on a acheté 1,000F au

Maroc' (you sell three grammes of hashish for a minimum of 100 francs [£12; $20], making it 33,000 francs a kilo for the stuff you bought at 1,000 a kilo in Morocco).

L'Événement du jeudi has the custom of inviting people with whom it does not necessarily agree to contribute short articles. On 6 October 1994, no. 518, one of the leading French theoreticians of free market economics, Guy Dorman, argued of one of the recent politico-financial scandals which had led to Alain Carignon, a former Ministre de la communication, to be arrested and put in prison to await trial, and another which had led to the resignation of the Industry Minister, Gérard Longuet, that it was the politicians and not the businessmen who were to blame:

> Ce n'est pas le dealer patron qui fait le drogué, mais le toxicomane député qui est en manque. (It's not the businessman who is the dealer who creates the drug addict but the drug-taking *député* who is suffering from withdrawal symptoms.)

The word is also used in a financial context for a dealer in international currencies, futures (the futures market, 'le marché à terme') or derivatives.

Disc-jockey n.m. The Toubon recommends 'animateur', which has the much wider sense of making sure that nobody is allowed to remain quietly alone when they are supposed to be enjoying themselves. It could not replace the phrase 'la victoire des disc-jockeys' in the description in *Le Point* for 19 November 1994, no. 1157, of how capitalism is winning back Saigon.

Doc's* n.m. Doc Marten's. Cf. above, 'baskets'.

Drag queen n.m. and f. In his review of the film *Priscilla, Queen of the Desert* in *Libération* magazine for 8 January 1995, François Reynaert praised the extravagant behaviour of cross-dressers and wrote that 'à côté d'une *drag* qui se respecte, une *girl* du Paradis Latin a l'air d'une pensionnaire de la Légion d'Honneur un jour du 11 novembre' (compared with a self-respecting drag queen, a girl at the Paradis Latin looks like a pupil of the boarding school for daughters of war veterans on parade on 11 November). See below, 'girl'.

François Reynaert argued that the vogue for drag queens was a product of 'les années SIDA', an example of the tendency of sexual privation to give rise to fetishism. He added, in praise of the drag queens, that

> Elles appellent de leurs voeux un monde qui soit non seulement gay [see below] mais surtout joyeux, ce qui témoigne enfin d'un grand coeur et d'un bel humanisme. God save the queens. (They call for a world which is not only gay but which is above all full of joy, an attitude which shows them to be generous-hearted and inspired by a genuine humanism. God save the queens.)

The French traditionally keep the masculine form of 'des travestis', and describe flamboyant homosexuals as 'des tantes' (aunties). If it is English visitors rather than the French themselves who make jokes about 'du camping avec de vraies tentes/tantes', this is because the expression 'to camp around' is not yet part of 'le franglais'.

Duplicate n.m. and adj. As in bridge and scrabble. Both games are popular enough in France to have regular columns in most newspapers. According to *Le Nouvel Observateur* for 28 July 1994, no. 1551, 40 per cent of French people regularly play scrabble, with

> chaque année, à la mi-juillet, un championnat 'du monde' des pays francophones. On y joue en duplicate, tous les joueurs reçoivent les mêmes lettres, et c'est chaque fois le meilleur mot – le plus cher – qui gagne. (Every year, in mid-July, there is a 'world' championship of French-speaking countries. You play in duplicate, all the players receive the same letters, and each time it is the best word – the highest score – which wins.)

The article explained that the game was developed from Lexicon in the 1930s by Alfred Butts, in collaboration with Jim Brunot. Butts then sold the copyright, but continued to play until he was ninety-three.

Event n.m. A reminder that 'le franglais' is not a recent phenomenon, especially in the language of sport, is provided by *Le Figaro* for 18 May 1921, writing that 'le match Cartier-Dempsey sera le grand event pugilistique de la saison' (the Cartier-Dempsey match will be the great boxing event of the season). Quoted in Louis Deroy, *L'Emprunt linguistique* (Les Belles Lettres, Paris, 1956).

Fitness n.m. On 20 January 1994, in an article in *L'Express* no. 2219 entitled 'Marie-Joëlle tout en fitness', the French woman interviewed described herself as an 'executive woman, une working girl et peut-être même une superwoman', and said:

> aujourd'hui, le has been et les ringards, ce sont ceux qui ne font pas de sport. (Today, it is the has-been and the people on the shelf who don't go in for sport.)

The word 'ringard' is relatively recent, and means old-fashioned. It is unlikely, when Marie-Joëlle concluded the interview by saying 'Français, je vais flasher le grand amour de ma vie', that she meant she was going to make an exhibition of herself; nor that she was thinking of drugs (see below, the first part of the entry 'flash'). What she meant is suggested in the second part of the 'flash' entry below.

Fix n.m. As in drug-taking; what you need when you are 'en état de manque' (suffering from withdrawal symptoms). See also 'sunlights' in IIc.

To be distinguished from 'fixe', in the sense of regular salary, as in 'Pour éviter de se trouver obligé de publier des livres pour gagner de l'argent, Albert Camus avait son fixe chez Gallimard comme administrateur' (To avoid ever having to publish books to earn money, Albert Camus had a regular monthly salary as an administrator with Gallimard.)

Flash* n.m. *L'Express* for 11 March 1993, no. 2104, reported that, if you took crack,

> une fois inhalée, la drogue atteint le cerveau en moins de

cinq secondes, c'est ce que l'on appelle le flash. (Once inhaled, the drug reaches the brain in less than five seconds, it is what is called the flash.)

The *Dictionnaire des Anglicismes* mentions *Le Nouvel Observateur* for 22 October 1973 as already using the word in this sense, and quotes the definition of Claude Olievenstein in *Il n'y a pas de drogués heureux* (Laffont, Paris, 1977): 'Sensation spécifique libérée par la drogue et qui envahit le corps' (specific sensation freed by the drug and which invades the body). See also the entry in IIc.

On 23 February 1995, in a discussion on female homosexuality, *L'Événement du jeudi*, no. 538 argued that it was a transient taste, 'passé l'adolescence où 90 per cent des filles flashent sur le prof d'allemand' (once adolescence is over, and when 90 per cent of girls get a crush on the German mistress).

Flipper* n.m. A pinball machine. An example of metonymy, the part for the whole, the lever used to send the ball up designating the machine itself. For the verb, see IIb.

Flirt n.m, and **flirter** v. Not in the Toubon. In French since 1879, in the sense of incomplete sexual relationships between young people. See above, 'boy-friend'. The person, male or female but always referred to in the masculine form, with whom 'on a l'habitude de flirter'.

In a political sense, 'il flirte avec le Parti Communiste' has the same connotations as in the English 'he is flirting with the communists'. When, on 7 February 1995, the American space-ship Discovery travelled for a few thousand miles in space close to the Russian space station Mir, Europe 1 described the operation as 'un flirt'.

Fun n.m. and adj. *Les mouvements de mode expliqués aux parents* Cobalk, Soral and Pasche) has a whole section on 'le Fun', which includes ostentatiously unfashionable activities such as going to all-in wrestling matches in the suburbs, collecting Mickey Mouse statues in plastic, and admiring 'la Funky Music'. It is also 'très fun' to go and see old American B movies, but only if they are dubbed into Italian, Spanish, or Portuguese.

There is also a radio station in Paris called Fun Radio which the government tried to ban in early 1994, thus – according to *Rivarol* for 17 March 1994 – increasing its listening public by 800,000.

In an article on 'La Séxualité des Ados [= adolescents]' on 21 April 1994, *L'Express* no. 2232, described a programme broadcast on Fun Radio every evening between 1900 and 2200 entitled 'Lovin' Fun'. This had the advantage of enabling French teenagers while 'les parents se vitrifient lentement' (literally, turn into glass; become couch potatoes (see 'pin-up' in IIc; go glassy-eyed) 'devant des Reality Shows' (see entry in IIc) to 'communier ensemble à cette grand'messe radio-phonique' (share in this radiophonic High Mass). One of the girls interviewed in *L'Express* for this article said:

> J'aimerais aller dans un planning [see IIa] pour l'avoir [= la pillule] gratos, mais j'ai un peu peur que mes parents apprennent cela. (I should like to go to a family planning clinic to get the pill for nothing, but I'm a bit afraid that my parents will find out.)

The article in *L'Express* pointed out that the advice given on Fun Radio by 'le Doc', Christian Spitz, author of a book entitled *Questions d'adolescents* (Odile Jacob, Paris, 1994) was very sensible, and contrasted it with the parental irresponsibility which it saw as the real cause of any problems encountered by teenagers.

On 6 October 1994, *L'Événement du jeudi* no. 518 gave details of the rivalry between Fun and Sky Radio, and described how the arrival of Tabatha Cash, 'cash comme l'argent', was enabling Sky to win by showing 'le Doc' to be old-fashioned and moralistic. Tabatha, 'sorte de James Bond girl du porno', gave very explicit advice. Sky Radio, *L'Événement du jeudi* reported, now had 1.3 million listeners.

The problem of preventing young people from being influenced by English or American popular culture was illustrated by two incidents which took place in the summer of 1994. The first occurred on 31 July 1994, the day before the Conseil

Constitutionnel was to draw the teeth of the loi Toubon, when 125,000 mainly young people went to hear Pink Floyd in the Bois de Vincennes, causing a five-hour traffic jam. The second was on 13 August 1994, when a festival which took place at Champs sur Tarentais, in the Département du Cantal, incarnation of 'la France profonde', included groups calling themselves 'Real Life Killers', 'Human Spirit', 'Back Sliders', and 'No-one Is Innocent'. As can be confirmed from any daily or weekly publication, the whole vocabulary of popular music is Anglo-American.

See above, 'acid jazz', 'country'.

Gay adj. In the sense of homosexual, in French since the 1970s; and the *Dictionnaire des Anglicismes* refers to the supplement to the *Oxford English Dictionary* to date its use in this sense in English as early as 1935. Not in the Toubon, though the adjective 'gai' is used in this sense. 'Gay Paris' – or 'Gay Paree' – goes back at least to the 1940s, and probably well before.

In France, as in England and America, disapproval of homosexuality tends to be a feature of the right. On 21 April 1994 *Rivarol* attacked the magazine programme 'Transit' on the television chain Arte for having presented

> des prêtres revendiquant hautement leur homosexualité, sous la houlette de l'abbé Perotti, créateur de l'association de chrétiens gay, 'David and Jonathan' (et surtout secré-'taire personnel de l'abbé Pierre, ce qui le rend intouchable) (priests boldly asserting their homosexuality, under the aegis of the Abbé Perotti, creator of the organisation for gay Christians 'David and Jonathan' (and, most important, private secretary to the Abbé Pierre, which makes him untouchable).

Abbé Pierre first became a public figure in 1952 when he launched an appeal in favour of the 'clochards' (tramps) who slept under the bridges in Paris and were badly affected by an exceptionally cold winter. He has since been associated with a large number of good causes, a fact which puts him perpetually on the side of the angels. See 'squat' in IIb.

Libération for 16 January 1995 talked about 'le gay pride', 'l'agriculture gay à la marinière lesbienne' (gay agriculture with a lesbian white sauce), and announced that the television chain Canal + was going to put on 'une nuit gay' in June.

Girl n.f. According to the *Dictionnaire des Anglicismes*, an abbreviation of the 'chorus girl', a term which the authors say is more frequently used in Britain than in America. Raymond Queneau gives the phonetic spelling of 'gueurle', and the term is a useful one. To describe the dancers at the Casino de Paris or the Folies Bergère as 'des filles' might be seen as an insult. Used absolutely, 'une fille' still sometimes has the sense of 'fille de joie' (prostitute). However, it might be equally misleading to describe them as 'des jeunes filles'. 'C'est une vraie jeune fille' means that a girl is unquestionably a virgin. See above, 'drag queen'. For the implications of 'girlfriend', see 'boyfriend' above.

Glamour n.m. *Le Point* no. 1152 for 15 October 1994 noted that the latest tendency in fashion went back to

> un glamour traditionnel, incarné par Jackie Onassis et Audrey Hepburn. Années 60, toujours (a traditional glamour, incarnated in Jackie Onassis and Audrey Hepburn, still the 1960s).

'La silhouette de Twiggy' was still very popular, as also were girls dressed up as boys.

Happening n.m. *L'Express* no. 2177 on 1 April 1993 commented of the student rebellion of 1968, 'L'affaire finit en happening'.

Hard adj. The Toubon gives 'facsim' for 'hard copy', together, more puzzlingly, with 'tirage', normally the word for the number of copies printed of a book or newspaper. 'Hard discount' is 'maxidiscompte', and 'hard discounter', 'maxidiscompteur'. The *Dictionnaire des Anglicismes* gives 'hard labour', 'hard(-)rock', 'hard-top' and 'hardware', though in the context of what the French conveniently call 'l'informatique'(everything to do with computers), and not as applied to weaponry.

In addition to being applied to drugs (where one also finds the term 'les drogues dures'), the adjective occurs frequently in a sexual sense, as in 'le porno hard', or 'le SM [sado-masochism] hard'. It can also denote extremism in politics, as in 'la gauche hard'. See below, 'soft'. Terms such as 'drogues douces' are nevertheless more frequent on the radio and in newspapers such as *Le Monde*. On 20 January 1994, the review in *L'Express* no. 2219 of the translation of Michael Korda's *Les Immortels* (*Charmed Lives*, Random House, New York, 1981) also offered another example (see 'star' in IIc) of how a 'franglais' word can coexist quite easily with very French expressions and cultural references. Describing Korda as 'un professionnel du best-seller', *L'Express* commented of his account of the affair between Marilyn Monroe and J. F. Kennedy that

> l'accumulation de scènes 'hard' transforme le livre en partouze au musée Grévin (the accumulation of highly explicit sex scenes makes the book into an orgy conducted in a wax museum).

'Une partouze' is a sexual encounter with a number of participants; 'le musée Grévin' is a waxworks museum in Paris comparable with Madame Tussaud's in London.

In an erotic sense, 'doux' cannot replace 'soft', as in 'soft porn', since it also means sweet, gentle and pleasant.

L'Express went on to comment on what it called

> l'étrange Amérique où, au nom de la liberté d'expression, deux 'cadavres exquis' sont engagés dans un peep show (strange America where, in the name of freedom of expression, two exquisite corpses are involved in a peep show).

The only meaning given in the dictionary for 'cadavre exquis' – placed in inverted commas by *L'Express* although 'peep show' is not – is a game of consequences, which cannot be the sense here. The word was used by the French surrealists to describe two categories of people whom they disliked: establishment writers who had just died, such as Maurice Barrès or

Anatole France; and living authors such as Jean Cocteau. See below for 'peep show'.

Hit Parade n.m. The recommended 'Palmarès de la chanson' is little used, perhaps because it is too specifically about music. On 7 August 1994, the Sunday edition of *Centre France*, a newspaper covering life south of Nevers and north of Martel, reported that *Business Age* had listed Paul Raymond, the owner of a chain of striptease clubs, as one of the richest men in England, with a fortune of £1,600 million and commented: 'La prude Angleterre n'est plus ce qu'elle était et, au hit-parade de la réussite, le porte-jaretelles devance l'ordre de la jaretelle' (Prudish England is not what it was, and in the hit parade of success, the suspender belt comes higher than the Order of the Garter).

See also above, 'blues'. See also 'hobby' and 'hooligan' in IIc for changes in French concepts of England.

Le Nouvel Observateur for 21 July 1994, no. 1550, also pointed out that 'au hit parade de la fraude, les vols de voiture occupent la première place' (stealing cars is the most popular crime).

In adj. See below, 'out'; see entry in IIa.

Junior n.m. Absent from the Toubon; and, more surprisingly, from the *Dictionnaire des Anglicismes*. In his second book of essays, *Noces*, Camus wrote enthusiastically in 1939 about his friend Vincent, 'champion de brasse junior' (junior breast-stroke champion) who had a healthily pagan attitude to life which led him to say, after he had had a woman for whom he had lusted for some time, 'ça va mieux'; a curious echo of the question which the French used to think that an English woman said to her husband after they had made love: 'Are you feeling better now, dear?'

In the 1950s, even before 'les enfants du baby-boom' (a term also in use in the 1960s; see above) had enjoyed their brief triumph of 1968, a number of expressions arose to describe anyone over forty: PPH (passera pas l'hiver); PPN (passera pas la nuit); pas coté à l'Argus' (too old for the old crocks market [for cars]). Since then, the introduction of 'la carte vermeille' (Senior Citizens card) has restored the balance, as has the popularisation of the term 'le troisième âge' (and of 'le quatrième âge); see below, 'senior'.

Kamikaze n.m. A rare example of a Japanese loan word, though one which obviously comes via English and American. The April–May 1994 magazine *Talents*, no. 10, talked about the phenomenon of cheating at examinations and described those who tried it, despite knowing the risks (permanent exclusion from all forms of higher education), as 'des kamikazes'.

I once had the unusual experience of sitting at dinner next to a man who described himself to me as a failed kamikaze pilot.

Look n.m. See also IIa. In a full-page advertisement for women's clothes, *Vendredi Samedi Dimanche* for 16 June 1994 described one garment as having 'un Look Army. Drôle et Sexy.'

Match n.m. In French as a sporting term since 1819, and widely used in other contexts, with the *Dictionnaire des Anglicismes* quoting *La Croix* for 1 October 1969 as writing of 'un match Allemagne–Grande-Bretagne qui commencera avec l'élargissement du marché commun' (a match between Germany and Great Britain which will begin with the extension of the common market).

Josette Rey-Debove and Gilberte Gagnon point out that 'match' cannot always be replaced by 'partie', since it tends to designate a competition between two teams ('un match de football'), while 'partie' denotes a contest between individuals ('une partie de tennis'). They quote John Orr's 1935 article 'Les Anglicismes du vocabulaire sportif' to the effect that 'match' is much more widely used in French than in English – 'le match de rame' for the Boat Race – and point to the odd way in which the French use the word 'matchmaker': in the sense of somebody who organises boxing matches, for example. The verb 'matcher' is more frequently used in the sense of 'to take part in a match' than in the English sense of to match two opponents against each other.

Miss. In French since the late nineteenth century, and since the 1930s in 'Miss France', 'Miss Univers, 'Miss Aquitaine', etc. According to André Thomas's *Dictionnaire des difficultés de la langue française* (Larousse, Paris, 1956), the word used absolutely means a governess; much as 'mademoiselle', in English, used to designate the French teacher in a girls' school.

New Age adj. The phenomenon known as the 'New Age travellers' has not yet hit France, perhaps because 'les lois contre le vagabondage' are stricter than in England. However, a review in *Talents* for April–May 1994 of a book entitled *L'anti-stress du chercheur de l'emploi* contains 'un recueil d'exercices pour "positiver le mental"'' (a set of exercises to make you think positively; 'mental' is not normally a noun in either French or English, so the word may qualify as an example of 'le franglais'). It also ends with the statement:

> bien sûr, on peut voir dans le chômage une occasion de training new age. (You can find in unemployment an opportunity for New Age training.)

Nightclubbing n.m. The term 'nightclub', as an anglicism for 'boîte de nuit', has existed since the 1930s. Under a headline 'Nuits Blanches' (nights when you don't sleep), *Libération* for 16 January 1995 promised to publish an account every Monday of 'le nightclubbing de la semaine', and gave details about how one could spend one's time at 'Flashback' or 'Too Sexy'.

Out adj. *Le Point* no. 1124 for 2 April 1994 reported that

> la poignée de main est complètement 'out' pour les jeunes Italiens, selon Meo Zilio, professeur de linguistique à Venise. Les jeunes se saluent désormais plus volontiers d'une tape sur l'épaule ou sur l'avant-bras. Les plus 'in'

utilisent le 'give me five' des basketers américains, ou le salut de rappers (bras tenus vers le haut, en se frappant les mains). (Shaking hands is completely out for young Italians according to Meo Zilio, Professor of Linguistics at Venice University. The young now tend to greet one another by tapping on the shoulder or on the fore-arm. Those who are really with it use the 'give me five' of American basket-ball players, or the zappers' greeting [clapping their hands high above their heads]).

For a long time, 'le shake-hand', a term first attested in French the late eighteenth century, was seen as 'très British', presumably in contrast with 'le baise-main'.[2] As Emma Bovary is about to bid her first farewell to young Léon, she holds out her hand for him to shake with the words 'à l'anglaise, donc'. English people coming to France are still taken aback during their first few days by the insistence of the French on shaking hands in the morning with somebody they have seen the day before.

See 'up' and 'down' in IIa; and for other examples of the semiology of everyday life, 'autostop' in IIb, 'catch' in IIc and 'boots' above.

Overdose n.m. See 'boat people' in IIa. Also the verb 'over-doser', as when *L'Événement du jeudi* no. 436, 3 November 1993 (see above, 'black') wrote about the money made in the drugs business being taken from poverty-stricken young-sters who were delinquent at sixteen, 'déglingués' (drop-outs) at twenty, and could therefore be found lying 'overdosés dans un coin de cave' (overdosed in the corner of a cellar).

The word is used in a figurative sense by Michèle Fitoussi in *Le ras-le-bol des SuperWomen* to describe the dangers of getting too involved in what she calls 'une love affaire' ('fuir comme la peste une love affaire dans le service'; avoid like the plague a love affair with the people you work with). 'En cas d'overdose', she writes, 'la rupture ne sera pas aisée' (if you get too involved, it won't be easy to break off).

See below, 'shoot' and 'se shooter'.

Pedigree n.m. In French since the 1820s as a term applied to animals. Generally used ironically of humans, as when the *Petit Robert* for 1976 gives 'un comte très fier de sa particule et de son pedigree' (a count very proud of the 'de' in his name and of his pedigree). See below under 'rap'.

Peep show n.m. The 1993 Larousse French-English dictionary explains the term as 'stéréoscope pour images érotiques' but gives 'peep show' as the French equivalent for What the Butler Saw. In *Le ras-le-bol des SuperWomen*, Michèle Fitoussi quotes a poem by Alain Souchon, whom she describes as the model of 'le Nouvelhomme' (the new man), the antithesis of the traditional macho Gallic male, which contains the lines:

Je veux du cuir,
Pas du peepshow, du vécu,
J'veux des gros seins des gros culs,
J'veux du cuir.

(I want leather,[3] not in a peepshow, but real experience, big tits big arses, real flesh.)

Pin's* n.m. A pin-on badge, very popular in the early 1990s, especially with teenagers, who would often decorate their clothes with what seemed to be hundreds of the objects. As an advertisement in *National Hebdo* no. 452 made clear, the right-wing, correctly patriotic French for it is 'épinglette', a term also given in *Logiciel et épinglette*, compiled by Mamavi and Depecker. In 1993 you could buy one to proclaim your allegiance to the Front National for 360 francs (£40; $60) in gold and 170 in silver. A headline in *Nice Matin* for 3 May 1993, entitled 'Le Pin's est mort, Vive le Magnet' announced what it presented as the end of the fashion, and quoted Marc Delacroix, 'patron de la société lilloise Officiel' as saying that the manufacture of stick-on magnets had achieved a turnover (chiffre d'affaires) of 12 million francs 'sur le créneau accrocheur de . . . pin's publications' (on the attractive window of opportunity of pin's publications).

In an article in supplement no. 44 of the *French Studies Bulletin*, Autumn 1992, T. D. Hemmings observed that the craze among French teenagers for festooning their clothing with minute enamel badges of varied design and usually negligible artistic merit seems to have crossed the Atlantic in 1990 missing Great Britain.

It offers, in this respect, a physical parallel to the way certain American words turn up in first of all in France rather than in Britain (e.g. 'reality show'). The fact that the craze missed Britain is also a reminder of the fact that French intellectual fashions are also more easily exported when they go directly to Sydney or New York than when they have to be filtered through Oxbridge or London.

Dr Hemmings also points out that 'pin's' is to some extent a necessary spelling, however odd it might look to the Anglo-Saxon eye, since the masculine plural 'pins' means pine trees and the feminine plural 'pines' a set of phalluses. He also observes that

> the apostrophe *s* is identified in French as a mark of Englishness and has been exploited in a variety of contexts – mostly commercial – for over a hundred years, as examples such as Fouquet's and Maxim's show.

He points to other cases where the apostrophe is used in 'a punning or ludic' context, such as Créa'tifs for a hairdresser, Ghis' coton, specialising in cotton blouses' and O'Nett for a dry-cleaners. Like the form of 'filet o fish' at the MacDonalds in Lille, and the *Mister Minit* as the name of a key-cutting establishment, the spelling 'pin's' has what Dr Hemming nicely calls 'the exotic origin and character of the word so written'. At the same time, like other aspects both of 'le franglais' itself and of 'la querelle du franglais', words such as 'pin's' offer additional evidence to the ungodly of how right Frank Richards was when he wrote to George Orwell, in May 1940, in response to Orwell's essay on boys' weeklies:

> As for foreigners being funny, I must shock Mr Orwell by telling him that foreigners *are* funny[4].

Poster n.m. A frequent word for a poster depicting 'une pop star' or film idol. The more general term is 'une affiche'.

Pull* n.m. The normal word for a pullover. In *Le Dico français-français* (see above, IIa, note 3), Philippe Vandel explains in the chapter 'Comment parler comme ses grands-parents' (How to talk like your grand parents) that this is what they called 'un chandail', in the same way as they still call a T-shirt 'un tricot de peau', describe homosexuals as 'des invertis', and use the word 'ballot' for stupid (in the 1914–18 war 'ballot' was an insult serious enough to set off fist fights).

Ranger n.m.p. American-style soft army boots, as worn by the crack American troops, the Rangers, who scaled the cliffs above a Normandy beach-head on D-Day. The skinheads (see IIa) who threw a Moroccan into the Seine on 1 May 1995 were wearing them.

Rap n.m. **rapeur** n.m. What the *Oxford Dictionary of New Words* defines as

> a style of popular music . . . in which . . . words are spoken rhythmically, often in rhyming sentences, over an instrumental background.

and which developed in the youth culture of both black and white in the USA of the 1980s, came as quickly to France as it did to Britain. *Le Monde* for 5 May 1994 noted how

> les rappeurs français mettent tous en avant leur pedigree [see above] impeccable d'enfants de cités. (French rappers all put forward their impeccable pedigree as children of suburban housing developments.)

See 'country' and 'fun' above; also 'inner-cities' in IIb.

Relapse n.m. In an article on AIDS On 10 March 1994, no. 1530, *Le Nouvel Observateur* said:

> on voit s'amplifier le phénomène dit de 'relapse', c'est-à-dire l'abandon des moyens de prévention par les personnes marginalisées. There is an increase in the phenomenon known as 'relapse', that is to say, the giving up by those

living on the fringes of society of any attempt to protect themselves.'

The article in *Le Nouvel Observateur* also said that France, with 25,583 declared cases of 'le SIDA', and an estimated 200,000 people who were HIV-positive (des séropositifs), had the worst record of any European country. See below, 'safe sex'; and 'golden boy' in IIa. The normal French word for relapse in a medical context is 'une rechute'.

Right man in the right place See under 'leader' in IIa for Proust's use of the expression. In *Les Mots*, Sartre describes the delight he felt when, at the age of ten and a half, he finally went to school and came into contact with other children.

> Sec, dur et gai, je me sentais d'acier, enfin délivré du péché d'exister: nous jouions à la balle, entre l'hôtel des Grands Hommes et la statue de Jean-Jacques Rousseau, j'étais indispensable: *the right man in the right place* . . . à qui Meyre, feintant Grégoire, ferait-il sa passe si je n'avais pas été, *moi, ici présent, maintenant?* (Lean, hard and happy, I felt like steel, finally freed from the sin of existing: we were playing ball, between the Hôtel des Grands Hommes and the statue of Jean-Jacques Rousseau, I was indispensable, *the right man in the right place* . . . who could Meyre have passed the ball to, as he sold the dummy to Grégoire, if *I myself, me personally*, had not been there, *here and now*?

The oddest paradox about Sartre is that the autobiographical fragment *Words*, which he published in 1963 at the age of fifty-eight, should show such nostalgia for a normal childhood, such envy for what Thom Gunn calls

> All the overdogs from Alexander
> To those who wouldn't play with Stephen Spender.

Rock music n.m. The French use no other term; as also for 'soul', 'punk', 'heavy metal', 'grunge' and 'rap' (see above, 'country'). See also above, the entry on 'fun'.

Safe sex n.m. During the summer of 1994, 8,000 billboards

were put up in France with the slogan 'Préservatif. Fuck
Aids'. the campaign was sponsored by the SNCF, Radio
France and a large clothing firm. Its defiance of the loi
Toubon can be justified on linguistic as well as health grounds
(see above, 'relapse'): 'Fuck you' is 'Va te faire foutre', a less
vulgar as well as a less easily adaptable construction. *Le Point*
for 2 April 1994, no. 1124, reported that

> lors d'un récent forum sur le *safe-sex*, un garçon demande à
> quoi bon, puisque de toute façon on finirait par attraper
> le SIDA. (During a recent forum on safe sex, a boy asked
> what the point was since you were going to get AIDS
> anyway.)

The New York Times for 20 March 1994 reported Annie
Cohen-Solal, a former French cultural counsellor, as saying
that the term 'safe sex' could not be translated into French
which she described as 'subtle, precise, descriptive, a language
where the word is an object in itself'.

Scratches n.m.p. A word objected to by Étiemble, but still
used by *Monde* on 4 April 1995 when it wrote 'le disc-jockey
repand des scratches qui glissent le long des morceaux comme
des gouttes de sueur froide' (disc-jockeys put scratches on the
records which slide along the surface of the music like drops of
cold sweat). See above, 'disc-jockey'.

Senior n.m. Contrasted with junior (see above). An article in
L'Expansion no. 484, on 10 October 1994, pointed out:

> Les vieux ne sont plus les vieux. Dans le vocabulaire à la
> mode, ce sont des seniors. Plus nombreux, plus actifs et plus
> riches (le revenu par tête dépasse celui des actifs). (Old
> people are not old any more. Fashion now requires them to
> be called senior citizens. There are more of them, more
> active and richer, with a per capita income higher than
> that of the working population.)

'Les Seniors' also have their own radio station, Radio
Bleue, which broadcasts only French Songs, and the word is
also used for those holding a senior position. But see above,

'juniors', for alternative terms. In *La Voix du Nord* for 4 August 1994, 'Le Sporting Club hornaingeois' (= de Hornaing) advised its readers of 'la reprise de l'entraînement pour les seniors et les juniors demain Vendredi au Stade Jean Miot' (training begins again tomorrow, Friday, for seniors and juniors at the Jean Miot stadium).

Sex appeal n.m. Not in the Toubon. *L'Express* no. 2261, for 10 November 1994 reported Fidel Castro as saying of Margaret Thatcher's Memoirs:

> J'ai surtout apprécié le chapitre sur ses rapports avec Gorbatchev. Elle a fait preuve d'un remarquable sex-appeal – sur le plan politique – dans ses rapports avec lui. (I particularly liked the chapter on her relationship with Gorbachev. She showed a remarkable sex appeal – on the political level – in her relationship with him.)

See Étiemble's protest, quoted in the *Dictionnaire des Anglicismes* under the entry 'sexy', against the replacement by 'l'ignoble *sexy*' not only of the perfectly good French word 'désirable', but of all the nuances implied in

> charmante, charmeresse, charmeuse, séduisante, séductrice, attirante, capiteuse, piquante, stimulante, aguichante, affriolante, excitante, voluptueuse.

Very true; the fact remains that for a native speaker of English, the best word to describe Sharon Stone in *Basic Instinct* is 'sexy', and the French clearly think so too.

See also under 'sex-symbol' in IIc.

Sex shop n.m. In French since the 1970s. According to the *Dictionnaire des Anglicismes*, a false anglicism first used in the more permissive Scandinavian countries. As in certain states in the USA, French sex shops have booths where one can watch pornographic movies.

Sexy adj. See above under 'look' and 'sex appeal'.

Shoot* n.m., *se shooter*, v.intr. A shot of heroin or some other hard drug, or to inject oneself with drugs, not to shoot oneself 'se tirer une balle – dans la tête, le coeur, etc.'. The review in *L'Événement du jeudi* no. 514, 8 September 1994, was enthusiastic about the scene in *Pulp Fiction* in which Uma Thurma,

> défoncée à mort, est sauvée de l'overdose par un shoot en plein coeur (drugged to the eyeballs, is saved from death by a shot directly into the heart).

The word 'shoot' can also be used in a political context and is frequent both in football and in basket-ball, where it gives the noun 'shooteur', as when *Le Parisien* for 11 February 1995 announced that

> Levallois enregistre le retour d'A.-J. English, son shooteur américain, pour la venue de Montpellier, ce soir. (Levallois announces the return of A. J. English, its American goalscorer, for the match this evening with Montpellier.)

The argument about 'le voile islamique' (whether Muslim girls should wear the chuddar at school or not) was initially set off in 1989 by Ernest Chenière, the *proviseur* (headteacher) at a school in Creil. Since he had the dark skin of his native Antilles, the French West Indies, it was difficult to accuse him of racism, and he was on firm ground in saying that he was merely applying 'les lois de la République'. He did, however, have fairly robust right-wing views on the matters, and was reported in *L'Événement du jeudi* for 5 May 1994, no. 496, as saying that 'le socialisme a empoisonné le pays par shoots successifs' (socialism has poisoned the country by successive injections of drugs). He has since joined the Front National, but was beaten at the 'élections cantonales' of May 1994.

Sixties, seventies n.f.p. On 13 October 1994, no. 519, *L'Événement du jeudi* wrote:

> Plus fort que les seventies: les sixties. Aux adolescentes qui refusent l'air à la Joan Baez, reste l'option Bardot, forcément très prisée. Son must, le chignon banane, qui requiert plus de doigté dans l'exécution que le look – précédemment cité – qui donne aux filles l'air de leur mémé. (Better than the

seventies: the sixties. The girls who refuse to look like Joan Baez, can choose to be like Brigitte Bardot. Her must, the banana chignon, requires more skill to produce than the previously quoted look, which makes the girls look like their grandmother.)

It is clearly fashionable to use the English term rather than the French 'les années soixante, les années soixante-dix', perhaps because teenage fashion is dominated by English and American models. On 5 May 1994, *Vendredi Samedi Dimanche* devoted a special number to what it called 'Les seventies'.

Slip* n.m. A pair of man's underpants. Cf. Prouse on 'smoking' for dinner jacket. 'Un slip de bain' is a pair of swimming trunks. As N.C.W. Spence points out in his article on *faux amis* and *faux anglicismes* (IIb, note 1), this use of a word which has quite a different meaning in English – that of a woman's garment worn under a skirt – probably stems from a 'pair of slips' used in the sense of bathing drawers. 'The reduction of a plural form to the singular in French', he notes, 'is not uncommon (cf. *pyjamas* becoming *pyjama*, *shorts* becoming *short*, etc.).'

Sniffer v. As in to sniff cocaine. An article in *Libération* for 12 December 1994 on how well the Americans were surviving the strikes in the baseball and ice hockey industry commented how the French had previously seen them as so totally hooked as to be 'des sniffeurs impavides de popcorn' (impassive sniffers of popcorn).

Soft adj. Software is 'le logiciel', a word universally accepted. The adjective 'soft', used by itself – see above, 'hard' – is applied to drugs, to 'les soft drinks', and 'le porno soft'. It could also be found in May 1993 in an advertisement on the Promenade des Anglais in Nice for 'Celebrity',

> un cadre soft et raffiné pour prolonger la nuit autour d'un drink dans une ambiance musicale (a gentle, refined atmosphere to prolong the evening over a drink, with a musical background).

On 19 January 1995, *L'Express* no. 2271 wrote that with Edouard Balladur, France was being offered 'une version soft – et démocratique – de l'ordre moral: "Tête haute, mains propres . . . et hymen intact"' (an easy-going version of Moral Order: 'Head held high, clean hands – and an intact hymen'). 'L'ordre moral' is a term associated with French régimes which are conservative to the point of being reactionary: the one imposed by Adolphe Thiers (1797–1877) after the repression of the Commune in 1871; the Vichy regime of Philippe Pétain (1854–1951). The use of the adjective 'soft' is another example of how 'franglais' words can coexist very easily with very French expressions. For 'star system' see 'star' in IIc.

Speedée p.p. On 1 February 1995, the popular daily newspaper *Le Parisien* reported Michel Polac of saying of 'le zapping' (see below):

> le mode d'emploi est un exemple de stupidité de notre époque speedée (the way it is used is an example of the stupidity of our time, which is in too much of a hurry).

Stand n.m. The *Dictionnaire des Anglicismes* suggests that it is used in three senses: a stand for spectators in a sports ground; a stand where you buy food at a sports meeting; and a small table on which to stand a typewriter or till. I have found it more frequently in that of a shooting gallery (see 'boss' in IIa), and Jacques Prévert writes in his poem 'Fête Foraine' (Fun-Fair):

> Malheureux les conscrits
> Devant le stand de tir
> Visant le coeur du monde
> Visant leur propre coeur
> En éclatant de rire.

(Unhappy conscripts, standing at the shooting gallery, aiming at the heart of the world, aiming at their own heart, while bursting out laughing.)

Strings n.m.p. In *Le Dico français-français* (see above, IIa, note 3), Philippe Vandel in the chapter 'Comment parler faux jeune' (How to speak as if you were still young) illustrates the use of ultra as an adverb by the example 'elle met des strings ultra-transparents' (she put on ultra-transparent strings); garments which, like the transparent bikinis now on sale in Britain, leave nothing to the imagination.

Striptease n.m. Criticised by Étiemble, who prefers 'effeuillage' or 'chatouille-tripes, selon que l'opération est réussie ou non' (taking off the leaves or tickling up lust, according to whether the operation is successful or not). The word was good enough for Roland Barthes, who in 1957 devoted an essay to it in *Mythologies*, arguing that it produced the paradoxical effect of de-sexualising the woman performing it:

> la fin du strip n'est plus alors d'expulser à la lumière une profondeur secrète, mais de signifier, à travers le dépouillement d'une vêture baroque et artificielle, la nudité comme habit *naturel* de la femme, ce qui est retrouver finalement un état parfaitement pudique de la chair. (The object of the striptease thus ceases to be that of expelling a secret depth to the clear light of day, but that of signifying, through the removal of a baroque and artificial set of clothes, a state of nakedness as a woman's *natural* form of dress, an activity which corresponds, in the final analysis, to rediscovering a totally chaste vision of the body.)

The review in *Le Point* for 27 August 1994, no. 1145, of the film *True Lies* was enthusiastic about

> la ravissante Tia Carrere en James Bond girl ... et la troublante Jamie Lee Curtis, qui effectue une jolie métamorphose d'épouse rangée en espionne de choc. Son strip-tease est un morceaux de bravoure d'un film qui en compte tant. (the ravishing Tia Carrere as a James Bond girl, and the sexually disturbingly Jamie Lee Curtis, who cleverly changes herself from a model wife to a top-class spy. Her striptease is one of the many high points of the film.)

Surprise party* n.f.; also spelt *surprise-partie*. Another false anglicism, as well as a misnomer. You were always invited in advance (or not), and/or told the person in whose flat it was going to be held that you were coming. Dating from the 1920s, replaced in the 1950s by 'boum', 'surboum' and 'sur-patte'. Often served as a marriage market: 'Et dans le Paris des années cinquante, toute maîtresse de maison⁵ qui se respectait avait parmi ses invités à toute surprise-partie un Polytechnicien en grand uniforme. (And in the Paris of the 1950s, any self-respecting hostess had among her guests at any 'surprise-partie' a student from the École Polytechnique in full uniform.)

They were events which made you realise how right Clamence was, in Camus's *La Chute* (*The Fall*, 1956) when he said 'les devoirs de l'amitié nous aident à supporter les plaisirs de la société' (the duties of friendship help us to bear the pleasures of society).

tag n.m., **tagger** v., **taggeur** n.m. Like *zapper*, a good example of the difference between a 'franglais' word and a normal anglicism. *Tagger* is to adorn with graffiti, generally from aerosol cans. In *L'Express* no. 2177, 1 April 1993, the critic Angelo Rinaldi illustrated the reluctance of the French to see anyone but themselves writing about their literature by describing Dennis Hollier's recently published collection of essays by American academics on French literature as

> un panorama des lettres françaises brossé en Amérique par une kyrielle d'universitaires avec la délicatesse de tagueurs auxquels on aurait confié la Sixtine (a panorama of French literature drawn up in America by a choir of academics with the delicacy of touch of a group of graffiti artists entrusted with decorating the Sistine chapel with aerosol cans).

Tee-shirt n.m. One also finds the spelling T-shirt.

Tennisman* n.m. What effect would be produced if one simply said 'joueur de tennis' instead? It would change the meaning of the statement in *Le Point* for 16 May 1994, no. 1130, to the effect that les organisateurs de Roland Garros ont demandé à leurs ordinateurs de dessiner le tennisman de l'an 2000: il mesurera deux mètres, pèsera 80 kilos, et possédera une force herculéenne lui permettant de réussir deux aces par jeu. De quoi dégouter le fan le plus assidu. (The organisers of Roland Garros have asked their computers to design the tennis champion for the year 2000. He will be six feet seven inches high, will weigh 176 pounds (12½ stone), and will possess a Herculean strength enabling him to serve two aces every time. Enough to put off the most devoted fan.)

Although French people will admit to playing tennis only if they are at least of club standard, there is no way in which 'un joueur de tennis' would be as tall, thin and good as that. The expression would have to be 'top tennis player'. See 'recordman' in IIa, and the comment made (p. 173) by N. C. W. Spence (see above, IIb, note 1) on the considerable difference between the English a *rugby man* – a man whose favourite game is rugby – and the French 'rugbyman', a member of a rugby team. He quotes other examples of what he calls pseudo-anglicisms such as 'bluesman', 'clapman' (somebody with a clapper board in a film studio), 'crossman' (a cross-country runner), 'cycleman', 'cyclocrossman' 'karate-man', 'racingman' (member of an athletics club) and 'trotting-man'. In *Zazie dans le métro*, Raymond Queneau makes fun of this habit by using the slang term for a policeman, 'un flic', to coin the word 'flicman'.

Top model n.m. On 18 April 1994, *Le Nouvel Observateur* no. 1538 mentioned the name of Andie MacDowell, the star of *Four Weddings and a Funeral*, as one of the 'top models' who had begun their career advertising 'des fast foods'. On 15 July 1993, *Paris-Match* carried an article entitled 'Les amours des Top Models' (the love affairs of the super models) describing how 'd'Estelle Hollyday à Irma Bowie, elles s'enflamment toutes pour des rock stars' (from Estelle Hollyday to Irma Bowie, they all fall for rock stars).

'Top model' can be either masculine or feminine, a fact which would have fitted nicely into Jean Genet's intention to exploit the occasional lack of correspondence between sex and gender in French by writing a poem entitled 'Les amours du mannequin et de la sentinelle'. An article in *Le Point* for 20 August, no. 1144, compared 'les top models masculins' to the naked male statues of the Greek and Roman world, arguing that their physical perfection revealed

> davantage la volonté hégémonique d'un peuple tendant à s'imposer comme type supérieur de la race humaine plutôt que le soi-disant représentation d'une sensualité collective

– meaning, in plain English, that Greek and Roman statues were to be seen more as examples of cultural and political propaganda than as the expression of a generalised homosexuality.

In spite of this reassurance, the Toubon makes no mention of 'top models', either male or female. The term is too recent to figure in the *Dictionnaire des Anglicismes*, which does nevertheless give 'topless' – admitting that 'l'équivalent français *seins nus* est sans doute moins chic' (the French equivalent of 'naked breasts' is doubtless less chic) – and 'top secret'.

An intriguing article in *Le Point* for 27 August 1994, no. 1145, described 'Les élections de MISTER France' as having taken place 'en direct' (live) on the main French television channel, TF1, and added that, at the same time, Sophie Favier 'décernait le prix du Play-Mec' (was awarding the prize of the best 'Play-Bloke'). According to *Le Point*, 'le striptease des Chippendale' had aroused great interest, and the magazine *Madame Figaro*, 'peu suspect de penchants grivois' (not normally obsessed with sex), had earlier celebrated the arrival of spring 'en consacrant un "Special hommes" à un "Voyage au pays des top-models"' (devoting a 'Special number on men' to 'a trip to the country of top-models').

See also the entry 'top' in IIb. The adjective 'top' occurs in other contexts, as in the advertisement in *Vendredi Samedi Dimanche* on 5 May 1994 for 'Yvane. Voyante Top-Niveau'. The French are keen on astrology, and Europe 1 – like many English popular newspapers – devotes five minutes every morning to broadcasting horoscopes. There is also a review called Top Santé, and the word was used substantivally on *France-Inter* for 2 February 1995 to describe how 'les rugby-men français sont au top physique' (in top physical form).

The term more frequently used in English for Fiona Campbell or Claudia Schiffer is not 'top model' but 'supermodel'; as illustrated by the *Coronation Street* T-shirt of Raquel (see above, p. 49).

Top ten n.m.p. On 11 November 1994 *Libération* gave the headline 'Top Ten' for its report from the analysis recently published by *Fortune* on the top ten cities for business. Although Paris had four globes, the highest category for culture, it did not make it into the top ten on other grounds. 'Le Français,' wrote *Libération*, translating *Fortune*'s comments, was

> glacial avec les étrangers, les salaires et les loyers de bureaux sont scandaleux. (French people are icy with strangers, salaries and office rents are scandalous.)

Toss* n.m. When *Libération* for 1 August 1994 carried the advertisement for '3615: TOSS. Le minitel de Tossing' and promised: 'Rendez-vos secrets, plaisirs d'une nuit, tout est possible sur TOSS', it assumed that its readers knew the definition of 'tossing' given on p. 194 of *Les mouvements de mode expliqués aux parents* (Obalk, Soral and Pasche):

> pratique consistant à faire l'amour avec une personne qu'on ne connaît pas, avec qui on n'a échangé aucun mot, et qu'on ne reverra pas (practice of making love with somebody you don't know, with whom you have not exchanged a single word, and whom you will never see again).

When first launched, in April 1973, *Libération* was noted for its small ads, 'petites annonces', many of which were obviously aimed at enabling people with comparably eccentric sexual tastes to meet one another. This function has now been taken over by the 'minitel rose', which in 1987 made a profit of two *milliard* new francs (a milliard = 1,000 million); of this, 750 million went to the state in tax.

Tube* n.m. The normal word for a pop song. Not mentioned either in the Toubon or in the *Dictionnaire des Anglicismes*, perhaps because 'tube', in the sense of a glass tube, has been in French since the thirteenth century. Even when 'les 45 tours' existed, the French did not use the terms 'revived 45', 'rave from the grave', or 'golden oldie' – now hilariously old-fashioned in England – and do not seem to have had any equivalent for them.

Also, in the 1890s, a word for a top hat.

Turf n.m. Used in horse-racing since the 1820s. Also in prostitution, 'avoir plusieurs filles sur le turf' (to be running several girls).

Vamp n.f. Originally applied to the silent cinema actress Theda Bara, and old-fashioned for the *Dictionnaire des Anglicismes*. *Madame Figaro* for 15 November 1994 used the word to emphasise what Marilyn Monroe was not. Derived from 'vampire'. There is also a verb, 'vamper'; as well as 'vampiriser', to suck somebody's blood.

Zap* n., **zapper** v. Either to change channels or, less frequently, to turn the telly off, as when Philippe Sollers, reviewing Volume XIII of a newly published edition of Voltaire's letters in *Le Monde* for 19 February 1994, offered a cure for unhappiness. Take down any volume of Voltaire, Molière, Proust or Diderot, 'rien que des auteurs français' (nothing but French authors); 'vous vivez modestement, en zappant ferme votre télévision' (live modestly, shutting the television firmly off); and you will be rapidly convinced that 'tout est pour le mieux dans le meilleur des mondes possibles' (all is for the best, in the best of all possible worlds).

In the review of the French press on France-Inter on 23 January 1993, Serge July, the editor of the left-wing newspaper *Libération*, said that its readers were 'des zappeurs professionnels' (compulsive channel-swappers). The existence of the form 'zappeuse' suggests that the women's movement has been more successful on a purely domestic level in France than in Britain, where it is still often the man who sits with the control and switches channels, using what is called 'la télécommande' (remote control). See above, 'speedée', and the report in *Le Parisien* for 11 February 1995 of the decision of the publishing house Marabout to produce versions of the classics of French literature in which the important passages were highlighted. 'Grâce à un zapping très spécialisé', it wrote, 'vous aurez lu *Madame Bovary* en 130 pages au lieu de 372' (Thanks to a very specialised technique of channel-swapping, you will have read *Madame Bovary* in 130 pages instead of 372).

Zoom n.m. By analogy with the zoom lense of a camera, a piece of information picked out and presented to the reader of a newspaper. On 18 August 1994, the copy of *Le Provençal* bought at Vaison la Romaine offered in 'Le zoom de l'été' some statistics about bullfights in Spain, Portugal and the South of France. In 1993, there had been 630 corridas, 11,500 bulls or young bulls killed, providing 180,000 jobs and being watched by 7.5 million spectators. No significant change was expected for 1995.

NOTES

1 A young person of non-Caucasian North African origin born in France. The word *beur*, which became popular in the late 1970s, is a form of backslang (le *verlan*, le langage à l'envers): Arabe = beur.
2 'Ne se pratique jamais sur une main gantée' (Never if a lady is wearing a glove). A practice described as 'shocking' by Eric Mension-Ruigau in his *Aristocrates et grands bourgeois* (Plon, Paris, 1993), a book which reminds one that tea for the children, in the French aristocracy, is still 'un rallye-confitures', invariably 'surveillé par des "nannies" à l'impeccable accent british' (supervised by nannies with impeccable British – he could mean the east of Scotland as well as English – accents).
3 Presumably in the sense of tough flesh; not leather as for fetishists.
4 See *The Collected Essays Journalism and Essays of George Orwell*, London, Secker & Warburg, 1968, Vol. IV, p. 491.
5 Who was not, of course, allowed to attend her daughter's party.

PART III
FRENCH WORDS IN USE IN ENGLISH

Introduction

The conversation between the Saxon thralls Wamba and Gurth in the second chapter of Walter Scott's *Ivanhoe* offers an immediate explanation of why the use in English of words of obviously French origin has always been associated with prestige activities. Since the French-speaking Normans were conquerors, it was natural for them to give French terms such as 'beef', 'pork' and 'veal' to the various meats served at table. Since it was the task of the conquered Saxons to look after the beasts in the field, without necessarily being allowed to eat them, it was equally natural for them, in contrast to their masters, to talk about 'pigs', 'swine', 'calves' and 'oxen'.

The names for the various ranks in the British army continue to bear witness to the greater prestige of French, with the word 'private' standing out in significant contrast to 'corporal', 'sergeant', 'lieutenant', 'captain', 'major', 'colonel', 'brigadier' and 'general', and Simeon Potter comments in *Our Language* how the names of the 'more elegant occupations such as carpenter, draper, joiner, mason, painter and tailor' come from the French, while those of the humbler jobs such as baker, fisherman, miller, saddler, weaver and shoemaker are of Germanic or Anglo-Saxon origin.[1]

Words such as 'carpenter' or 'draper', like more abstract terms such as 'elegance' or 'esteem', are nevertheless loan words, not examples of an English equivalent of 'le franglais'. I have already suggested a definition of 'franglais' words as terms of English or American origin which have not been fully assimilated into French, and contrasted them with words such as 'détecter', 'impérialisme', or 'parlementaire'. Although these are included by Josette Rey-Debove and Gilberte Gagnon in their *Dictionnaire des Anglicismes*, there is a very good reason why they have not attracted the ire of Étiemble or been listed in the 'termes étrangers ou termes impropres à éviter ou à remplacer' in the 1994 *dictionnaire des termes officiels de la langue française*. They have been in the language so long that they are no more recognised as foreign intruders than the Italian-born actor Yves Montand or the Russian-born writer Henri Troyat. Yet while such obviously unassimilated French words as 'après-ski', 'baguette', or 'tête-à-tête' are in daily use in modern English, there has never been a serious attempt to ban them from the language. French has not lost the prestige which it acquired at the time of the Norman Conquest, and has remained the language of what, in this context, is significantly called the élite.

Since it is also the tongue used to evoke pleasurable and generally civilised activities, and to make distinctions involving a certain finesse, it is understandable that the French terms listed below should fall into the categories they do. It is almost as though the English cannot talk about food, social relationships, or the more elegant and expensive types of enjoyment without using words which remain French in their pronunciation as well as in their morphology. Since it is almost equally impossible, as the words listed in Part II tend to suggest, to talk in French about drug-taking, pop music and a life-style associated with working-class adolescents without using 'franglais' words, it is not surprising that certain members of the French political and cultural élite should have tried to ban them. If, in English, expressions such as 'à propos' or 'hors de combat' were regularly used by football hooligans, then the proposed introduction in July 1994 by Anthony Steen, Conservative MP for South Hams, of a law banning all French words from the English language would not have been quite so obviously a joke aimed at Jacques Toubon, and might not have been rejected, as it was, by 149 votes to 49.

Anthony Steen also made the suggestion that since it would take about three million workers all their time to search and eliminate all words of French origin from the English language, the adoption of his bill would have the additional advantage of considerably reducing the number of people unemployed in the United Kingdom. Although this was a slight exaggeration, alert readers will not fail to spot omissions in the following list. On 25 May 1994, Mr John Brownjohn wrote to the *Daily Telegraph* to say that he had already collected 1,452 words of obviously French origin currently in use in English, and mentioned as examples not only 'fiancée' and 'doctrinaire' but also 'avenue', 'balustrade' and 'cigarette'. I have included only those which are more obviously French, and am aware that some of some of the words in my list can be placed in a different category. This includes the invaluable bidet.

a History, politics and diplomacy

agent provocateur, aide-mémoire, amende honorable, ancien régime, après moi le déluge, attaché, au-dessus de la mêlée

bloc des gauches, bon plaisir, bourgeois

cadre, canaille, canard (to evoke a fact frequently reported in the newspapers but actually false, such as the view that Eskimos have no generic word for snow), carrière ouverte aux talents, carte blanche, cause célèbre, chambre introuvable, chargé d'affaires, chauviniste, clientèle, cordon sanitaire (originally devised by the father of Marcel Proust), coup d'état (de main, de maître)

démarche, détente, droit de seigneur

élan, élite, émeute (as when the policemen in *The Pirates of Penzance* sing: 'When you're threatened with émeutes, / And your heart is in your boots'), éminence grise (Neil Kinnock is said to have described Glynis as his 'éminence rouge'), entente cordiale, épater les bourgeois, esprit de corps

fin de siècle, folie des grandeurs, force majeure

gendarme, glacis, grognard, guillotine

hors de combat

interdit de séjour

jeunesse dorée, journée révolutionnaire, jusqu'au boutisme

lèse-majesté, lettres de noblesse

matériel

noblesse oblige, nouveau riche

petit bourgeois, plus royaliste que le roi, politique du pire, en poste, pourparlers, protégé

raison d'état, rapprochement

sans-culottes

terreur blanche, trahison des clercs, tranche (as in sum immediately available for expenditure over a period, out of a global allotment)

ultra

b *Food, drink and fashion*

à la carte, à la mode, apéritif, après-ski, au pair

baguette, bistrot, bon appétit, bon viveur, bonne bouche, bouquet garni, brioche

café, chaise longue, chic, chicken suprême, chinoiserie,

coq au vin, coupé, haute couture, crème brûlée, crème fraîche, crêpe de chine, crêpe suzette, croissant, croupier

dernier chic, dernier cri, demi-monde, divertissement, douceur de vivre, dressage

eau de toilette, eau de vie, éclair, entrée

filet mignon, flâneur

garçonnnière, gourmand, gourmet, grisette

homme moyen sensuel, hors d'oeuvre

les jeux sont faits, joie de vivre

liqueur, de luxe

maître d'hôtel, maîtresse de maison, menu, midinette, mille-feuilles

pâté, pâté de foie gras (when the loi Toubon was first mooted in France, *The New York Times* for 17 March 1994 pointed out how silly it would be to pass a law in the United States requiring it to be translated as 'fat liver paste'), pâtisserie, pièce de résistance, plat du jour, pousse-café

quiche

salade de crudités, salade niçoise, salade russe, salade verte, salon, soirée, soufflé, soupçon

Table d'hôte, trousseau (as in *Trial by Jury*: 'Doubly cruel of him to do so, / For the maid had bought her trousseau')

c Art, literature and language

anti-roman, anti-théâtre, argot, art déco, art nouveau, artiste, avant-garde, avant-propos

beau idéal, beau ténébreux (e.g. Clark Gable as Rhett Butler, any actor as Mr Rochester), belle dame sans merci, belle époque, belles lettres, bon mot

cabaret, chef d'oeuvre, cinéma d'auteur, claque, comédienne (as in 'Marilyn Monroe was a marvellous comédienne in *Bus Stop* or *The Seven Year Itch*'), compère, connoisseur, coup de théâtre, cri de coeur

débutant, dénouement

en trompe-l'oeil

film noir

grande dame

dumb down?

haute vulgarisation (making the findings of advanced thinkers accessible to the layman)

impromptu

jeune premier

matinée, mélange des genres, monstre sacré (Sarah Bernhardt, Marlene Dietrich), mot juste nature morte (still life), nouveau roman

passé (out of date), pièce à thèse, poète maudit, précis

roman à clef

succès de scandale, succès d'estime

vernissage, vers libre (Fowler recommends 'free verse')

d Intellectual, physical, social and sexual behaviour, personal characteristics and intellectual distinctions

adieu, ambiance, amour propre, arriviste, art de vivre, au courant, au revoir

bête noire, billet doux, blasé, bon voyage

cliché, comme il faut, coquette, courtisane, coûte que coûte, crime passionnel

déjà vu, de haut en bas, de rigueur, de trop, délicatesse, demi-monde, démon du midi (male menopause), double entendre, drôle (as in Sir Humphrey's ironic 'Very drôle, Minister')

embarras de richesse, embonpoint (as when designating what Jeeves calls 'a gentleman of full habit', or Sartre implies when he speaks of 'un tailleur dicret pour messieurs mûrs'), enfant terrible, entre nous, esprit d'escalier (remembering a witty riposte too late), esprit de finesse (contrasted by Pascal with the 'esprit géométrique'; intuitive as opposed to scientific knowledge), expertise[2]

fait accompli, faute de mieux, faux naïf (Fowler acknowledges 'no real equivalent'), faux pas,[3] femme fatale, fiancé, finesse, flair, folie à deux, folie des grandeurs, frisson, fracas

gauche (in the sense of socially clumsy), gaucherie

habitué

idée fixe, impasse, ingénu(e), insouciance

je ne sais quoi, jeu d'esprit, jolie laide, juste milieu

largesse, louche

malade imaginaire, malaise (a certain malaise among the backbench Tories), malentendu, manqué (he is an actor manqué), mariage blanc (unconsummated), mariage d'amour (followed by 'une lune de miel'), mariage de raison (followed by 'un voyage de noces', as in Mauriac's *Thérèse Desqueyroux*), ménage à trois, mésalliance, misanthrope

naïf, nostalgie de la boue (a hankering after low life, often sexual, either experienced or imagined), nouveau riche, nuance

par excellence, parvenu, pêle-mêle, père (as in Muggeridge *père*), petite (as in the song 'Riding down from Bangor': 'Enter village maiden/beautiful, petite'), pis aller, politesse

raconteur, raison d'être, raisonneur, rendez-vous, roué, RSVP

sang-froid, sans peur et sans reproche, sans souci, savoir faire, savoir-vivre, soi-disant (condemned by Fowler), svelte

tête-à-tête, touché, le tout Leeds (ironic, as in 'le tout Paris')

venue, vis-à-vis, voyant, voyeur

NOTES
1 See Simeon Potter, *Our Language*, Penguin Books, Harmondsworth, 1950, p. 37. In two cases, the terms for the military ranks do not coincide. 'Le major' in French is the medical officer, and the word used in an educational context means the student who comes out first in the competitive examination marking the end of the period of study at one of the *grandes écoles*. It is 'le commandant' who is the equivalent of the English major, and Mérimée's *Carmen* makes it clear that Don José, who is 'un brigadier', is a fairly lowly non-commissioned officer.

2 Invented by Dryden, but then borrowed by the French themselves, though used nowadays in the sense a valuer's report. See T. E. Hope, 'Language and Stereotype. A Romance Philologist's Parable', an Inaugural Lecture, *University of Leeds Review*, 1971.

3 Invented by Dryden and adopted by the French themselves. See 'expertise', above.

Bibliography

This bibliography is divided into three sections: the press; dictionaries; and other works.

THE PRESS

Most of the examples are taken from the following French newspapers and magazines, here presented in alphabetical order with an indication of their general political tendency.

L'Action Française. Originally established by Charles Maurras in 1894 at the time of the Dreyfus case, and the voice of the extreme, still royalist right in France. An influential daily in the 1930s, now published weekly.

La Croix. A daily newspaper inspired by a liberal-minded Catholicism.

L'Événement du jeudi. Established in 1984 by Jean-Fraçois Kahn with the support of a number of small shareholders. A weekly magazine of centre left persuasion.

L'Expansion. Established 1987. A monthly review specialising in business and economics.

L'Express. A weekly magazine founded in 1954 to support Pierre Mendès-France, and originally slightly left of centre. Since its purchase in 1977 by James Goldsmith, and then in 1986 by the CGE, it has moved to the centre right.

Le Figaro. One of the oldest French newspapers, conservative and traditionalist, founded in 1826. Since 1978 it has also published a weekly *Figaro Magazine*, and since 1983, *Madame Figaro*, both of which are aimed at readers with high purchasing power.

France Soir. An evening paper, with the largest circulation of any Parisian-based daily paper.

L'Humanité. Founded in 1904 by Jean Jaurès. The official newspaper of the French Communist Party.

Libération. A daily paper of robustly left-wing persuasion, originally established in 1973 and, after an interval, revived in 1981 by Serge July.

Le Monde. Established in 1944 by Hubert Beuve-Méry, with the support of Charles de Gaulle. Published daily, in the evening. Moderate, centre left. Its weekly selection, obtainable only by subscribers from overseas, is similar to the *Guardian Weekly.* It also published *Le Monde Diplomatique*, *Le Monde de l'Éducation* and other monthly supplements.

National Hebdo. A weekly paper expressing the view of Jean-Marie Le Pen's Front National.

Le Nouvel Observateur. Originally *France-Observateur*, a weekly, left-wing magazine founded in 1950 by Gilles Martinet. Changed its name to *Le Nouvel Observateur* in 1964, under the direction of Jean Daniel. The major organ of the French intellectual left.

Paris-Match. An illustrated weekly paper founded in 1928. Although famous for its photographs, it also contains much useful information, and has been known to express some fairly robust conservative views. Its continued existence, when contrasted with the demise of *Picture Post*, underlines the same difference between French and English reading habits as does the success of *L'Express*, *Le Point*, or *Le Nouvel Observateur* compared with the difficulties of the *Spectator* or *New Statesman and Society*. What the French call 'des magazines d'information' (see 'news magazines' in IIc) fulfil the same function as the serious Sunday newspapers in England.

Le Parisien. A relatively low-circulation Paris morning paper.

Le Point. A weekly magazine founded in 1972, somewhat to the right of *L'Express*, and which recruited several of its best-known columnists, particularly Jean-François Revel, when *L'Express* was taken over by James Goldsmith.

La République du Centre. Covering the area around Clermont-Ferrand. Not easy to find elsewhere, and mentioned less frequently than *Le Dauphiné libéré* or *Ouest-France* in the 'Revue de Presse'.

Talents. A monthly magazine established in 1993 and aimed at students in higher education.

Vendredi Samedi Dimanche. A recently established mass-circulation weekly, cheaper than *Paris-Match*, and aimed at a younger readership.

20 Ans. A monthly magazine aimed, as its title implies, at adolescents.

La Voix du Nord. The main paper of the Lille area. Solidly socialist and, like other French provincial papers, rich in the odd, incidental news items known in French by the untranslatable expression 'des faits divers'. As Roland Barthes pointed out in 1957 in his *Mythologies* (Éditions du Seuil, Paris), the structure of the classic 'fait divers' is characterised by the Latin construction 'cum . . . tum': at the very moment when he was going to give his dog away, it saved his life.

L'Yonne Républicaine. A daily paper available in the area around Poitiers.

A feature which most clearly distinguishes the French from the English press is the size and importance of provincial newspapers. I have consulted these only when the happy accidents of foreign holidays have brought me into contact with publications such as *La Voix du Nord, La République du Centre,* and *L'Yonne Républicaine.*

I am conscious of having only scratched the surface of all the social and linguistic implications of 'le problème du franglais', and would suggest as a future research topic a detailed and systematic study of the frequency with which 'franglais' words recur in different newspapers in France, perhaps at periods separated by ten-year intervals. It would be particularly interesting to see how frequently they recur in the French newspaper with the widest circulation, *Ouest-France.*

DICTIONARIES

1 Official Government Publications

Dictionnaire des néologismes officiels, Commissariat Général de la Langue française, Journal officiel de la Langue française, Paris, 1989.

Dictionnaire des termes officiels, Commissariat Général de la Langue française, Journal officiel de la Langue française, Paris, 1993.

Dictionnaire des termes officiels de la langue française, Délégation Générale de la Langue française, Journal officiel de la République Française, Paris, 1994.

Logiciel et épinglette: Guide des termes francophones recommandés, comp. G. Mamavi and L. Depecker, Délégation Générale de la Langue française, Documentation française, Paris, 1992.

2 *Standard Dictionaries Consulted*

Dictionnaire des Anglicismes: Les mots anglais et américains en français, comp. Josette Rey-Debove and Gilberte Gagnon, Les Usuels du Robert, La Société du Nouveau Littré, Paris, 1980.

Dictionnaire Hachette de notre temps, Hachette, Paris, 1994.

Petit Larousse Illustré 1995, Larousse, Paris, 1994.

Petit Robert Alphabétique et Analogique de la Langue française, Les Usuels du Robert, Paris, 1992.

OTHER WORKS

Chiflet, J. L., *Sky Mr Allgood: Parlons français avec Monsieur Toubon*, Éditions Mille et Une Nuits, Paris, 1994.

Colignon, J-P., *La cote des mots*, Le Monde Éditions, Paris, 1994.

Étiemble, [René], *Parlez-vous franglais?*, Gallimard, Collection 'Idées', Paris, 1964, 1973; reprinted 1991.

Fitoussi, M., *Le ras-le-bol des SuperWomen*, Calman-Lévy, Paris, 1987.

Gordon, D. C., *The French Language and National Identity*, Mouton, The Hague, Paris, New York, 1978.

Hagége, C., *Le français et les siècles*, Odile Jacob, Paris, 1987.

Hagège, C., *Le souffle de la langue*, Odile Jacob, Paris, 1992.

Hope, T. E., *Lexical Borrowings in the Romance Languages: a critical study of Italianisms in French and Gallicisms in Italian from 1100 to 1900*, 2 vols, Blackwell, Oxford, 1971.

Luthi, J. J., Viatte, A. and Zananini, G., *Dictionnaire général de la Francophonie*, Letouzey & Ané, Paris, 1988.

Mackenzie, Fraser, *Les Relations de la France et de l'Angleterre d'après le vocabulaire*, Droz, Paris, 1939.

Merle, P., *Dictionnaire du français branché*, Seuil, Paris, 1986.

Obalk, H., Soral, A. and Pasche, A., *Les mouvements de mode expliqués aux parents*, Robert Laffont, Paris, 1984; reprinted in Livres de Poche, 1985.

Saint-Robert, Philippe de, *La Cause du français: Du service de la langue française à la naissance de la francophonie*, Éditions La Place Royale, Collection 'Contradictions', Paris, 1987.

Thody, P. M. W. and Evans, H., *Faux Amis and Key Words: a Dictionary-Guide to French Language, Culture and Society through Lookalikes and Confusables*, Athlone Press, London, 1985.

Thomas, George, *Linguistic Purism*, Longman, London and New York, 1991.

Tullock, Sarah (comp.), *The Oxford Dictionary of New Words: a Popular Guide to Words in the News*, Oxford University Press, Oxford, 1991.

Vandel, Philippe, *Le dico français-français*, Éditions Jean-Claude Lattès, Paris, 1993; reprinted in Livres de Poche, 1994.

Index (to Part II only)

As in the body of the text of Part II, an asterisk * is a reminder that the word either does not exist in that form in English, or that it is used by native speakers of English in a sense which is different from the one which it has taken on in 'le franglais'.

The symbol † indicates that the word is recorded either in the *Petit Larousse Illustré 1995*, or in the *Petit Robert* for 1992, or, in a large number of cases, in both. The *Petit Robert* tells its readers, where this is possible, when the words it defines first entered the French language. I have reproduced this information, where available, by including in my index the entry date given by the *Petit Robert*. This occasionally differs slightly from the date given in the *Dictionnaire des Anglicismes*.

The Larousse is a national institution whose annual edition is reviewed in many national newspapers and magazines. It sets out to include, as it says, 'les créations du français vivant, de la langue d'aujourd'hui' (the creations of living French, of the language of today) and aims to present its readers with 'une sorte de consensus minimal sur la langue acceptable, et acceptée, par tous les usagers du français' (a sort of minimum consensus on the French language, acceptable to all users of French and accepted by them).

The *Petit Larousse Illustré* also gives, where appropriate, the official equivalents recommended in the Toubon for terms of English or American origin. It consequently contains a large number of the words discussed in *Le Franglais: Forbidden English, Forbidden American: Law, Politics and Language in Contemporary France*; and should be the first book consulted by readers wishing to make any further study of 'le franglais'.

The rich man's Toubon is, obviously, the *Dictionnaire de l'Académie Française*. However, the most recent edition to appear, the eighth, did so in 1932. The 'quarante immortels' preparing the ninth edition have so far reached only the letter 'E', and it will be interesting to see what happens when they reach 'I' and come to 'impact'. Although not mentioned either by Étiemble or in the Toubon, it was regarded as late as 1980 by one of my French-speaking colleagues as acceptable only in the purely physical sense. 'The impact of the industrial revolution', she insisted, could be correctly translated only by 'le bouleversement apporté par la révolution industrielle'. On the morning of 30 March 1995, it was used seven times on France-Inter to speak of 'l'impact des grèves sur les transports parisiens'.